Development Intervention and Programme Evaluation

Development Intervention and Programme Evaluation

Concepts and Cases

Edited by
Vijay Padaki

Sage Publications
New Delhi/Thousand Oaks/London

First published in 1995 by

Sage Publications India Pvt Ltd
M-32 Greater Kailash Market I
New Delhi 110 048

Sage Publications Inc
2455 Teller Road
Thousand Oaks, California 91320

Sage Publications Ltd
6 Bonhill Street
London EC2A 4PU

Published by Tejeshwar Singh for Sage Publications India Pvt Ltd, phototypeset by Pagewell Photosetters, Pondicherry and printed at Chaman Enterprises, Delhi.

Library of Congress Cataloging-in-Publication Data

Development intervention and programme evaluation: concepts and cases / edited by Vijay Padaki.
p. cm.
Includes bibliographical references.
1. Economic development projects—India—Evaluation. 2. Economic development projects—India—Evaluation—Case studies. I. Padaki, V. (Vijay)
HC435.2.Z9E444 338.9—dc20 1995 95–8277

ISBN: 0–8039–9240–8 (US-hb) 81–7036–469–8 (India-hb)
0–8039–9241–6 (US-pb) 81–7036–470–1 (India-pb)

Sage Production Editor: *Niti Anand*

Once were we dependent
on the Landlord man
who ruled over our lives
over our lives
    We were taken then to a friend
    with pots of money to lend
    with money to lend
Then were we dependent
on the Moneylender man
who ruled over our lives
over our lives
    We were taken then to a friend
    with a helping hand to lend
    with a hand to lend
Now are we dependent
on the Knowledge bearing man
who rules over our lives
over our lives
    As friends help other friends
    so must we to ourselves tend
    so must we our own selves tend

Ballad of a village minstrel

Contents

List of Figures

Acknowledgements

It started with the invitation from the Development and Educational Communication Unit of ISRO in Ahmedabad in the beginning of 1988. The (then) Director, Kiran Karnik, had circulated the paper 'Social Institutions in Development Strategy' among his colleagues. It was felt that the paper provided, perhaps, a valid framework for the exercise on hand then, namely a review of the Kheda Communications Project. What came out of that extended visit was not only another way of looking at the project. In their wish to share the experience with others, DECU actively encouraged the idea of a larger exercise to review the field of programme evaluation itself. A project proposal was prepared. We were on. Kiran took a personal interest in every phase of the two year project. According to the project contract with ISRO, he was, technically, the co-director of the project, but it was so like Kiran to define for himself the role of Moral Support Director at the DECU end, a job he executed admirably.

The Editor was a Visiting Professor at the Department of Management Studies, Indian Institute of Science, Bangalore, when its programmes of work were being revised and reoriented towards the management of resource systems. The new programmes of work required a background in the policy sciences. The opportunity to engage in a project to review experiences in programme evaluation seemed timely. Amulya Reddy, who was Chairman of the Department at the time, readily approved the DECU idea, and took an active interest in the project. Amulya's participation in the workshop phase of the project was particularly helpful.

Vanaja Ramprasad joined the project as an associate. She provided valuable support in the literature survey leading up to the working paper, and in the conduct of the workshop.

In 1989, the Editor was invited by the Institute for Social and Economic Change, Bangalore, for a three year term as Honorary

Visiting Professor at the Social Services Management Unit of the Institute. Vinod Vyasulu, who headed the Unit, had himself been a participant in the workshop phase of the project. The case studies were completed during this visitorship at ISEC, and the support from Vinod and the SSM Unit was most readily available when needed.

A special note of appreciation for those who volunteered the case studies: K. Ramakrishnan at Bharathiar University, C.R. Bijoy at the Rural Health Centre in Thadagam, Subhash Joshi and B.S. Bhatia at DECU/ISRO, Sharada Jain and her colleagues associated with the Women's Development Project in Rajasthan through the Institute of Development Studies in Jaipur, K.S. Jagadish at ASTRA (Application of Science and Technology for Rural Areas), Indian Institute of Science, and Sandeep Virmani at Jan Vikas. Their patience with the demands of the project co-ordinator was remarkable. Their contributions to the subject of programme evaluation through this volume may be regarded as truly significant.

The two day workshop was the crucible in which the ingredients from the working paper could be reformulated towards viable alternatives in future practice. The proceedings were rich in content, exhilarating in experience. Neither quality lends itself to adequate transcription in third person reports. Yet, it was recognized early in the workshop that the participant mix was an important factor in the richness of output. It was particularly gratifying that most invitees could come. Some who could not, helped from without. A complete list of all those associated with the project appears elsewhere in this volume.

Padma Raju has provided the quietly efficient secretarial support throughout, from the first project proposal to DECU to the final manuscript for publication. It is such a nice feeling to know that the hundreds of bits of paper, fed into her desk in various scrawls, will somehow come out neatly ordered the next day.

There has been a long gap between the completion of the project and the publication of this book. It is easy to list reasons for the delay out there. It must be admitted, however, that the Editor must take the final responsibility for that and any other errors of omission and commission in the publication.

Vijay Padaki

One

Introduction: Towards an Alternative Methodology in Programme Evaluation*

Vijay Padaki

Another Look at Programme Evaluation

This publication is meant to serve two purposes: first, to share a line of thinking that has emerged in an on-going programme of work with the larger body of professionals; secondly, to present a case for deliberate research efforts towards exploring alternatives in the methodology of programme evaluation, in the special context of development interventions.

It is becoming increasingly clear to all concerned with programme evaluation that the available repertoire of tools and techniques of its methodology has severe limitations. Further, a mechanical execution of evaluation, with these limitations, often does more harm than good. The solution appears to lie not in more efficient implementation of the same, as is commonly believed, but in explorations of valid alternatives in methodology.

A concerned group of professionals—administrators, researchers, change agents—deliberated on the predominant issues in programme evaluation in the development context, and identified avenues for exploration of just such an alternative methodology. Their findings are summarized in this book.

---

* From programme to publication.

The publication should interest readers in all of the constituencies represented above. In our professional engagements with voluntary/non-governmental organizations (NGOs) in development programmes, we are constantly reminded of the paucity of material of Indian origin which can effectively relate to their working context. Early drafts shared with a sample of NGOs indicated that the publication might help fill the void. A large readership in the NGO community will be the happiest outcome of the entire effort.

The Programme Whole and the Parts

The first, tentative proposal for work in this area was prepared in 1986 and was titled 'An Evaluation of Programme Evaluation Research'. The focus on review and the urgent need to reflect on our experiences with programme evaluation (PE) was clear.

Purposeful interventions through development programmes require both (*a*) an understanding of the development process and (*b*) a valid methodology to assess the consequences of the intervention. It has often been observed that while the Indian experience in development is impressive, the enrichment of the theory–methodology cycle has remained wanting, largely on account of inadequate ploughback for research, poor exchange, and weak networking across the pools of experience.

A sustained programme of work to help correct the inadequacies must therefore recognize the multiple objectives of:

* Promoting professional interaction
* Encouraging documentation
* Seeking refinements in methodology
* Aiding theory building
* Facilitating professional communication/publication

The tasks to be undertaken for accomplishing these objectives can be viewed in at least two time frames: the short-term, taking one to two years, and the long-term, extending beyond two to three years. Table 1.1 sets out the distribution of tasks against such objectives.

There is a pragmatic basis for the separation of the short-term from the long-term. At the start we must accept the exploratory

Table 1.1: **A Programme of Work in Programme Evaluation**

Objectives	*Short-term*	*Long-term*
Professional Interaction	Workshop exchange among reserachers and practitioners	Creation of a forum for continuous exchange
Documentation	Immediate work on select case studies	Compilation of case leads and full case studies
Methodology	Descriptive review—for the state of the art	Prescriptive—aimed at varied system levels, operational contexts, objectives, etc.
Theory Building	Hypotheses from select case studies on functional role (or otherwise) of evaluation act	Towards purposive and integrative fit in development theory, intervention theory
Publication/ Communication	* Review monograph * Handy guidelines	* Text-cum-case book * Handbook/sourcebook * Training package/course

nature of the programme and, therefore, the uncertainty regarding outputs from the exploration. Thus, discoveries in the short-term will themselves influence pursuits in the long-term. Secondly, the tasks in the long-term are necessarily diversified. It will be impractical for one research centre to undertake all of them. A collaborative effort through a purposeful network of interested groups will be called for.

What follows is a description of the specific projects undertaken in a programmatic manner for the short-term.

The programme was supported by the Indian Space Research Organization through its Development and Educational Communication Unit (DECU). It was directed by the Editor of this volume, who was then a Visiting Professor at the Department of Management Studies, Indian Institute of Science, Bangalore.

Reflection and Re-examination

Two phases of work were visualized. Broadly, the first aimed at a review of the PE experience so far, to seek an alternative framework that had at least a priori validity in the context of development interventions. The second phase sought to test the validity of the alternative framework in a set of case studies. It was felt that work in both phases would be best undertaken through a process of planned, purposeful, professional interaction with all the interest groups.

Phase One: Workshop

This phase of work focussed on a workshop on PE in the following steps.

Project 1—Literature Review

An extensive literature review was undertaken, with the 'output' from the review exercise envisaged in two steps:

Step 1: A working paper for the workshop which simultaneously

1. reviewed the premises of PE, and
2. raised questions and issues for the practice of PE in the special context of developing societies.

Step 2: An expanded review, in the nature of a monograph, to be completed after the workshop.

Project 2—Workshop

Step 1: Preparatory

* Participants for the workshop were identified and invited over three months in advance.
* Participants from the following three types of backgrounds were sought:
    - Field; i.e., project/programme implementors.
    - Research; i.e., academics/researchers in development studies.
    - Development administration; i.e., functionaries from funding agencies, both governmental and non-governmental.
* The early identification of the participants facilitated exchanges even before the workshop; e.g.:

- o Comments on a draft outline for the working paper.
- o Draft case leads from the participants.
- o Comments on workshop structure/schedule.

* The working paper prepared for the workshop, titled 'Development Intervention and Programme Evaluation', was sent three weeks in advance to all participants.

Step 2: The workshop, 27–28 September 1988

The deliberations over the two days were as planned:

* Presentation of the working paper.
* Lead discussions on the working paper.
* Open discussions on emerging issues, priorities.
* Two workshop syndicates to examine more closely:

1. *Conceptual* issues in development interventions
2. *Methodological* issues in PE

* Integration of recommendations from the two workshop syndicates.

Step 3: Follow-up case studies

Several case leads were brought to the workshop and presented. A select number of case leads were identified for follow-up documentation into full-scale case studies.

Phase Two: Case Studies

On the basis of the workshop deliberations, a detailed note was prepared on how to proceed with the task of preparing full case studies from the leads.

The case studies were completed by the end of 1989. The output visualized from this phase of work was a concepts-cum-cases publication, incorporating an expanded version of the earlier working paper, the workshop proceedings and the cases.

The Workshop Focus

Programme evaluation can be undertaken at several *system levels* of organization—from a single village school to the Ministry of Rural Development. The focus of the workshop was on two system levels:

1. A *project* or *programme* which attempts intervention at the level of an entire community.
2. The *agency* that functions in the intervention, comprising two or more projects.

As examples, we might examine (*a*) the impact of a new income generating activity introduced by an NGO on a group of villages, or (*b*) the impact of the NGO on its operating environment. (Or both.)

This delimitation was considered practical, and was consistent with the definition of scope as spelt out in the working paper:

* The problems in *developing societies*, with special reference to the Indian experience.
* Within the above, special attention to PE in the context of planned *intervention* programmes, rather than the monitoring of various on-going socio-economic processes.
* Within the above, special attention to interventions in *states of deprivation*, attempting to meet basic needs, rather than on interventions for incremental changes in reasonably well-served needs.
* Within the above, special attention to system levels reasonably *within the control of programme administration*, e.g., a project, a programme consisting of several similar projects, the agency itself that undertakes such projects, rather than large country level programmes involving multiple agencies.

The Development Context

Is PE methodology universally valid? When a development worker finds the textbook method in PE 'irrelevant' to the task on hand, what exactly does it mean? How exactly does the 'development context' differ from the context in which the PE methods originated, rendering them ineffective? How basic are these differences? In other words, do we need refinements in available methodology, or will we need an alternative methodology?

PE as an aid in *policy analysis* is seen in the following sequence of events:

1. Visualization of a desired state (health, sanitation, education, income, etc.).
2. Recognition of the state not appearing on its own—existing institutional/market forces loaded against it.
3. Articulation of public policy to reach the desired state, envisaging both policy instruments and policy agencies.
4. Manipulation or modification of existing institutional/market forces by policy implementation.
5. Assessment of policy impact; i.e., outcome vis-à-vis the desired state.

In the sequence of events above, the important assumptions are:

* Given a good project appraisal and 'systems analysis' at the start, it is possible to devise a policy that will alter social phenomena in the desired direction.
* The intervention called for is primarily the correct policy instrument, backed by the organizational facility of a policy agency for implementation and monitoring.
* In the first few cycles of events in the new system it is possible to debug the system of flaws that might have occurred due to shortcomings in the appraisal.

In much of the available literature, on policy analysis in general and on PE in particular, we can see that the above assumptions are indeed valid; but only in 'that' context, that is, the 'developed' societies from where the literature on policy analysis and programme evaluation is drawn. Why do they become unreliable, if not invalid, in 'this' context?

The development context can be seen as genuinely different. A historico-political analysis reveals how and why it is different, and in what ways the difference invalidates conventional PE methodology.

The working paper identified eight important features of the development context that rendered PE methodology originating in a 'developed' socio-economic context ineffective. The workshop groups readily endorsed the analysis.

In summary, the eight features were:

1. Development interventions generally attempt to provide a new service, meeting basic needs, as distinct from the modification/improvement of an existing public system.
2. There are usually powerful, vested institutional and market forces that act as filters and counter-currents.
3. There is an absence of appropriate social institutions to 'take over' and aid rapid diffusion after intervention.
4. The quantitative indices in PE are often deceptive in not revealing the inequitable, lopsided outcomes of the change process.
5. The protective–nurturing role of the change agency over an extended, indefinite period appears inescapable.
6. The required complementarity between the regulatory function and the development function in interventions is often missing, with an emphasis on one at the expense of the other.
7. The role of the NGO sector in the development effort remains scattered, and the vast potential from an appropriate networking is unutilized.
8. There are several dysfunctional, iatrogenic, effects from interventions because of inadequate systemwide support systems.

Thus, it appears abundantly clear that the difference in context between a developed and a developing society is far beyond the conventional notion of 'resources'. Indeed, we often equate 'context' with 'resource position'. Alternately, we may be required to view *social institutions as resources* too. All development interventions require appropriate social institutions to sustain the processes introduced. The institutions might exist, they might not; they might be functional, they might be dysfunctional; they might be existing institutions that can be mobilized usefully; they might be institutions developed anew.

Part I

Concepts

Two

The Development Context*

Vijay Padaki and Vanaja Ramprasad

Overview

A Review Exercise

Among the numerous ways in which the intellect of the human species is manifest in overt behaviours are two that draw special attention:

* Active manipulation of one's environment to control future outcomes.
* Enquiry into the outcome process to better control future manipulations.

Together, these two characteristics of human cerebration constitute the core elements of the elaborately formalized activity that we call science and technology. When channelized into one set of procedures in one type of manipulation of the environment, we have the formal discipline called programme evaluation (PE).

Action and enquiry may therefore be seen as dialectical, complementary, mutually supportive, spirally reinforcing and so on, but in sum as inevitably bound.

---

* A working paper to review theory and methodology in programme evaluation.

When action and enquiry are put together in a formalized procedure, as in PE, that act itself is an operation on one's environment. Sooner or later we are compelled to reflect on what we have done in the name of PE, where it has led us, what we have got out of it, and what else we might expect from it. This review of PE is thus best regarded as the natural phase of enquiry following a spell of professional practice. It is not the first of its kind. It certainly cannot make the mistake of regarding itself the ultimate.

The Scope

The subject of PE is extraordinarily vast, especially when we consider all the areas of application as well. Our interest in the present review exercise is narrowed down by design through the following steps:

* The problems in *developing societies*, with special reference to the Indian experience.
* Within the above, special attention to PE in the context of planned *intervention* programmes, rather than the monitoring of various on-going socio-economic processes.
* Within the above, special attention to interventions in *states of deprivation*, attempting to meet basic needs, rather than on interventions for incremental changes in reasonably well-served needs.
* Within the above, special attention to 'system levels' reasonably *within the control of programme administration*, e.g., a project, a programme consisting of several similar projects, the agency itself that undertakes such projects, rather than large country level programmes involving multiple agencies.

The Working Paper

The principal function of the working paper is to generate discussion in a workshop to follow. It must (*a*) aid a proper articulation of certain questions that might have occurred to all of us at one time or another in various developmental projects and programmes, and (*b*) enable the workshop to then seek alternative approaches to the task of programme evaluation.

It is important for the working paper to be truly *eclectic*. It must neither represent a chosen point of view, nor become a vehicle for another point of view in itself. On the other hand, it must identify the typicalities of difficulty encountered in many PE tasks and the underlying assumptions of the tasks that may be linked to the difficulties.

It is not to be expected that either the working paper or the workshop will lead to one ideal PE model. However, the methodology adopted for evaluating the outcome of a development effort cannot be independent of the theory adopted for it. The linkage might be stated explicitly or it might be implied. If these theory–methodology linkages are revealed, an important purpose would be served. Going further, if we detect clusters of methods around theoretical assumptions we would have done better. If in the process we identify gaps and sources of inadequacy in the development process, it would be a bonus from the workshop.

Following from the above, the working paper has concentrated on questions rather than on answers, on description rather than on prescription. It has attempted to deal with difficulties that are in the realm of 'issues', rather than the purely technical problems of the tools and techniques employed in PE practice, such as the reliability index of a survey instrument or the social desirability error in a questionnaire.

Finally, although the working paper has been prepared after an extensive literature review—books, research papers, journalistic articles, case studies—it is not put together as an academic paper, with notes, references and footnotes. Such a construction would not serve the purpose of the workshop. The paper can indeed be expanded into a monograph; but that must come later, and must include the proceedings of the workshop.

Quick Recap: PE as Generally Understood

On Terms Used

Practices in evaluating an on-going intervention programme draw heavily from the branch of social science research called *evaluation research*. The need for application of evaluation research is felt when programme effects are not directly discernible, but surface in diffused patterns. Evaluation research broadly encompasses the different stages of programme formulation, the analysis of the programme within the context of its objectives, assumptions, activities, the theoretical rationale, the prediction of 'benefits' and 'costs', and the assessment of outcome. Implicit in this approach is the expectation of specific outcomes, perhaps in quantitative terms. Evaluation methodology has been developed over the years to provide tools and measures to serve the purpose of public accountability. *As a management tool*, therefore, evaluation cannot be separated from the process of planning, implementation, monitoring and review, associated with the whole life-cycle of the project.

The term evaluation covers a wide range of activities and different terms have been used to differentiate between evaluation carried out during a project's lifetime and evaluation conducted later. Although differences in usage are common, the following distinctions should be useful:

Before	*During*	*After*
* appraisal	* concurrent evaluation	* ex post facto evaluation
* feasibility	* project monitoring	* summative evaluation
	* process evaluation	* impact evaluation

The term appraisal is better applied to the analysis before the project is undertaken and the term programme (or project) evaluation for the analysis either during or after the project's formal lifespan. However, there is little agreement in the literature on whether programme evaluation refers only to the formal, specific, activities of a project or to its larger overall impact.

An appraisal is meant to guide the decision on whether or not to proceed with an investment proposal. The appraisal procedures also provide the criteria by which to accept or reject a proposal and decide between alternative investment propositions. One of the appraisal methods that gained rapid importance during the sixties was the technique of cost-benefit analysis (CBA). The main concern of such a technique was to predict the 'profitability' of a project by comparing the project's expected costs with its expected benefits. Notwithstanding the fact that the perspective of CBA was essentially financial, and best suited to a private enterprise, a further sharpening of the technique took into account the direct and indirect costs to society and was referred to as social cost-benefit analysis. In spite of the obvious value of the concept, SCBA has been accused of hiding behind contrived techniques of quantification, and being thus unusable in actual practice, especially by non-experts.

On the other hand, evaluation relates to accountability and the requirements of future planning and decision-making. In assessing the outcome, whether during or after a project, the evaluation also attempts to establish to what extent the observed outcome can be attributed to the project, whether it could be attributed to the factors within the boundaries of the programme or to factors outside the programme. It is here that PE also displays its ancestry as a *research tool*—drawing on concepts, methods and tools from diverse disciplines, and feeding back methodology to diverse applications within the general quest for a methodology which can infer causal associations among identifiable and measurable variables.

One area of application where PE has served simultaneously as a management tool and a research tool in an integrated manner has been in policy analysis, i.e., in the enunciation and modification of public policy. Thus evaluation research is often viewed as integral with the policy process, and PE as the component of evaluation research more specially concerned with assessing outcomes from policy interventions for the purposes of (*a*) establishing outcome, (*b*) estimating causal associations, and (*c*) guiding modifications in policy or control systems.

Underlying Meanings and Assumptions

We have so far examined the denotative meanings of terms associated with PE. There are, understandably, the connotative meanings too that frequently cause problems in practice, especially if the parties involved—the funding agency, the project agency, the beneficiaries, the professional analyst—have varied exposures to evaluation research. As can be appreciated, words like 'appraisal', 'monitoring', and 'evaluation' conjure up images of unhelpful intrusions by unfeeling professionals into well-intentioned efforts. Indeed, many would object even to the term 'programme', referring to its connotation of being something inposed from outside. Not surprisingly, project proposals and project reports resort to a great deal of wordplay, creating new catch-phrases, new definitions, reflecting more often than not the needs of the change agents, rather than the needs of the beneficiary system. (Connotations of the term 'beneficiary', too, are often disliked!)

What appears important for our review task is to accept at the start that in any developmental intervention,

* the *criteria* adopted for assessing change are inseparable from the articulation of *objectives*, explaining in turn the costs and benefits in a programme; and therefore,
* there are *value positions* underlying the intervention that must influence the content and methodology of PE as well.

Thus the feedback from PE serves to either reinforce or, in a truly open system, alter the prevailing value position. Figure 2.1 across depicts the cycle of events.

In sum we might observe that every intervention task, by any agency, with any value position, calls for the articulation of:

* The kind of change desired
* The means by which the change is to be brought about
* The indicators by which the change is to be recognized

Recognition of the core requirements of *articulation*, *unambiguity* and *internal consistency* is essential. Giving the activity a label like 'Management by Objectives' might appear perfectly logical to the administrator, but it tends to complicate matters for the many others involved in the effort.

The Development Context Re-examined

We have already seen that the subject matter of PE has benefitted from developments in many fields, the common concern in all of them being the assessment of change and the explanation for changes assessed. PE as a specialized discipline has developed by

1. drawing on the experiences in different fields;
2. abstracting these experiences into general principles, concepts and models; and
3. feeding back these abstractions into professional practice in the fields.

When a development worker finds the textbook method in PE 'irrelevant' to his task, what exactly does it mean? How exactly does the 'development context' differ from the context in which the PE methods originated, rendering them ineffective? How basic are these differences? In other words, do we need refinements in available methodology, or do we need an alternative methodology?

Figure 2.1: **POLICY CYCLE**

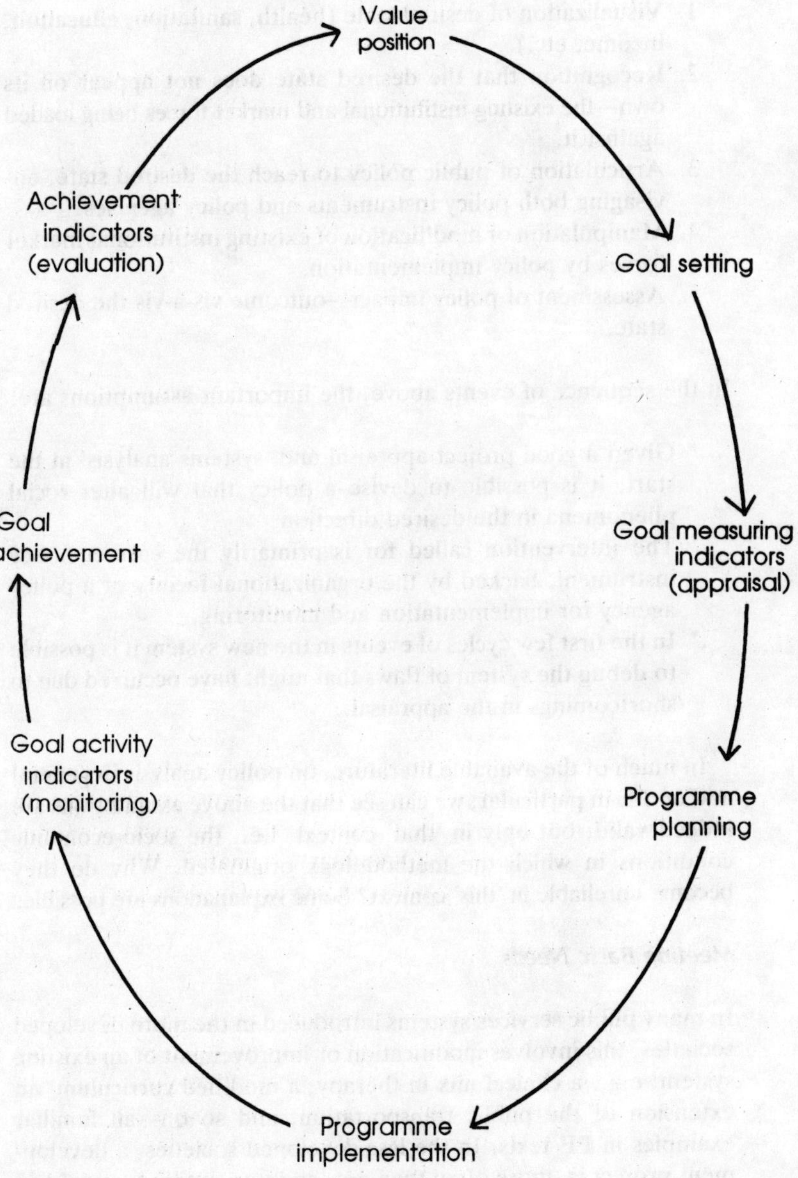

PE as an aid in *policy analysis* is seen in the following sequence of events:

1. Visualization of desired state (health, sanitation, education, income, etc.).
2. Recognition that the desired state does not appear on its own—the existing institutional and market forces being loaded against it.
3. Articulation of public policy to reach the desired state, envisaging both policy instruments and policy agencies.
4. Manipulation or modification of existing institutional/market forces by policy implementation.
5. Assessment of policy impact—outcome vis-à-vis the desired state.

In the sequence of events above, the important assumptions are:

* Given a good project appraisal and 'systems analysis' at the start, it is possible to devise a policy that will alter social phenomena in the desired direction.
* The intervention called for is primarily the correct policy instrument, backed by the organizational facility of a policy agency for implementation and monitoring.
* In the first few cycles of events in the new system it is possible to debug the system of flaws that might have occurred due to shortcomings in the appraisal.

In much of the available literature, on policy analysis in general and on PE in particular, we can see that the above assumptions are indeed valid; but only in 'that' context, i.e., the socio-economic conditions in which the methodology originated. Why do they become unreliable in 'this' context? Some explanations are possible.

Meeting Basic Needs

In many public services/systems introduced in the more developed societies, this involves modification or improvement of an existing system; e.g., a clinical mix in therapy, a modified curriculum, an extension of the public transportation, and so on—all familiar examples in PE texts. In the less developed societies, a development project is, more often than not, an intervention to provide a new facility, attempting to meet a basic need, calling for a whole new class of social behaviour. (In marketing management terms, this is the basic difference between brand switching within a product category and initiating new consumer behaviour in a new product category.)

Filters and Counter-Currents

The existing institutional/market forces that had prevented the desired state from occurring on its own in the first place are so powerful, so *systemic*, that they beat the new system, i.e., they successfully foil the interventions of policy. In other words, a mere monitoring role for the policy agency is generally inadequate to ensure change. (There is a great deal of analysis available on the 'dual society' phenomenon in most developing societies, certainly of the Indian scene, and should not need special elaboration here.)

Absence of Facilitating Institutions

In a more developed society, when a policy intervention is made to promote social behaviour in a desired direction, it can be assumed that existing social institutions will 'take over' soon after in dissemination and diffusion of the change. These social institutions may pertain to the market, the academic system, the civic administration, the media, community traditions and so on. In a less developed society, the social institutions for effective diffusion are typically weak or non-existent *for the new behaviours* promoted by the interventions. An 'appropriate' technology is introduced to create jobs and income. An organizational set-up is created around the new activity which even succeeds in 'imparting' new skills in the handling of new machines and tools. But in no time at all the condition of the machines deteriorates rapidly, and both productivity and quality suffer. Typical explanation: The maintenance culture was not internalized. In other words, the new behavioural pattern around the new economic activity did not get 'institutionalized'. Similar setbacks are observed in all types of intervention for development. The intervention provides the *technical artefacts* for some overt behaviours to change. It does not provide in most cases for (*a*) several related behaviours to change correspondingly, and (*b*) for the set of changed behaviours to be reinforced and sustained over time.

Licensed Trespassing

The last two conditions often combine in a yet more pernicious problem in the development context. Because of inadequate institutionalization, not only is the change from the intervention poorly diffused—and the potential benefit from it inadequately realized—among the people for whom it was conceived, but the very vested interests that were to be kept at bay by the policy intervention find ways to 'muscle in' on the opportunities created for the disadvantaged, and take away the benefits for themselves. Whether it is the ration-card for essential commodities or an improved wood burning stove, the working of the system ends up serving the needs of the better off more effectively, contrary to the original intentions of the intervention. In all such cases, 'evaluation' would rather refer to the numbers benefitting, which will always be there, often large, rather than the equitable distribution of the benefit.

Extended Agency Role

Following from the above, the typical assumptions of intervention, namely, self-sufficiency, withdrawal and replication, appear very unrealistic. The intervening agency, be it governmental, quasi-governmental or NGO, finds itself compelled to play a protective–nurturing role for a long, even indefinite, period. Is this 'wrong'? 'Bad'? Or is it only natural in the given historical context?

Regulatory and Developmental Functions

Should we accept the legitimacy of an extended protective role for the intervening agency in the special context of underdeveloped social institutions, we may regard the two principal approaches to this role as complementary rather than in conflict: the 'regulatory' role, typically played by the governmental agency, and the 'developmental' role played by many an NGO. Too much of either without the other, and we may not have the emergence and stabilization of genuine, purposeful, new social institutions appropriate to the development objectives. We may have, instead, only continued dependence on the agency itself. *The development of appropriate social institutions thus appears the superordinate task in all development programmes*.

Role of NGOs

Following from the above, we must accept that in developing societies the NGOs have a monumental role to play, far beyond mere welfare services. However, it must also be recognized that the NGO role in development is currently diffused, and the vast potential from an appropriate network unrealized.

Programme evaluation, correspondingly, can serve two important purposes, at two levels of organization:

* Given a policy framework, including the roles for policy regulation agencies, the actual implementation of programmes needs participation from the NGO sector on a huge scale. And PE here must ensure the fulfilment of programme level objectives and performance criteria; i.e., *PE for programme and organizational effectiveness*.
* But what PE feedback does policy-making receive? There is tremendous scope for channelizing PE data from the numerous programme streams, through an appropriate design, into this level of policy analysis, i.e., *PE for policy effectiveness*.

Treatment Induced Disorders

Finally, we must recognize one other important difference in the development context as it pertains to interventions—the unforeseen, unwanted consequences of the intervention. In medical parlance, iatrogenic disorders (i.e., treatment induced disorders) can be regarded as being either

* secondary, i.e., the physiological links with the treatment for the main disorder are casual/incidental; or
* primary, i.e., the new signs and symptoms are systemically linked to the starting disorder, *making it a more complex dysfunction*.

In social dysfunctions, too, we can think of vicious circles that perpetuate the condition. In a given condition of inequitable distribution, for instance, we may find that the 'side effect' of an intervention was the inadvertent reinforcement of inequalities—the rich getting richer at the expense of the poor. Thus, a purely technique-oriented 'management' plan of action in a context of injustice, inequality and exploitation may only result in more 'efficient' injustice, 'maximized' inequality and more 'effective' exploitation, to be viewed ultimately as the price to be paid for the gain in some 'objective' economic index.

In referring to the differences in context affecting the course of events in a development project most observers would readily recognize the difference in the *resource position* while undertaking the project—the seed monies, the capital budgets, the working capital funds, the technology that can be mobilized, the levels of education and skills and so on. Indeed, we often equate 'context' with 'resource position'. On the other hand, the analysis that we have attempted here suggests that there is far more to context than a conventional resource checklist. Alternately, we may be required to view social institutions as resources too. All development interventions require appropriate social institutions to sustain the processes introduced. These institutions might exist, they might not; they might be functional, they might be dysfunctional; they might be existing institutions to be mobilized usefully; they might be institutions developed anew.

Context and PE Methodology: Some Issues

If we accept that the unique historico-political contexts of developing societies present certain unique problems in ensuring desired outcomes from interventions, it should not be too difficult to see how certain recurring questions in PE might in fact be related to these contextual uniquenesses.

The Non-Occurrence of Expected Outcomes

When bonded labour does not get freed, when a minimum wage is not paid, when neither the food nor the work targets are achieved in a food-for-work programme, when there is a lock on the door of the schoolhouse the year round, *what* do we evaluate and *why*? Were the agencies concerned ineffective, were the control systems weak, were the methods adopted faulty? Or was there, perhaps, a systemic condition that guaranteed a 'failure' even at the start?

The Occurrence of Non-expected (Undesirable) Outcomes

This is the dysfunctional iatrogenic effect referred to earlier. When the benefits go to the wrong parties, or when existing anomalies are aggravated by the intervention itself, what exactly does PE evaluate?

Macro-Influences on Micro-Outcomes

As part of an employment generation programme the state government releases outright grants and arranges bank guarantees for soft loans to new cottage industry units. A voluntary agency assists a group of households to go ahead with a clay tile-making unit within the provisions of the scheme. Within about a year both the cottage industry and the voluntary agency discover: (*a*) the newer ceramic tile-making technology has become far more cost-effective due to changes in the duty structures, and (*b*) the traditional uses of clay tiles are rapidly disappearing due to wholesale changes in style in the general sphere of construction. The first question before PE now is: Which system should be evaluated? The governmental agency, the bank, the cottage co-operative society, the NGO? Whatever the focus, and whatever its rationale, the next question is: Which function should be evaluated? The 'marketing' function, i.e., the failure to create new markets for the product or new uses for it? The 'finance' function, i.e., cost control, cash flows, etc.? The 'technical–production' function, i.e., in terms of productivity, quality and waste? Or do we ask what is happening 'out there' in licensing policy that so many ceramic tile units have come into being in such a short time?

Outcomes Not Sustained

In programme after programme, in every sphere of developmental intervention, with every conceivable model or strategy, the outstanding common feature of outcomes is that in an alarmingly large number of cases the achievements are not sustained. The problem is manifest in different ways and reported in different terms; e.g.:

* Dramatic change in the first year, but backsliding later.

* The agency departed, and everything returned to the original condition.
* So much time and effort is required to keep the achievements propped up.

To regard all these cases as comprising a high 'failure rate' would perhaps be uncharitable, even simplistic. While we cannot claim to have a duly researched explanation for the phenomenon, at least the starting hypotheses would be:

* A small percentage of these cases can probably be explained by microlevel processes, such as a sort of Hawthorne effect (i.e., the very act of attending to a chronically underattended group brings about short-term changes).
* A larger percentage of these cases can probably be explained by the macrolevel processes, such as the absence of appropriate social institutions (or the presence of negating social institutions and vested interests).

The outcome situations listed above are meant to illustrate the general problem of the *context* influencing the process of development interventions on the one hand and their outcomes on the other hand. It is not claimed to be an exhaustive listing. We may consider other types of difficulties and even attempt a more purposeful classificatory scheme for them. For the present, from the review so far, we might note at least two broad categories of conditions in the societal context which can affect the course of development interventions:

* The realm of political economy of the society, through such macroparameters as choice of technology, investment priorities and geopolitical alignments.
* The adequacy or otherwise of social institutions to sustain the development process in the directions taken.

In turn, these conditions may be seen as the principal sources of the conceptual and methodological problems in PE.

Beyond Context: More Issues

So far we have identified some issues in PE that arise on account of the more direct bearing that features of the societal context seem to have on the development process. They also manifest themselves as pitfalls in PE practice.

There are also some recurring difficulties in methodology, some unanswered questions, some unarticulated questions. These difficulties might be regarded as universal, not specially manifest in the development context. Nevertheless, it is quite important to come to grips with them in development interventions.

Short-term vs. Long-term Outcomes

The time perspective adopted for PE may be very important; i.e., the distinction, often not made, between the immediately observable effects of an intervention and effects over later cycles of events. Consider the introduction of the 'Amul model' milk cooperative in two very similar villages in the same district:

* First order effects in approximately six to eight months, similar in both villages: a rise in household incomes.
* Second order effects in about fifteen to eighteen months. Village 1 typically ploughs back disposable income into cooperative operations. Village 2 diverts it to other consumptions, notably in cloth/clothing, popular durables, liquor.
* Third order effects in about twenty-five to thirty months. The two villages differ significantly in indices of health and education. There is, further, higher economic insecurity in Village 2, bringing in older moneylending practices that were thought 'eradicated' earlier.
* Fourth order effects in about thirty-six to forty months. A voluntary agency documents important differences in 'quality of life' in the two villages.

Which PE over the forty months was more 'correct'? More 'valid'?

Integration among Outcomes

In the example above, it must be clear that as we move up from indices of change in the first cycle of events to later cycles,

* more and more spheres of community behaviour get inter-related, i.e., integrated into institutionalized patterns of behaviour;
* community values are invoked in upholding these larger wholes of behaviour patterns.

In the beginning, for instance, there is only the common *belief* in both communities that the milk co-operative is worthwhile. By about the second year we have the same belief in both communities, but as ingredients in two quite different *attitudes* to expenditure from profit. Later, the two sets of beliefs and attitudes are seen as parts of two quite different *values* regarding community life.

Is PE capable of (*a*) sensing the integrated wholes, and (*b*) subjecting them to systematic assessment, or does it stick to single dimensions, one at a time, in a limited repertoire?

Product Outcomes vs. Process Outcomes

A related problem area in PE is also a major challenge in the development context. Once a programme is formulated, an operational definition of the objectives of the programme is usually discernible, sometimes implied, sometimes made explicit. These are, typically, the *product* outcomes, conceivable in numerical terms—e.g., the number of children matriculating, the increase in crop yield, the caloric intake and so on. Few programmes visualize or deliberately plan the assessment of *process* outcomes—the less observable and not so easily quantifiable states of self-sufficiency, increased confidence, decreased prejudice, intergroup co-operation and so on.

Two common assumptions in the distinction between product and process outcomes are:

1. Process outcomes are necessarily 'qualitative' (vs. products necessarily quantifiable).
2. Process outcomes are invariably 'subjective' (vs. products invariably objective).

Both these assumptions may need serious re-examination.

Whose Need? Conflicting Expectations of Outcome

'We see things not as they are but as we are.' PE too cannot really be independent of the perceptual scheme, the eye of the beholder. The principal interest parties in evaluation would be:

* The donor agency—governmental or NGO.
* The implementing agency, programme/project holders—again, governmental or NGO.
* The beneficiaries, people themselves.
* The professional evaluation researcher—internal or external.
* Perhaps the tax-payers too, if they could have a say.

Can their perspectives be the same, especially in the articulation of *objectives* and *criteria*? What happens when a donor agency calls for an evaluation, and the project agency calls in an outsider professional to undertake the task, and the three have quite different criteria, based on the more fundamental differences in conviction of what constitutes development?

Technology and Social Organization

A development programme introduces both:

* *A technical system*—materials, tools, techniques.
* *A social system*—organizational forms, roles, relationships, deemed appropriate to implement the technical system.

What we have as the intervention programme is really the *composite package* in which the technical and social components are indistinguishable—the immunization programme, the fisheries development programme, the rural transmission programme, and so on. When things go awry and we see dysfunctional outcomes, are we evaluating:

* The technology?
* The social organization?
* The composite package?

Is it possible, for instance, that the same (or modified) technology deployed with an alternative social organization might have had more purposeful outcomes?

System Levels of Change and Assessment

The guts of any intervention programme, it is said, are in changed behaviours. But *what* do we observe as behaviours relevant to change, and *how* do we assess them?

The methodological problem here arises from the fact that the behavioural characteristics of a group are not arithmetical aggregates of the individual parts. Thus the 'family planning behaviour' is relevant as a concept at the 'system level' of the couple, and not at the level of either the man or the woman separately. Likewise, 'teamwork' and 'authoritarianism' are concepts that are understood best at the system levels of group and community, rather than as sums of individual predispositions. Young fieldworkers are always amazed when an opinion is expressed consistently in individual meetings, but the consensus in the group meeting turns dramatically otherwise. (And vice versa.) Much of the 'data' gathered by us in the field by conventional tools and techniques is really at the system level of the individual. The statistics of central tendencies from a number of individuals do not necessarily pertain to the characteristics sought at the levels of group, intergroup and community behaviours.

Manifest Levels of Change

When do we say that the 'input' from a programme has 'worked'? The literature in training evaluation has something significant to say about this, and PE practice may find useful parallels in its own efforts to define and assess change. It is said that change may be assessed at four different *manifest levels*:

* Reaction; i.e., what the people concerned say, how they felt about the programme, how they perceived it—useful data, but no guarantee that there will be any difference in changed behaviours.

* Learning; i.e., the observable/measurable difference in levels of actual knowledge, skills, understanding and so on—something more than the mere opinions at the first level, but still no guarantee for changed behaviours.
* Performance; i.e., actual changes in behaviour, from one practice to another, or in an entirely new area of practice—but still incomplete, because the actual desired outcomes may be beyond 'performance' alone, dependent on other systems, other groups.
* Outcome; i.e., when the *system objectives* are fulfilled—increased earnings, decreased inequality, greater self-reliance and so on.

Internal vs. External Validity

Since one important function in PE is to establish a causal association between programme inputs and the observed outcomes, the question of replicability of the change process is inevitable. The continuing debate on the question reveals two typical positions taken.

Case Specific Intervention: The position taken is: 'We do not know enough about the change process in large, complex social systems. This intervention is specific to the case at hand, aimed at a specific problem area, with a specific diagnosis. We can legitimately judge only whether the specific goals identified were accomplished or not, according to the specific indicators identified.' This refers to the internal validity of the intervention.

Generalization in Interventions: 'Social programmes are expensive, and undertaking them is a great responsibility. It is important to minimize groping and coping with uncertainties in such programmes. We need evidence of causal associations for the class of interventions of which this programme is one specimen. Has it worked elsewhere, and will it work in other similar cases?' This refers to the external validity of the intervention.

Some Grey Areas: Other Issues

In the issues examined so far we might have noticed a possible two-way classification:

* Primarily methodological issues, but with implications for concepts in evaluation research.
* Primarily conceptual issues, but with implications for methodology.

There are some other questions in PE that are difficult to fit into the two-way classification. These are in the realm of development theory and, perhaps, professional ethics. There may, in fact, be no single criterion to hold these issues together in one category. They might be examined separately too.

Choice of Programme and Criteria of Success

In development (as in any other intervention—therapy, industrial reconstruction, education, training), is it possible that we tend to take up, consciously or unconsciously, those cases in which we perceive a greater probability of success? Is there a 'theory' of development behind such a choice? What are the ideological and philosophical implications of such a force at work in a society? Can PE criteria be the same for interventions in low risk ('more likely to benefit') as well as high risk ('disadvantaged') cases?

Professionalization in PE

It is often argued that for a truly objective and constructive role, PE must be organizationally separate from the project implementation, e.g., as quality control is separated from production. It can be a specialized cell within the project agency or even an outsider specialist service. The counter-argument demands attention too: If PE is not an organic part of the development intervention, it can be prostituted. It must rely on the project agency to direct it on criteria and measures, and may therefore be oblivious to alternatives in criteria, observations, measures, interpretations. In other words, professionalization of PE itself might result paradoxically in its becoming a handmaiden to the project agency. The implications appear particularly significant when large governmental programmes carry a stated 'development' objective, but in reality amount to welfare/relief/alleviation actions. PE is almost invariably in terms of 'targets' of disbursement and the statistics reported tend to endorse the 'success' of the programme. But has 'development' taken place? Or has it in fact been retarded? Or worse, have we ensured by accident or design that the continued dependency serves some other purpose?

Participatory Methods

The connotative meanings of the term participation tend to be generally positive, acceptable, appealing, and consonant with a broader democratic value system. However, a closer examination of the more specialized terms, such as participatory research, participatory evaluation, and participatory development, reveal that within that general predisposition there are in fact several different ways in which the terms are used with several important distinctions among them. Some questions that arise from these differences are important.

* At what level of practice is the 'method' truly participatory?
  - At the level of tools/techniques that elicit the *responses* of the people concerned?
  - At the level of *involvement* of the people concerned in the development process? Including the planning process?
  - At the level of *empowerment* of the people concerned to develop themselves?

  It must be evident that all three levels of operation exist in actual practice among the large and growing number of project agencies adopting participatory methodology.
* A related question is: Is participation an end or means? If the latter, then means to what ends?
* Following from the above: Can there be a reasoned social cost benefit analysis of a pure process-oriented intervention, such as the empowerment of a beneficiary group?
* Finally, the larger theoretical question: Can participation be, perhaps, oppressive? In other words, when the ends of an intervention programme are predetermined, i.e., the 'desired' states in health, education, skills, etc., is there real self-determination in the beneficiary group? Further, what if self-determined ends of the beneficiary group are unacceptable to the agency? Does intervention then provide participation or a 'sense of participation'? Precisely because the general rubric

of participatory methodology is so rich in content, and so promising as a model, we need to understand it more wholly.

Value Conflicts in Interventions

In an earlier section we regarded the possible consequences of conflicting expectations of outcome of different interest groups, i.e., the PE task finds itself in multiple value fields. An equally difficult but less easily identifiable situation arises when there are value conflicts *within* the same field. For instance:

* One part of a community development project reinforces one value position, say, *competitiveness* ('achievement motivation'), including a manipulative world-view, and it conflicts with another value position, say, *co-operation*, including openness/authenticity in community transactions.
* The project agency belongs to an ideological/religious group that does not permit participation in the family planning component of a larger community health programme.

Identity Conflict in the Project Agency

The starting condition for an NGO to come into being in the first place is usually a combination of (*a*) dissatisfaction with the 'mainstream', and (*b*) conviction in an alternative approach or methodology. 'To be different' is therefore an important motivation force that keeps the prime mover of the NGO active. On the other hand the NGO depends considerably on external funding. And meeting the criteria set forth by funding agencies, governmental or private, amounts to 'conforming' to the expectations of another party, a conflicting motivational force. The conflict is a very real one, with very real, serious consequences. The problem is compounded when the NGO accepts funding from multiple sources, with different, conflicting criteria. Conforming, then, combines with compromises on stands taken, positions held, methods upheld and so on. For instance, a donor agency introduces an emphasis on 'gender' in its funding policy. Predictably, the project proposal from the NGO then includes a section on gender in its statement of objectives or action plan or in a questionnaire design. In another project proposal sent to another agency there is a section on income generation around a craft that actually leads to greater gender inequality. To call this phenomenon a bandwagon rush might be convenient, but it would be a somewhat unsympathetic verdict if we do not separate the more opportunistic proposals from the conflict-ridden ones.

Where do We Go from Here?

Theory in Practice

If we regard this review exercise as a fresh examination of theory and methodology in programme evaluation, the reaction might well be: 'Theory in programme evaluation? We can take a look at methodology, because we do face difficulties in assessing changes sought, but where is the theory in PE?' The question reflects the viewpoint that PE is nothing but a technique repertoire, and that the right technique mix for a given evaluation task is all that matters. If we recall that 'there is nothing so practical as good theory', we will see that PE practice, too, calls for theoretical support of two types:

* Within measurement. Establishing the validity of measures employed—the question of *what* we are assessing through the numbers and indices before us.
* Between measurement and objectives. Establishing the relevance of the measures for the objectives and concepts of development adopted—the question of *why* we are seeking these numbers and indices.

When PE seeks to assess, for instance, the extent of improvement in the community's standard of health, and chooses, say, the infant mortality rate as an index for the purpose, there are two theoretical premises for the choice of the index:

* It is a valid index of the community's health.
* It is a relevant index of the development process, *via* a health programme.

Likewise, another programme may adopt 'emergent local leadership' as an appropriate criterion. What do we observe, and how do we convert that into a numerical index of this leadership? And why?

If we recognize the intimate (and inevitable) bond between theory and method for purposeful practice, then the real sense of the term *methodology* might be better appreciated, including the need for *internal consistency among specific tools and techniques employed*.

The task before us in the review of PE practice may also be seen as stemming from the inadequacies perceived (and dissatisfactions experienced) in actual practice. The most pressing concern is usually regarding the compatibility between assumptions of development and the ways to assess outcomes from interventions for that development.

Levels of Abstraction

When an agency expects a benefit for a targeted group from specific project inputs, what might be the *intervention rationale*? Different projects and agencies reveal different extents of abstraction regarding the rationale. For convenience we might identify three distinct levels of reasoning, ranging from the more 'peripheral' to the more 'central' in abstraction:

* Assumption—usually at the level of simplistic positions about what ought to be done.
* Theory—usually at the level of conviction of what should work.
* Ideology—usually at the level of values, or conviction of what is right.

The level of abstraction in intervention rationale is really an attribute of the *agency*, manifest in its projects and programmes in various ways. For instance, activity specific statements with several differences between projects is probably a reflection of a relatively 'peripheral' position, while consistent reference to certain desired states in society over several projects and programmes is more likely a 'central' position.

Is level of abstraction manifest only in intervention rationale? Is it possible that there will be *corresponding* levels of abstraction in the (*a*) expected outcome and (*b*) methodology adopted? For instance, a project may seek

* 'product' outcomes, or
* 'process' outcomes, or
* the emergence of appropriate social institutions as outcomes.

Do these expectations of outcome correspond, perhaps, to the levels of abstraction in intervention rationale?

Towards an Integration

In Figure 2.2 we have attempted to depict the theory–methodology framework, incorporating the levels of abstraction, in four lines of manifestation. The framework is not necessarily complete. The main purpose of the figure is to suggest that there must be some compatibility across concept, criteria, comparison and time frame (among other things) in terms of the level of abstraction. Too 'central' a level in methodology would be an overkill for a project with a simplistic assumption about its purpose. On the other hand, a project with a strong ideological base—possibly one of several endeavours of the agency—would have no patience with the peripheral offerings in methodology.

Theory–Method Clusters?

In Figure 2.2 we see how crucial the *expected outcome* is in the total intervention–evaluation framework:

* It seeks clarity of *concept* in the intervention.
* It sets *criteria* for change.
* It seeks certain kinds of *comparison*, in a certain *time frame*, to establish change.

However, much of our earlier analysis has suggested the significance of context both in shaping interventions and in evaluating outcomes. The intervention rationale in Figure 2.2 might itself be a function of several factors operating in the given context.

In other words, the actual content of PE assessment may be viewed in terms of a 'method mix'. The attributes that can comprise a method mix are not difficult to identify. Figure 2.3 combines the ideas above to depict (*a*) how the criteria in PE might be influenced

Figure 2.2: **A FRAMEWORK FOR PE METHODOLOGY**

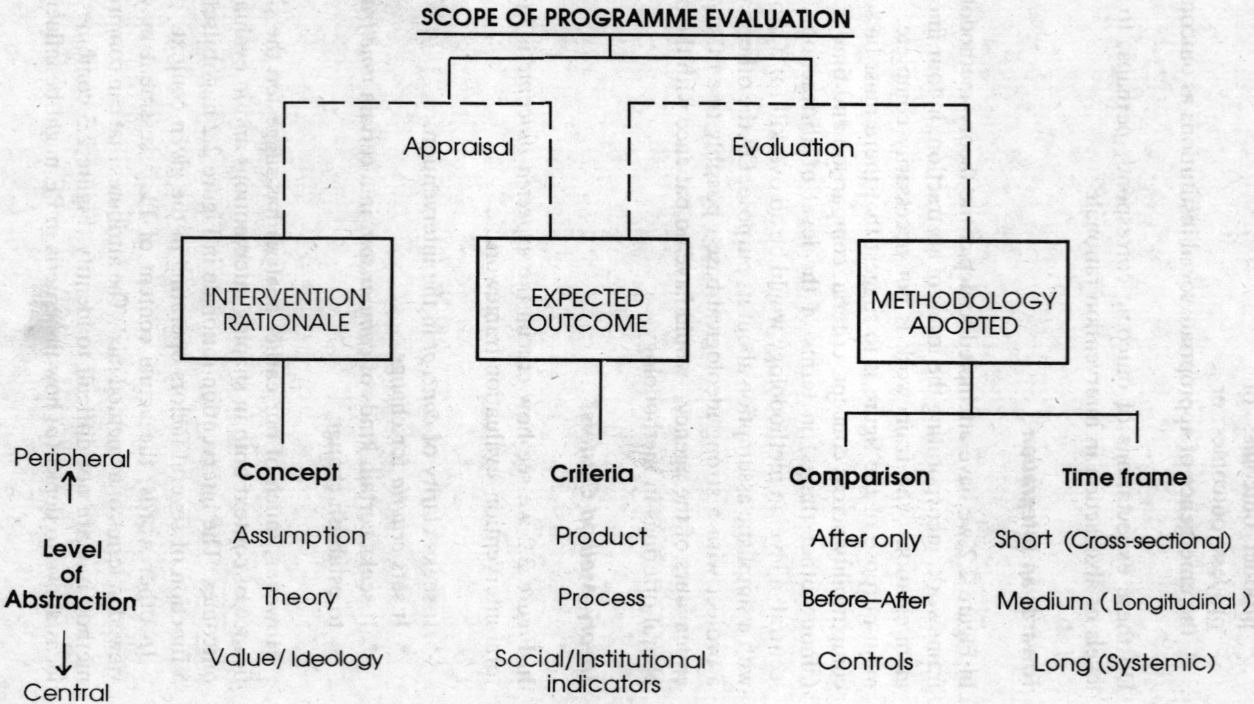

Figure 2.3: **CRITERIA AND METHODOLOGY IN PE**

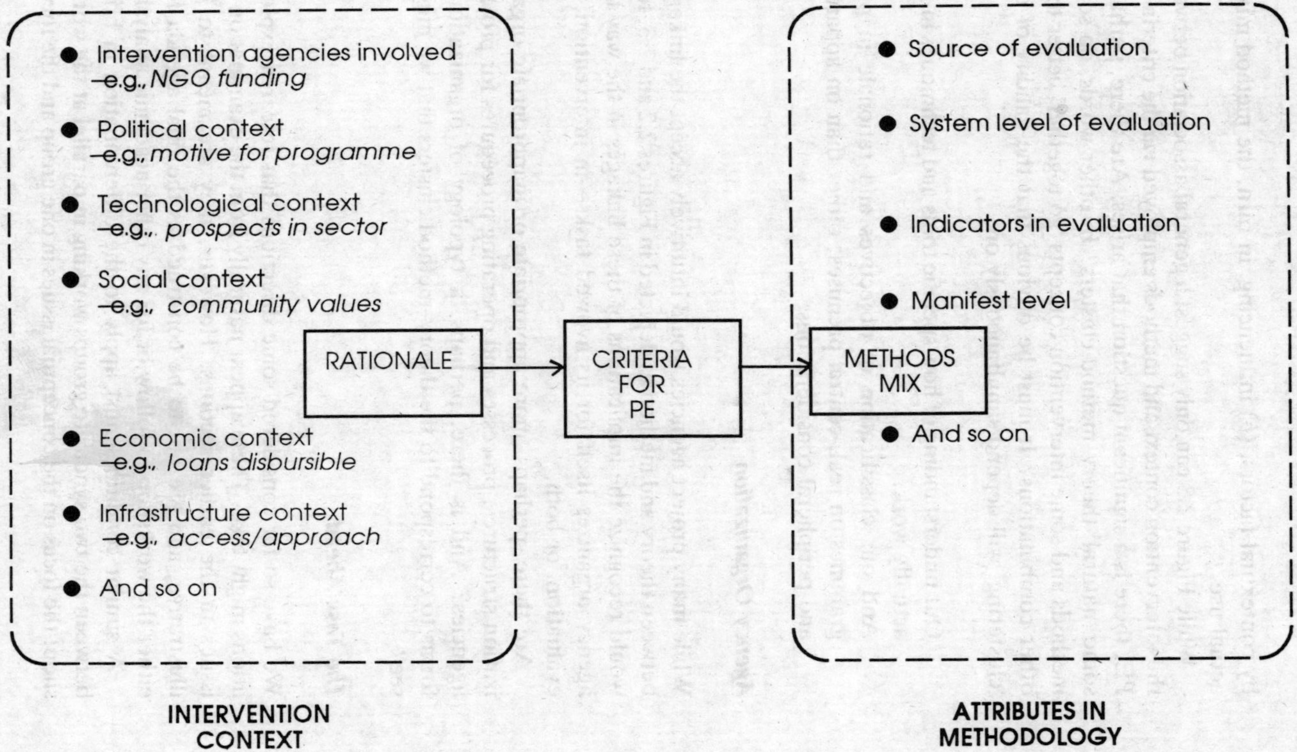

by contextual factors, (*b*) influencing, in turn, the method mix in actual use.

While Figure 2.3 can only suggest a general association between the intervention context and methods employed *via* the criteria for PE, there is a significant question that arises: Are there, perhaps, some 'natural' theory–method clusters? In other words, do some methods and some intervention concepts 'go together' better than other combinations? It must be obvious that the validity of our 'clustering' will depend simultaneously on:

* Our understanding of how specific tools and techniques in PE actually work.
* And our classification of objectives and rationale in programmes on real, central premises, rather than on apparent and peripheral considerations.

Agency Organization

While many project agencies would intuitively accept the linkages between theory and method as depicted in Figures 2.2 and 2.3, few would recognize the implications of these linkages in the way the agency organizes itself for its avowed tasks—in intervention, in evaluation, or both.

Are there, perhaps, more appropriate or inappropriate organization structures, processes and operating procedures for project agencies? And is there, perhaps, a typology of organizational forms to correspond to the theory–method clusters that we might see?

The Task Ahead

We have so far considered some directions that research explorations might take. These appear naturally from the examination of issues in the earlier sections. However, they are meant to be illustrative, and are not to be construed as the final agenda for either the workshop to follow or for any other academic analysis.

A similar condition must apply to the differentiation in brief between the two syndicate groups working in parallel at the workshop: the focus on the conceptual issues in one group and the focus on methodological issues in the other group are only the starting points for an ultimate integration. Each must examine the conclusions in its own sphere for their implications in the other sphere. What comes out of this search for integration is best seen at the workshop itself.

Three

Exploring Alternatives in Methodology*

Vijay Padaki

Intervention and Evaluation

The Theory–Methodology Bind

The re-examination of PE methodology and the search for alternatives must consider simultaneously:

1. The contextual features identified as significant in the intervention.
2. And the concept of development itself towards which the intervention is initiated.

The workshop recognized the theory–methodology bind early in its deliberations. The two syndicate groups working thereafter had the following common premises:

* *What* we look for in PE and *how* we go about the evaluation task cannot be independent of the underlying assumptions in a programme of what constitutes development.
* The value premises of a development programme are discernible in both the *content* and the *process* of the development

---

* Summary of proceedings of the workshop to review theory and methodology in programme evaluation.

programme. PE methodology which claims to be value neutral also has a high probability, ironically, of being 'co-opted'; i.e., of evaluating a programme from the given (limited) perspective, rather than examining all options, all consequences.

* It is possible to visualize and spell out an *alternative framework* for the development process which attempts to curb the destructive and dysfunctional outcomes seen in many programmes today and, at the same time, seeks a social transformation with defined, purposive objectives.
* Such an alternative framework will include at least two important and complementary features:

  ○ *Alternative value premises* to guide the content and process of development programmes.
  ○ An *alternative methodology* that is valid for the content and process sought.

With the groundwork accomplished, the workshop proceeded with more detailed explorations in two parallel streams: conceptual and methodological issues. What follows is a summary report of the two syndicate groups in the workshop, and the implications for action from their integration.

Figure 3.1 is a diagrammatic representation of the events leading up to the action implications presented.

Résumé of Syndicate One: Conceptual Position

* The group began with an examination of the concept of evaluation. It was clear that this concept was inseparable from the concept (and the underlying assumptions) of development, which in turn demanded an examination of such questions and issues as:

  ○ Trends in social transformation
  ○ Basic needs versus minimum needs in defined groups of people
  ○ Control and use of resources for equitable outcomes
  ○ Ecological balance in development

Figure 3.1: **WORKSHOP PROCESS SEARCH FOR MEANINGFULNESS IN DEVELOPMENT INTERVENTIONS**

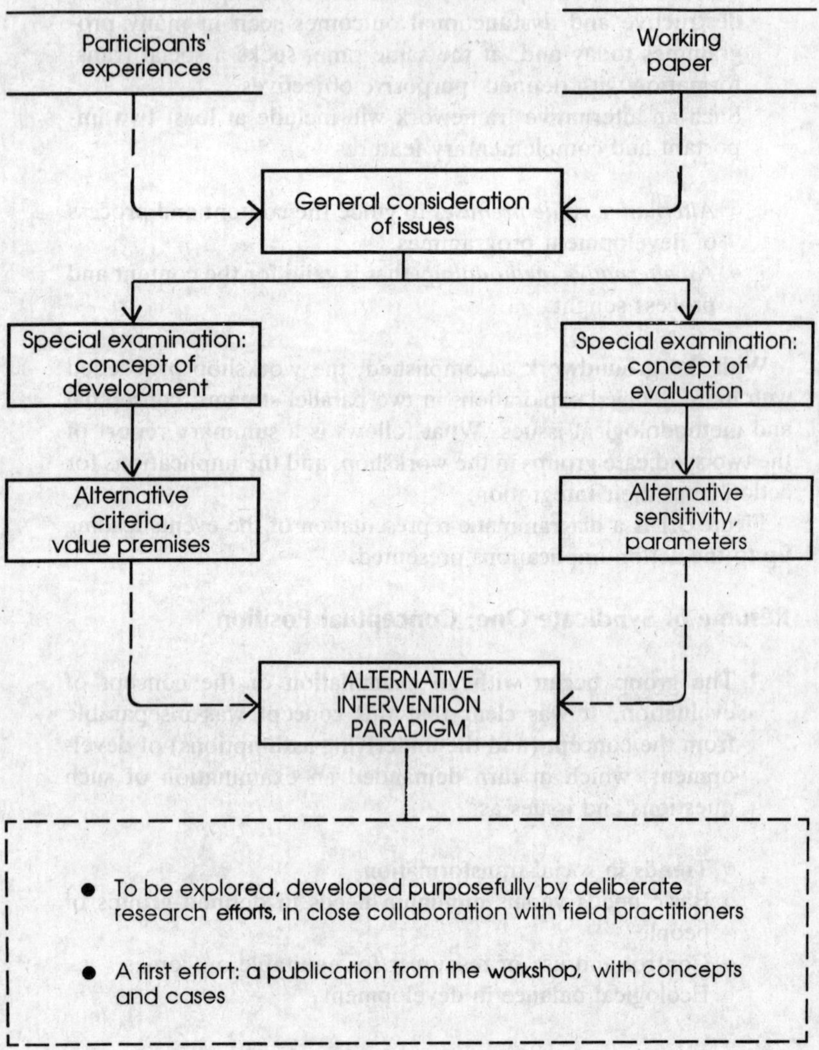

The concept of *sustainable development* appeared sufficiently wide to include most of the concerns noted.

* The nature of social transformation in sustainable development will call for, on the one hand, a serious re-examination of the objectives and their rationale in several nationwide programmes and, on the other hand, an undeniable emphasis on *empowerment* and self-determination at different levels of social organization.
* Evaluation was seen as *integral to the process of social transformation*. In other words the objectives of PE had to be consistent with the objectives of the development intervention, aiding it in (*a*) improving the content of a programme over cycles of work, and (*b*) providing feedback to policy for other, similar, programmes.
* Following from the above, while the specific information needs of parties involved in the development programme might be different, e.g., the change agency (NGO or governmental), the beneficiary community, or the funding agency, it should be possible to aim at *compatibility* across the different information systems. This calls for a deliberate effort towards a shared vision of the development process.
* One obvious way to achieve the compatibility will be to visualize the entire evaluation exercise and all its facets *at the time of programme formulation*, rather than on a piecemeal, as-and-when basis.
* The *NGO role* is likely to continue to be important in the diffusion of the visualized development process. The role may be in different capacities, e.g., on their own, assisting in the implementation of governmental programmes, or as adjunct organizations providing technical/support services. In any capacity, their contribution to programme planning and, therefore, to evaluation design must be recognized as valuable.
* The issues raised in the working paper, stemming largely from the special contextual features in a developing society, are very real, influencing both the process of social transformation and PE practice in significant ways. Yet, there is no explicit treatment of these issues in any formal training for PE. *There is an urgent need for academic material and*

pedagogical aids to prepare PE professionals with the alternative perspective.

* The group consolidated the above observations in a perspective statement titled 'The Development Vision', which is reproduced below.

The Development Vision

Development is a complex, multifaceted process of social transformation, including as necessary conditions:

* The satisfaction of basic needs, starting with the needs of the neediest.
* The capability to resist the forces of destruction and inequality inherent in many forms of modernization.
* Increasing knowledge and awareness of the macroenvironment, simultaneous with the concern for local, regional and national issues.
* Voluntary participation in, and control of, programmes and projects of economic development by local people, and thereby a reduction in dependence on remote and external bodies.
* Ecological harmony, in that resources are conserved and pollution controlled in the interests of the long-term sustainability of the development process.
* The accrual to local people of the benefits of large projects, in a process in which such benefits then spread outwards to the region and nation.

These, it is reiterated, are the necessary, not the sufficient, conditions for development, which above all is a process of empowerment of the people.

The concept of PE must therefore be integral with the desirability of these features in any developmental intervention, and the need to assess the extent to which they are achieved or negated in the programme.

Further, since interventions involve several interest parties, such as the beneficiary group, the funding agency, the facilitator NGO, the policy analyst, the taxpayer, etc., *the challenge before social science research for development is the building of a knowledge base and dissemination for a shared vision of the development process.*

Résumé of Syndicate Two: Methodological Position

There were two broad stages in this group's deliberations. In the first stage, the group attempted to identify all the conditions and variables that influence the content and conduct of PE. The object of this exercise was to examine the extent to which the content of programme evaluation might inadvertently be method-bound or contextbound. In the second stage the group examined illustrative cases and experiences to seek generalizations towards innovative alternatives in methodology.

Conditions in Conventional PE

The term *methodology* is not to be equated with a method or technique in research. It is best understood as a composite of tools and techniques, the nature of data collected, the analysis attempted, and the inferences sought—all internally consistent in rationale, for a given set of objectives and the context of enquiry. Thus a survey research methodology has an internal consistency for a given context, which is different from an ethnographic methodology, with its own internal consistency, in its own contextual conditions.

The appropriateness of tools and techniques in a PE methodology would be determined by several contextual conditions, such as:

Interest Group Represented

* Programme administration
* Funding agency
* Beneficiary group
* 'Taxpayer' (other than the beneficiary)
* Special interest group
* 'Independent' or 'professional' PE agency

Stage of Programme

* Formulation
* Concurrent
* Summative
* Feedback to policy

Assumed Role of the Evaluator

* Reporter
* Observer
* Facilitator
* Participant

System Level of Analysis

* Group of individuals
* Community
* Village
* Taluka
* Higher system levels

Nature of Programme Input

Several classificatory schemes may be applied, with a focus on the *primary activity* chosen for intervention, e.g., health care, education, technology, community organization, etc. However, as far as the effects on PE content were concerned, it was found convenient to simply dichotomize all cases of programme input into (*a*) conventional (or typical) and (*b*) atypical, i.e., inputs demanding innovative devices and indices.

Temporal Frame for Assessment

* Cross-sectional vs. longitudinal
* Short-term change vs. long-term impact

World-view as a General Factor

It was seen that a prevailing world-view could also influence the content and conduct of PE. It may be:

* Articulated or implied
* Consciously or unconsciously applied
* Strongly held or flexible

In fact the world-view may be manifest to different degrees in one or more of the other variables already identified.

Is there a valid classification of world-views? Would the classification differ significantly from the categories of 'value system' or 'political ideology'? Would the classification correspond ('correlate') with a typology of PE methods? It was seen that these and similar questions were important, but it was impractical to seek answers to all of them in the workshop. Indeed, a classification of world-views might itself be determined by a world-view, and might therefore tell us more about the classifier than about what was being classified. It appeared pragmatic, however, to visualize a *method mix* that had a more natural fit with the *context mix* provided by the variables considered so far. The working paper, too, had suggested a similar association. The significant question then would be: Are there some natural theory–method *clusters*? In other words, do some methods and some intervention concepts 'go together' better than other combinations? For instance:

* If the intervention discards the concepts of risk and probability of success ('bankable proposition'), and opts to meet the basic needs of the neediest through an income generation activity, would indices derived from the concept of 'growth', (such as market penetration) be helpful?
* If the intervention is a 'blueprint' and 'targeted' programme—not to be faulted just because it is so—would a participatory technique implying self-determination be helpful?

The Development Image

'The eye cannot see what the mind does not know.' An alternative development vision, as proposed by the first workshop syndicate, can be companioned only by an alternative image.

It became increasingly clear that the wide repertoire of indices available in 'conventional' PE were held together by a common set of contextual conditions. They produced, correspondingly, a common image. They had emerged in a given historical context, meeting the requirements of PE in that context, and yielded the corresponding tools and techniques. Development interventions, as defined and examined in the workshop, are in contexts with genuinely different, unique features. They make special demands on methodology, including the constituent tools, techniques and analyses. The alternative methodology must therefore have as its central concern

An Alternative Sensitivity

to various characteristics of the development process in that context.

All evaluation focusses on certain defined *attributes* in the phenomenon under study. Tools/techniques developed for the study are required to possess the sensitivity to detect and assess the attributes in question. It is entirely feasible to identify some *essential* attributes in the development process to which the alternative methodology must be sensitive. The group identified the following attributes as a sampler, and substantiated each of them with (*a*) actual field illustrations and (*b*) possible ways to assess changing states in them.

Historical/longitudinal Process in the System

In social dysfunctions (as much as in individual afflictions), symptomatology is purposeful only if viewed in a longitudinal time frame, i.e., historically. The intervention as well as the evaluation must be sensitive to the realities of past and present vested interests, the perpetrating mechanisms, and the institutionalized forces in the perpetration.

Future Courses from Trends in the System

A community being freed from bonded labour might have the same needs of sustenance as a community of tribals being relocated following a dam construction project. However, since they have arrived at the state of deprivation from two different routes, their responses to any standard 'treatment' are likely to be quite different too.

The Systemic Effects of Interventions

Social interventions rarely, if ever, produce simple, unidimensional, cause-and-effect changes. Unforeseen effects, though numerous, are often kept out of PE on grounds of their being outside the given brief. In the development context, it must be admitted at the start that project appraisals and systems analyses have several imperfections. Valid generalizations are few, and tested models mythical. Under the circumstances, the *action research* path is unavoidable. The very origins of action research were in a theoretical perspective that can be called, for convenience, the systems view.

Social Institutions to Sustain Planned Change

Social interventions set up (*a*) technical systems and/or (*b*) social organizations. The survival, growth and effectiveness of the induced changes depend on a 'superordinate' system, the appropriate social institution. More often than not, the intervention does not envisage the setting up or strengthening of the institutional forms, over and above the specific organization for the specific programme input. The organizational set-ups are designed to deal with the operational objectives. Social institutions uphold the community's value system. Until the operational objectives become consonant with an accepted value system as well, the required institutional form may not emerge, and the programme may not get too far.

The Role of the Beneficiary Group in the Intervention Process

For the beneficiary group as well as for the intervention agency, it is crucial to know the effort being made by the community to develop itself. This effort may be visualized on an active–passive continuum, although the initiative itself might have originated from outside.

The Process Outcomes from the Intervention must have Far Greater Priority in PE than the Product Outcomes

Motivation, confidence, leadership emergence, group cohesion, value shifts—these and similar process parameters in the development programme are the crucial attributes for assessment. For the continuity and long-term sustenance of the programme, these assessments may in fact be more reliable than the numbers and statistics connected with the product outcomes. Social psychological research literature, in particular, appears to offer several valuable leads to develop valid methods in these directions.

Optimality of Resource Use in the Programme

Many programmes, at least in the initial years, amount to the mobilization of a tank squadron to kill a fieldmouse. The statistics of the dead mouse are all that matter. Could there have been a simpler, safer, more ecologically sound method, one which used and developed local resources?

Two reminders should be useful before we pass on. The attributes of social change listed above are a suggested sampler, and not purported to be a complete list. Secondly, we have seen that each of these attributes is indeed real, relevant to the PE task, and systematically assessable. The key word is sensitivity.

The Challenge Before Social Science Research for Development is to Develop Tools and Techniques to Meet These and Similar Requirements of Alternative Sensitivity.

Pointers for Research and Action

We shall begin by reminding ourselves of the principal objective of this workshop report:

> To facilitate recognition of the unhelpful character of much of conventional PE methodology in the special context of development, and to promote innovation towards alternatives in PE practice.

From the review of PE experience and the workshop discussion so far, it seems possible to tease out three general lessons. We shall enunciate these first, and then consider an illustrative sample of specific experimental measures that may be taken up in following them.

Lesson One

Improvements and innovations in programme *evaluation* methodology must be matched by improvements and innovations in programme *management*, including the policy aspects of management. An alternative PE methodology will be incompatible with a conventional programme administration.

Lesson Two

There is a tremendous need to provide agencies in development administration, including governmental agencies, with a more comprehensive appreciation of programme evaluation methodology, especially the scope for innovations in a development context.

Lesson Three

There is a tremendous need for social and behavioural science researchers to undertake work in the area of PE innovation towards valid alternatives in PE methodology, and for the social science institutions to encourage such research pursuits.

Now, let us consider an illustrative sample of actions that follow from the above:

1. An intervention programme has, typically, three or more interest parties involved:

    * The programme administrator—often also the funder, often a governmental agency.
    * The programme implementor—often an NGO, sometimes another governmental agency.
    * The researcher–analyst agency—often in an advisory, adjunct, capacity.
    * The beneficiary group—often identified by the programme administration in advance, along with programme content.

The operational (or 'instrumental') objectives of the groups may differ naturally. So would their specific information needs differ. But can the *goals of the programme* be different for the different agencies involved?

A good *programme organization* is thus a prime requirement for effective development intervention. The organization must promote processes of consonance across the interest parties. The desired organizational processes must be ensured well in advance through appropriate structures, including innovations in organizational design.

2. One important process in development interventions, in the best sense of action research, is *open analysis*, including increasing levels of process awareness among all parties concerned. The quality of organizational communication and the nature of information flows must benefit from structural innovations.
3. Many different types of information are needed for the various tasks in PE. They may originate in specific quarters, in specific terms. Organizational structures must promote the communication processes of *dialogue, joint interpretation, and shared decision-making*. Organization for PE must be integral with programme organization.
4. Underlying any PE procedure—as well as a larger management information system (MIS)—is an assumption of *accountability*. Although seldom made explicit, the presumption is that accountability is to 'he who pays the piper'. Let us examine an alternative set-up. Let us propose that the programme is accountable to the people—the beneficiary group. What, then, would be the consequences for

   * organization structures,
   * MIS,
   * data collection and information processing,
   * PE methodology?

5. Whoever might be the various interest parties in a programme, and whatever their number, the *nature of information* that must flow for PE should be of two broad types:

   * To benefit the programme itself (typically through concurrent modes).

* To provide feedback for policy and generalizations, to benefit other programmes (typically through summative modes).

Since the exact purposes are different, the information content can also be different. The audiences are different too—typically, the beneficiary group and the programme implementor for the first, and the researcher–analyst and the programme administrator for the second. How does a programme make the different types of information processing, with their different methods, compatible facets of one PE system?

6. Following from the above, it will be seen that in a given programme, the total PE system will comprise *four broad types of information*, requiring four somewhat different types of methods, tools and techniques.

		End Use	
		For Administration	*For the Programme*
Methods	Standard/ Conventional	(1)	(2)
	Innovative/ Alternative	(3)	(4)

Viewed this way, it must be clear that every programme organization can invest resources formally in the development of quadrants (3) and (4).

7. Explorations such as the above, however valuable in themselves, may remain scattered and underattended, especially since programme implementation is typically through diverse NGOs. *Networking* among various development programmes would ensure (*a*) information consolidation and (*b*) generalizations for policy. An apex agency can play a very useful role in providing the institutional facility for such a networking, at least for the government sponsored programmes.
8. The methodology debate in PE commonly deals with such *dichotomized positions* as:

* Subjective vs. objective measures
* Qualitative vs. quantitative indices
* Process vs. product outcomes
* Internal vs. external assessment

Further, we *assume* an intercorrelation among these dichotomized pairs; e.g., that a process measure is necessarily qualitative and (therefore) necessarily subjective. Is this true? Must it be so? Are there not research procedures to establish the objectivity of qualitative assessments? And do we not know of quantitative assessments reeking of subjective biases? Fresh research in PE methodology must expose the unquestioned and fallacious bases of such notions, even as it rigorously develops reliable and valid measures as alternatives.

9. The *qualitative–quantitative* divide, especially, is a non-issue, even for those trained in the natural sciences. For in reality, in all scientific endeavour, *definition* and *measurement* form a dialectic couple, the one refining the other in a continuous cycle of events. No sophisticated measurement, in any scientific discipline, came off a tree. It began somewhere, some time, inevitably, as a good *description* of the phenomenon under study. What made it a respectable measurement system over time was a deliberate investment in research efforts to put the cycle into motion. In PE methodology, this will require an appreciative partnership between the researcher and the administrator.
10. A useful beginning is from *case research*. A large pool of well-researched case studies provides not only experiences for others to learn from, but also throws up leads and hypotheses for more focussed investigations.

    A 'case bank' would be invaluable. Case studies can serve both the purposes of

    * substantiating the relevance of specific techniques to the methodology for chosen criteria, and
    * revealing the inadequacies of techniques in mismatches between criteria and measures.
11. An area of growing significance for PE in the development context is all that is encompassed by the term *participatory*

methodology. Within the general rubric are discernible several streams of thought, several premises, as well as several questions and issues. If participation provides refreshing options for an intervention methodology, can it not provide a complementary research methodology that finds a legitimate and respectable place in programme administration and PE?

Perhaps we should stop here. The list of researchable and actionable areas can be very long indeed. It is not the objective of this report to provide an exhaustive list. That must come from the field. The working paper referred to earlier raised many questions. The workshop could do justice to only one subset of those questions. Yet, the emerging research agenda is long and formidable. There is tremendous scope. There is room for many to work simultaneously. There is a great need to undertake such work by design rather than by accident. There is some urgency to get going.

Appendix 3.1

The Workshop: Some Reflections by the Group

The subject was programme evaluation. There remains an undercurrent of uneasiness among most users of PE—researchers and fieldworkers—that a certain preoccupation with action tends to make one believe that we may do without evaluation. Might it not be applicable to the workshop exercise too?

The criteria for this stocktaking can only be our *expectations* from the workshop. It would be useful to recall these one by one and reflect on the achievements and shortfalls.

The *data* for the stocktaking is necessarily (*a*) subjective and (*b*) informally gathered—grave shortcomings by professional PE standards. However, this is compensated to some degree by (*a*) the absence of 'stakes' in the programme or 'threats' to future courses, and (*b*) our own endeavour to reflect on the workshop processes willingly, rather than as a requirement from outside.

Expectation 1: The *subject of PE* appears too specialized, too narrowly focussed. Yet, because of its intimate bind with any planned intervention, the assumptions of evaluation cannot be separated from the assumptions in development. The workshop had to reveal, and reinforce, this essential unity.

This was achieved to a great extent. In the second half of the second day the woods did appear more recognizable over the trees of technique and design which drew heavier attention in the first half of the first day.

Expectation 2: Academics/researchers and activists/fieldworkers have *two quite different perspectives*, different vocabularies. However, the twain can meet, must meet.

This too was achieved to a great extent. (In spite of the initial risk of the working paper appearing abstruse!) Indicated rather strongly by the patience with which either party heard the other—instead of polarizing into camps, as usually observed in such gatherings—and by their recognition of the truly complementary effort required to make the 'alternative methodology' work. The offer of case leads from activist participants was also a good indicator.

Expectation 3: The *workshop methodology* is as much a research mode as a conference mode. As a semi-structured enquiry, it can provide (*a*) a good reflection of the state of the art in a given area of effort, and (*b*) new leads and creative options for further work that might not occur to individual participants working by themselves. For this, it is very important that the proceedings are not steered in any desired direction, even subtly or unconsciously.

Achieved to a great extent. The alternative framework that emerged may be regarded as authentic, original, and in no way preconceived. Doubtless the output is yet rough, needing much elaboration and refinement, but its potential significance to social science research in India cannot be overlooked. An analysis suggests a few 'factors' that might have contributed to the success of the workshop methodology:

* The working paper. It was comprehensive. It pinpointed problems/issues that all recognized as familiar, but relegated to the subconscious. It was eclectic, yet concerned with action, dissatisfied with directionlessness.
* The working paper was only a starting point. It was not 'defended'. It demanded prescriptive alternatives from the participants themselves. (These features of the working paper were by design, not by accident.)
* The complementarity of analyses in the two syndicate groups was aided by the half-time conference of the two spokesmen, reporting back to their groups. (As a matter of fact, the deliberations in the group on methodology gelled rapidly only after the reporting.)
* Choice of participants, i.e., the criteria adopted for inviting participants to the project, emphasizing the task of strengthening interfaces.

Expectation 4: The idea of splitting into *two syndicate groups* was:

* To allow more intensive discussions in smaller groups.
* To cover more ground in limited time through a division of responsibilities.

But what should be the basis for the grouping? It might be said that the dichotomies we commonly observe—theory vs. practice, concept vs. methodology, analysis vs. action, etc.—were unhelpful to good PE, and should therefore be avoided. On the other hand, it could also be argued that these dichotomies had, perhaps, a common perceptual basis. Why not take it that the very act of seeking alternatives in PE methodology from polarized positions may reveal the limitations of those positions? The need for bridges would be felt.

We cannot talk of an 'achievement' in degree here. We can only reflect on the relevance of the concept–methodology bases for the two syndicate groups. In other words, it made sense. Again, some factors that might have helped:

* The deliberate brief to each group—including periodic, gentle reminders—to not only focus on the chosen thrust, but also examine the implications for the other side.
* The deliberate 'matched sample' basis for the grouping, ensuring heterogeneity rather than specialization within the two groups.

There were some shortcomings too. Some expectations that were not met:

1. We did not arrive at the theory–method clusters that we thought we would. The discussions in the two syndicate groups revealed that it was well within their experience to articulate and frame such a taxonomic scheme. If they chose not to, it might be a disappointment for the workshop organizers, but it must also be viewed as a more realistic reflection of the prevailing preoccupations and priorities among PE professionals. On the other hand, the 'alternative framework' that did emerge is both valid and a good indicator of felt needs, even if it is a long way before it can be developed into a full-fledged methodology.
2. We had insufficient participation from governmental agencies. Two participants happened to bring in the government perspective because of positions held previously, but it was not the cap worn.
3. We had no participant from a non-governmental funding agency. Two invitees from this quarter had to drop out just before the workshop date.
4. The case leads were by and large thin, inadequately prepared. The lesson was clear. The case method may mean more to the researcher than to the programme functionary. However, once the assistance was provided in the actual case studies, the end-products blossomed beautifully.

Appendix 3.2

EXAMPLE OF AN EVOLVING P E METHODOLOGY
From observation to analysis in a community development project

Stage/ duration	Nature of Stimulus	Nature of Observation	Nature of Analysis
(1) Approx. 2-3 weeks	Unstructured	Unstructured diary notes	Nil
2) Approx 5-6 weeks	Ad hoc meetings. 'inverted funnel' interviews	Incidents anecdotes, frames of reference	Content analysis
3) Approx. 10-12 weeks	Weekly get-together/review	Critical incidents, frequencies against categories	Trends in frequencies
4) Approx. 10-12 weeks	Role play, simulation	Prevailing states in -Locus of control -Individual/group orientation - Rationalization other defenses	Shifts in attitudes/ values
5) –	Participatory review	Confrontation/ analysis/consensus	- Achievement against own targets set - Correlation to shifts in values.

Appendix 3.2

Participants in the Programme Evaluation Workshop

Ahmedabad: 27–28 September 1988 (Positions at the Time of the Workshop)

1. K. Ramakrishnan. Professor, Management Studies, Bharathiar University, Coimbatore.
2. Kishore Saint. Executive Director, Ashoka Foundation; Ubeshwar Vikas Mandal, Udaipur.
3. Vinod Vyasulu. Head, Social Services Management Unit, Institute of Social and Economic Change, Bangalore.
4. C.R. Bijoy. Rural Health Centre, Thadagam, Coimbatore.
5. Mohan Rao. Centre for Social Medicine and Community Health, Jawaharlal Nehru University, New Delhi.
6. Kiran Desai. VIKSAT, Nehru Foundation for Development, Ahmedabad.
7. S. Rajagopalan. Joint Secretary, Karnataka State Council for Science and Technology, Bangalore.
8. V.R. Gaikwad. Professor, Centre for Management in Agriculture, Indian Institute of Management, Ahmedabad.
9. Pandurang Hegde. Chipko–Appiko Movement, Sirsi (Karnataka).
10. Meera Shah. Programme Executive, Aga Khan Rural Support Programme, Ahmedabad.
11. Binoy Acharya. Participatory Research in Asia, New Delhi.
12. B.C. Muthayya. Director, Psychology Division, National Institute of Rural Development, Hyderabad.
13. H.R. Prakash. Director, ARTIC, Kotturu (Andhra Pradesh).
14. S.K. Deshpande. Development Officer, National Bank for Agriculture and Rural Development, Bombay.
15. P.J. Contractor. Director, Jan Vikas, Ahmedabad.
16. T.S. Kannan. Formerly Chairman and Managing Director, National Small Industries Corporation, New Delhi.

17. Gurinder Kaur. Independent researcher/consultant, development studies, Ahmedabad.
18. Amulya K.N. Reddy. Chairman, Management Studies, Indian Institute of Science, Bangalore.
19. Vanaja Ramprasad (Project Officer). Development Resources, Bangalore.
20. Vijay Padaki (Project Director; co-convenor of workshop). Visiting Professor, Management Studies, Indian Institute of Science, Bangalore.
21. K.S. Karnik (Co-convenor of workshop). Development and Educational Communication Unit (DECU), Indian Space Research Organization, Ahmedabad.
22. B.C. Agrawal. Development and Educational Communication Unit (DECU). Indian Space Research Organization, Ahmedabad.
23. Subhash R. Joshi. Development and Educational Communication Unit (DECU), Indian Space Research Organization, Ahmedabad.
24. B.S. Bhatia. Development and Educational Communication Unit (DECU), Indian Space Research Organization, Ahmedabad.
25. N. Kalyanraman. Development and Educational Communication Unit (DECU), Indian Space Research Organization, Ahmedabad.
26. Arbind Sinha. Development and Educational Communication Unit (DECU), Indian Space Research Organization, Ahmedabad.

Other Professionals Associated

27. Sharada Jain. Institute of Development Studies, Jaipur.
28. R. Venkatesan. Financial Specialist, Co-operative League of the USA, New Delhi.
29. K.S. Jagadish. Convenor, ASTRA, Indian Institute of Science, Bangalore.
30. Darryl D'Monte. Editor, *The Times of India*, Bombay.
31. Pravin Visaria. Director, Gujarat Institute of Area Planning, Ahmedabad.
32. Barry Underwood. Regional Representative, OXFAM, Ahmedabad.
33. Parmesh Shah. Co-ordinator, Aga Khan Rural Support Programme, Ahmedabad.
34. D.K. Subramaniam. Centre for Computer Science and Automation, Indian Institute of Science, Bangalore.
35. Abhijit Sengupta. Indian Administrative Service, Secretary (Finance), Government of Karnataka, Bangalore.

Readings

Essays on Individual and Programme Perspectives in the Development Process

Four

Lessons from ASTRA's Experience of Technologies for Rural Development*

Amulya Kumar N. Reddy

A Personal Introduction

After almost two decades in the field of electrochemistry, I felt that, like most of the work in advanced institutions of education, science and technology, my own work was largely irrelevant to India's poor, the majority of whom live in villages. I also felt that I should reorient my efforts towards technologies for rural development. Such a viewpoint found sympathy from many other colleagues at the Indian Institute of Science. This shared vision led in 1974 to the formulation and implementation of the ASTRA programme through which it was hoped that the application of science and technology would become a weapon (or *asthra* in Sanskrit) in the interests of the poor.

However, the attempt at working in rural areas quickly revealed my serious shortcomings. I was born and raised in a city and therefore knew virtually nothing about life in villages; I had received

* This paper is based on a keynote address first delivered at the Rural and Community Services Centre, The Tata Iron and Steel Co. Ltd., Jamshedpur, on 4 March 1987, and then developed for the Valedictory Address to the Workshop on Rural Development organized by the Asian Institute of Technology, Bangkok, and the Institute for Social and Economic Change, Bangalore, on 9 July 1988, at the Institute for Social and Economic Change.

a Western type of education and approaches; and I came from a family of professionals, and was a member of the elite, and therefore found it very difficult to see the world through the eyes of the poor.

All this meant that I had to undergo a great deal of unlearning (in addition to learning) to be able to function in rural areas. Thus far, my learning experience has spanned fourteen years of which the first nine were as the Convenor of ASTRA, and the remaining years have involved its community biogas plant project at Pura village, Kunigal taluk, Tumkur district, Karnataka.

Many lessons have emerged from this experience. Since these lessons may be of some use to others wishing to make similar efforts, they are set down below.

Lesson 1: *Rural people may be poor and illiterate, but they are not irrational*. In fact, the poorer they are, the more does their survival depend upon their rationality, i.e., upon a proper evaluation of costs and benefits. And, in the attitude to returns and risks, they invariably take the worst case scenario more seriously than the best case scenario because the former can lead to total ruin whereas the latter only means marginal improvement. For example, their choice of traditional seed varieties in preference to high yielding varieties is often dictated by the fact that the latter can give lower yields than the former if the inputs are not in the optimum range; as the nursery rhyme goes: 'When she was good, she was very very good, but when she was bad, she was horrid.'

Lesson 2: We must therefore proceed with the assumption that, given the options within the range of awareness of the people, *the technological choices of the people are rational*. For example, the draught animals in many parts of the country are fed well only during the ploughing season because most of their traditional year-round functions—water lifting, oil extraction, cane crushing, etc.—have been usurped by pump-sets, oil-mills, cane crushers, etc. Another example is the fact that the load-bearing capacity of bullock carts is kept low because the average pay-load is only about 250–300 kg.

Lesson 3: *We must understand rural rationality if we want our technological suggestions/recommendations to be accepted*. For example, if smoke from their wood stoves (*chulas*) is essential to control termite attack on thatched roofs, then it is unlikely that smokeless stoves will be accepted unless they are accompanied by a solution to the termite problem, for instance, a termiteproof roof.

Lesson 4: *We must first be students if we want to be successful teachers*. Information must flow both ways—from the people to rural technologists, and from rural technologists to the people.

There are several important steps in this information flow process.

Step 1: *Scientific study of the lives of the people*: This step is crucial because most rural technologists know more about London or New York than about villages 20 km from their institutions. Hence, there is no option other than starting from scratch.

Step 2: *Identification of felt needs, rather than perceived needs*. For instance, villagers are completely aware of the fact that thatched roofs (*a*) leak, (*b*) catch fire, (*c*) are attacked by termites, (*d*) harbour insects and rodents, and (*e*) need constant maintenance. If asked (for instance, through a questionnaire), they may express their perceived need for a tiled or RCC (reinforced cement concrete) roof because those are the only alternatives that they have seen and are aware of. But, their *felt* need is really for an improved roof that does not have the defects of thatched roofs. An understanding of felt needs is essential therefore for working out the design criteria for improved technologies.

Step 3: *Presentation of options to the people*. Before a major effort is launched on the development of new technologies, it is vital that the various technological options be presented to the people and their preferences elicited.

Step 4: *Technology selection*. If the intention is ultimately to disseminate the technology and to ensure that it does not remain a museum piece, it is imperative that the final decision on the selection of the technology is made by the people and not by the technologists.

Step 5: *Technology generation*. The arduous task of research and development (R & D) has to be taken up at this stage.

Step 6: *Technology testing*. This important step consists of testing out the technology in the field and getting the reactions of the potential users.

Step 7: *Technology finalization*. The feedback from the field is used to improve/modify the product/process before the technology is finalized for diffusion.

Step 8: *Technology dissemination*. The process of disseminating the technology has to be a multi-institutional effort involving rural users, development agencies, technologists, financial and/or credit institutions, etc.

Lesson 5: *Start with the people, and end with the people!* Unfortunately, it is possible for scientists and engineers to get so involved with Steps 5 and 7, i.e., technology generation and technology finalization, that they forget all the other steps in which the people (who are the prospective real users of the technology) have a crucial role to play. This process of bypassing the people is even more easy when the technology dissemination consists of simply transporting a device/equipment (for example, a photovoltaic module or a biomass fuelled engine-cum-generator) and installing/erecting it in a village. What these blinkered scientists and engineers disseminate may be rural technology, but it will certainly not be technology for rural development. For, *there cannot be development without the involvement of people.* It is wise therefore to keep on asking: '*Where are the people?*'

Lesson 6: *Women are often the best agents of disseminating technologies for rural development.* Even where technologists work with the people, the tendency is to restrict popular involvement to the men. This gender bias is often difficult to avoid because most scientists and engineers are men, their technologies are often male-oriented, there are social taboos discouraging direct interactions with women, rural women do not come forward to articulate their views in the presence of their men, etc. But, with many,

many technologies, once the women are seized of it, the dissemination takes off. Thus, once the women began to have a vested interest in the delivery of dung to the Pura community biogas plant, the operation of dung collection and delivery has been running smoothly.

Lesson 7: *The steps involved in the two-way information flow of Lesson 4 are quite similar to those involved in satisfying the demands of urban middle- and upper-class consumers*, but the terminology is usually different. In the case of the generation and dissemination of technologies for the middle- and upper-classes, the following steps are usually distinguished:

> Market Survey → Consumer Preferences ('the customer is always right!') → Identification of Market Demand → R & D → Test Marketing → Productionizing → Manufacturing → Marketing

Lesson 8: All this, which is considered so self-evident in the case of affluent customers, is completely ignored in the case of the poor. This bias is perhaps there because the poor do not have the purchasing power to articulate their demands through the market mechanism and be rated as 'consumers'. *But, because people are poor, we must not ignore their likes, tastes, preferences and needs*. For example, Janata houses for the poorest sections tend to ignore the way in which the spaces in traditional houses are used by villagers.

Lesson 9: *We must curb our market tendency to develop technologies in response to imaginary and imagined needs identified in remote and alien settings*. For example, a number of 'modern' designs of bullock carts were developed with the capacity to carry 1000–2000 kg of load even though such high loads do not arise frequently in typical rural situations except, for instance, in the catchment area of a sugar factory.

Lesson 10: *Traditional technologies are optimal solutions for the challenges of the past and therefore must not be ignored as sources of innovation—they have evolved through a long process of the natural selection of innovations*. For example, computer analysis has shown that the geometry of traditional bullock carts represents an optimum solution.

Lesson 11: *Though traditional technologies were optimal solutions in the past, almost all of them are suboptimal and inadequate today* because of changed expectations, resource availability, materials and circumstances. For instance, in the past when the country was heavily forested, teak may have been an optimum material for constructing the highly stressed wheels of bullock carts, but today teak has become such a scarce material that it is a costly and therefore suboptimal solution.

Lesson 12: On the other hand, *the so-called 'modern' technologies, which are only bad xerox copies of Western technologies, are invariably inaccessible to the poor*. For example, the poor cannot afford a modern roofing technology such as RCC.

Lesson 13: *It is therefore a Hobson's choice for the poor—on the one hand, traditional technologies are inadequate, and on the other hand, modern technologies are inaccessible. To permit the poor to escape from this dilemma, scientists and technologists must generate new options, each more effective than the traditional, and more accessible than the modern*. Ideally, the options should constitute a hierarchy of technologies with upward compatibility. Then, with rising incomes, the poor can climb from a cheaper less cost-effective option to a costlier more cost-effective option. Only in such a situation will the people have genuine choices. Thus, the roles of rural technologists should be those of option generators and choice wideners. For example, in the matter of cooking fuels and stoves, rural technologists can widen the options of villagers so that they can also choose improved (smokeless and fuel-efficient) wood stoves or biogas cooking.

Lesson 14: *But the ultimate choice of technology must be made by the people, because technology choice is too important to be left to technologists and other 'experts'*. These experts have made monumental errors even in the industrialized countries (for instance, the Concorde supersonic passenger plane or the US breeder reactor). And, our countryside is littered with the blunders in the choice of technology. Rural technologists, like all technologists with careers, fortunes and fame linked with technologies, have clear-cut vested interests in the technologies that they push—they are neither as unbiased nor objective as they claim or as they are portrayed.

Lesson 15: *In generating technological options, there are three approaches for technologists*:

1. Cheaper Western technology
2. Develop ab initio an alternative technology
3. Transform traditional technology

For example, in the case of low-cost building technologies, the approach of cheapening Western technologies may consist of developing fibre reinforced materials, that of ab initio alternative technologies, geodesic domes, and that of transforming traditional technologies, compacted unfired mud-blocks.

Lesson 16: Even though it is a hitherto untapped source, the *transformation of traditional technologies is a rich source of, and promising route for, technologies appropriate for rural development*. The transformation of traditional technologies involves an understanding of their scientific basis, followed by qualitative changes achieved through marginal improvements.

Lesson 17: As a consequence of the whole process that has been outlined above, *the technologies that are developed are likely to be region specific, location specific and culture specific*. And, the local culture may have many surprises. This is probably why Gandhiji is reported to have advised one of the most creative architects in India, Laurie Baker, 'When you design for the poor, restrict yourself to materials that are available within a radius of 10 miles!'

Lesson 18: *Any fool can make a thing complicated, it takes a genius to make it simple*. The end-product may have to be, or may turn out to be, simple, but the thinking that goes or went into its development can be quite sophisticated. In fact, there is a desperate need for wise ideas and ingenious solutions. Rural technologies are neither trivial nor second-class because they invariably pose the extremely tough challenge of having to be 'zero-cost'.

Lesson 19: In the case of most rural technologies (stoves, windmills, biogas plants, wood gasifiers, etc.), *there is a marked difference between the first generation of unsuccessful devices* (which were often the result of the enthusiasm of unqualified amateurs) *and the second generation of successful devices* (which emerged from the creative efforts of qualified professionals).

Lesson 20: *Thus, the penetration of the countryside with rural technologies involves a learning curve*—in the initial part of the curve, there is a very slow penetration of the potential 'market', then a rapid climb, and finally a saturation. Unfortunately, most plans of development agencies forget this learning curve and prescribe linearly increasing targets.

Lesson 21: During the initial part of the learning curve, *there has to be intense back-and-forth interaction between the lab and the field.* The feedback from users in the field must lead to modifications and improvements in the product/process, and the modified/improved product/process needs further 'test marketing' in the field. As a result of this interplay between technology generation and dissemination, and between technologists and potential consumers of the technology, the penetration of the market is necessarily very slow during this phase.

All these points are generally ignored when technology dissemination is planned and implemented. In fact, there is a general tendency for technology generation and technology dissemination to be thought of as two distinct non-overlapping sequential stages with the generation ending when the dissemination begins, and the generators washing their hands off the technology dissemination process.

Lesson 22: There are four main mechanisms for the dissemination of rural technologies:

1. The market
2. The top-down approach
3. The bottom-up approach
4. The franchising approach

And it is very important that the appropriate mechanism is chosen.

Each of these has its advantages and disadvantages. The market is an excellent allocator of resources, but it ignores three extremely important aspects: equity, the environment and the long-term. In particular, the rural poor are by and large outside the market because they do not have the requisite purchasing power to articulate their demands via the market.

The top-down approach—favoured so much by bureaucracies—seems the obvious route when there is clarity at the top; but it underrates the central role of popular participation in technology selection and finalization, and of the strengthening of self-reliance.

The bottom-up approach starts with popular participation, but may suffer from the inadequacy of technical expertise.

The franchising approach, in which a centralized technology generating-cum-development agency franchises local groups/entrepreneurs, may be able to combine the advantages of the large and the small, the public and private initiatives and the technologists and the grassroots workers.

Lesson 23: *Of the various technologies contending for dissemination, the ones that get successfully disseminated (i.e., penetrate the 'market') are those that simultaneously solve several problems.* Charles Berg who enunciated this 'theorem' illustrated it by stressing that energy-efficiency improvements were introduced into the US steel industry during a period of declining energy prices because those improvements were accompanied by other useful characteristics. The Berg theorem is very relevant to rural technologies too. Thus, of the various designs that have been tried for improved wood stoves, the ones that have succeeded (for example, the ASTRA Ole) have been those that simultaneously eliminated smoke, cut down cooking time, and reduced fuel consumption.

Lesson 24: *The technologist must ensure that all the objectives in a rural user's list are included in his/her design criteria.* If the technology designer can achieve the simultaneous inclusion of all the rural consumer's objectives in the technology, then it does not matter whether the consumer's ranking of the objectives is different from that of the designer. This is what seems to have happened in the case of the ASTRA Ole. Whereas the designer's priorities seemed to have been (*a*) reduction of fuel consumption, (*b*) smokelessness, and (*c*) cutting down cooking time, the rural user's priorities were quite the opposite: (*a*) smokelessness, (*b*) cutting down cooking time, and (*c*) reduction of fuel consumption.

Lesson 25: *If the designer cannot meet all the user's objectives simultaneously but only in stages, then it is imperative that the designer's sequence must be the same as the user's priorities, otherwise the implementation may run into problems*. This is what happened to ASTRA's community biogas plant at Pura. The villagers wanted the biogas to lift and pipe drinking water, generate electricity for lighting homes and provide cooking fuel, but they did not stress this order of priorities. Neither did the ASTRA workers pick up the signals—they sought to provide cooking fuel first. The villagers went along with this effort out of solidarity, but the available dung could not provide biogas even for one complete meal (let alone two meals) and the biogas plant had to be stopped for some time. Subsequently, when the plant was restarted at the request of the villagers, drinking water was taken up as the first priority, as desired by the villagers, and the project has taken off again.

Lesson 26: Notwithstanding any successes with the generation and dissemination of rural technologies, *technology alone cannot remove poverty, redress injustices, prove a panacea to solve development problems*. Technology is only a subsystem of society, and the development of society hinges not only on technology, but also on the other crucial subsystems. Technology is only an instrument for the development of society. Like all instruments, it must be specifically chosen and/or designed to fulfil its intended function. But the will to use the instrument, and the skill to wield it effectively, do not depend so much on the instrument as on the users of the instrument. Thus, technologies are a necessary but not a sufficient condition for rural development. It is also essential that the political structure and the socio-economic framework both be committed to development goals. Rural technological missions will succeed only when they are part of successful societal missions. *Rural technology has therefore both power and limits—it is an essential requisite for development, but it cannot be a substitute for economic, social and political change.*

Lesson 27: However idealistic and romantic it may appear, it must be stressed that *technologists must approach rural work with empathy* *and affection for the people*. Otherwise, they tend to be afraid of the people and hide behind the walls of their rural centres. If they do not have these positive feelings, they are not able to look forward to interacting with the people (even when they are in groups). Then, *the poor tend to conclude that their poverty is being used as a resource for professional gain.* Even if the people do not get something back in return from the interaction, the feelings with which technologists make efforts are extremely important in the eyes of the people. Given the right attitude, the people are far more understanding of technical failures (which are the usual precursors of success) than the so-called educated who cheer when the satellite goes into orbit and jeer when it falls into the sea.

Science and technology too stand to gain from these feelings of empathy and affection. The forging of an emotional bond with the people may result in the catharsis, redemption and the resurrection of science and technology which have become so amoral, immoral and violent. At that stage, the poor shall inherit science and technology and therefore the earth.

Lesson 28: The perspective guiding rural technology is also vital. Rural technology is not merely a matter of expediency; it is not a transitory measure or a tactical device to cope with the current predicament of the poor in the countryside. *Rural technology is a path to a new society. It is an instrument for development*. And development must be seen as a socio-economic process directed primarily towards the satisfaction of basic human needs starting from the needs of the neediest, particularly in the locations of development projects. In addition, development must involve the strengthening of an endogenous self-reliance based on social participation and control. Finally, if this development is to be sustainable over the long-term, it must be in harmony with the environment.

Five

Social Institutions in Development Strategy*

Vijay Padaki

There are two key words in the title of this essay: institutions and strategy. In popular usage these terms have a number of different meanings. We shall see why a correct understanding is of great value to all development programmes. In the process, we may need to ask afresh what the development effort is all about. We may need to distance ourselves from the projects and programmes and view them from the top of a hill.

The essay is developed on the following lines:

* A historical analysis of development programmes and a classification of programmes/approaches.
* Programme objectives and achievements as limited facets of an institutionalization process.
* A correct view of social institutions—including the difference between developing organizations and developing institutions.
* The tasks ahead, illustrated through two capsule case studies.

---

* Revised version of a paper first presented at the Tenth Third World Studies Conference, University of Nebraska, October 1987. Reproduced in Chary, S.N. and V. Vyasulu (eds.), *Managing India's Planning*, vol. 2, Printwell–Rupa, 1992.

I

It has often been observed that while the Indian experience in development is vast and rich, particularly in the NGO sector, the sharing of this experience among all the persons, groups and organizations concerned is limited.

The need for information and exchange is hardly ever denied. Some networking does exist, through federal structures and co-ordinating organizations. Individuals and groups in various development programmes do keep in touch with each other, at least in like-minded clusters. Yet, the total output from all such exchanges remains limited, scattered, disproportionately small to the ongoing effort, and far too varied in quality for systematic analysis. Figure 5.1 represents the cycle of events for continuously developing field actions in and a knowledge pool on the subject of development. The three 'poles' enclosed in a dotted perimeter represent the somewhat specialized tasks that must be undertaken in an academically rigorous way. However, they work only with a purposive give-and-take relationship with the field professionals at pole 4. The isolation of a development programme may thus be viewed in terms of weak linkages with poles 1 and 3. The reasons for these linkages being weak are worth looking into, but are outside the scope of this paper. We need only note here the familiar unhelpful gap between 'research' and 'action'. One consequence of the gap appears to be a paucity of strategic perspectives in development programmes beyond the here-and-now preoccupations of project administration.

II

The content of a particular programme for a given 'target population' is only partly determined by the assessment of local conditions. The options for activities are equally likely to be determined by a starting concept of what constitutes development. Development workers may differ in the elegance with which their ideas are articulated: assumptions, premises, theory, ideology. Nevertheless, a starting conviction does exist, influencing the content of the programme of action.

Once a programme is conceived, an 'operational definition' of the objectives of the programme is usually available, whether or

Figure 5.1: **DEVELOPMENT PRACTICE AND KNOWHOW**

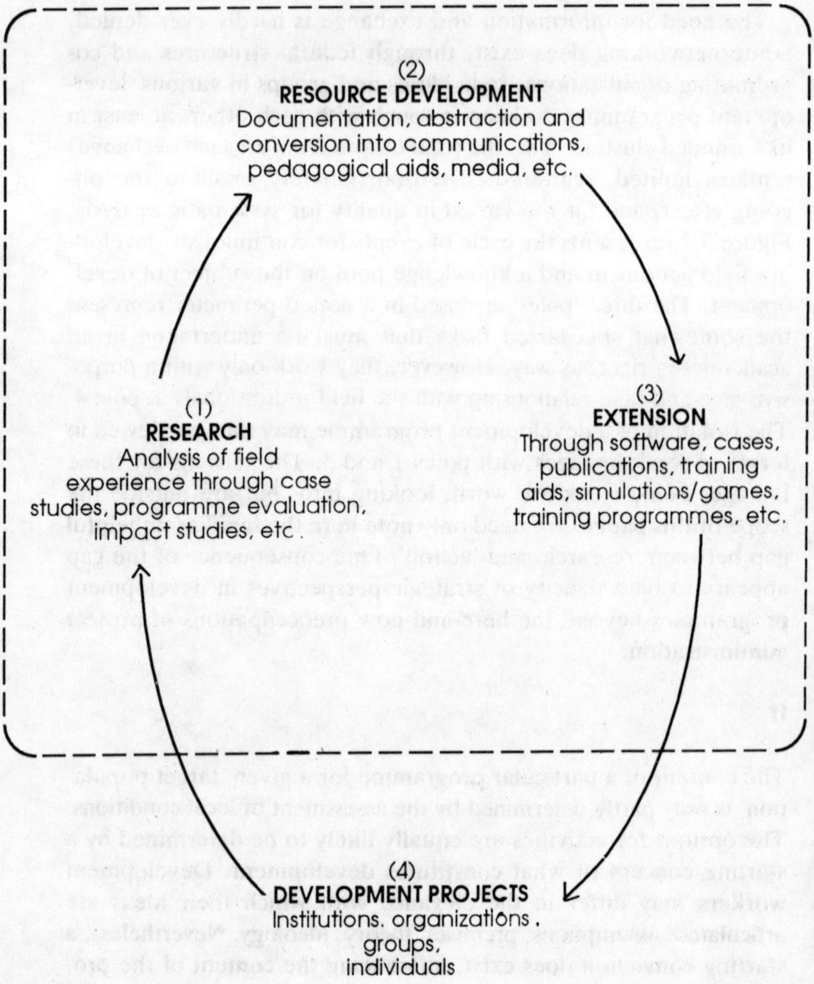

not the agency actually puts them on paper. The desired products of the programme are visualized as 'indicators' and, where possible, are listed in numerical terms: the number of children matriculating, the increase in crop yield, the caloric intake, and so on. Few programmes visualize or seek *process* outcomes—the less observable, not easily quantifiable states of self-sufficiency, increased confidence, decreased dependence, quality of inter-community communication and so on. Either way, we have in most programmes an apparent internal consistency across:

1. Development ends conceived (theory)
2. Preferred intervention (action)
3. Outcome(s) observed (assessment)

The interventions chosen by development agencies do exhibit some clustering by their similarities and differences. An analysis of cases from diverse programmes in India suggests a taxonomic scheme in which a development programme may be characterized by its position on four dimensions:

1. Nature/source of funding
2. Ideological position
3. Form of organization adopted
4. Primary intervention strategy

Let us examine one of the four dimensions in slightly greater detail, namely, the primary intervention strategy. A historical trend is discernible. Four broad intervention strategies have enjoyed widespread adoption over the last forty years or more. They have appeared in the following order.

Providing Infrastructural Facility

Housing, electricity, installing pumps, constructing roads, opening a health centre, etc.

Initiating Economic Activity

Employment/income generation through traditional or new skills, as in weaving, packaging, food processing, subcontracted assembling, etc.

Sectoral Focus in Programmes

As in education in earlier years; then in appropriate/alternative technology, community health, etc.; and in more recent years, women's programmes and ecology/environment related projects.

Organizing People

Building local organizations and movements, and facilitating their entry into sectoral programmes of the community's own choice—the current 'paradigm' widely adopted by most change agents.

Some development programmes do have two or more of these interventions together. However, there is almost always a discernible *primary* intervention, revealing a prioritization in the efforts, consistent with the starting ideas about development in the agency concerned.

Three important observations follow: First, no matter what the starting focus might be, the development process is seen only when the three other facets come into play some time or the other, and are integrated into the effort. In other words, the 'primary' intervention is best regarded only as an appropriate gateway.

Second, the development of the *system* concerned (village, community, region) makes interdependent demands on all four fronts, which might well be regarded as the *four task dimensions* in any development effort.

Third, while the choice of gateway for the primary intervention might, perhaps, be associated with a theoretical or ideological position taken, the need for integration among the four task dimensions appears independent of theory or ideology. In other words, any development agency, with any starting action plan, will sooner or later have to recognize the interdependence of that dimension with the three other task dimensions, whether or not that agency itself is to be actively involved in all task dimensions.

The integration across the four task dimensions appears crucial to the success of the development effort. On closer examination we find that such an integration amounts to the *institutionalization* of a new set of behaviours by the social system.

What is easily overlooked in our development efforts is the time frame within which certain ends of development are sought. Since most, if not all, developing societies are post-colonial independent nations, they would like to accomplish as much as possible in as little time as possible to 'catch up' with the higher standards of living in other societies. For this, they do not have models in history to fall back upon. The models available, largely from the advanced societies, have one feature difficult to reproduce quickly in the new setting: appropriate social institutions for translating development ideas into development practice. Social institutions *evolve* over time, and tend to be consistent with the values being pursued and upheld by separate facets of the society's productive forces.

III

The origins of any institutionalization are: (*a*) the experience of a set of behaviours as purposeful, and (*b*) the need to protect and promote those purposeful behaviours. The natural consequence of such stirring in motivated behaviour is the creation of an *organization* that permits, after all, an organic survival and growth of these behaviours in that environment. Soon, however, the organization itself requires protection and promotion, along with other, similar organizations that have arisen, created by various other groups of people, with similar purposeful ends in view. At this stage a more abstract organizational form is called for: the social *institution*. This 'superordinate' organization must simultaneously (*a*) provide sustenance to the various constituent organizations, and (*b*) permit variations in pursuits in the individual organizations within a growing body of commonly accepted norms and conventions. In this way, both conformity and innovation are rendered socially acceptable in the interests of the long-term survival and growth of the organizations concerned. Thus it was in the oldest forms of food gathering or procreative behaviours; thus it has been in the evolution of the later institutions of religion, politics or industry.

In an organic sense the sequence *New Behaviours–Organizations–Institutions* seems logical, even essential, for the 'health' of the organizations created. The emergence of a stable, purposeful, institutional frame is also the appearance of a structural facility in the social system. An institutional structure facilitates such interactive processes among the constituent organisations as:

* Information exchange
* Optimization of gains
* Conflict resolution
* Joint lobbying/action
* Strategic planning
* Public awareness/education
* Promotion

We might note briefly here that viable social institutions may be seen in two broad varieties—the 'vertical' and the 'lateral'. Vertical institutions are federal structures for bringing together organizations with the same/similar activity: for instance, the apex co-operative holding together a large network of self-help groups. Lateral institutions hold together dissimilar but interdependent organizations around a common economic activity. The *social ecology* of the bullock cart in Box 5.1 is an example. At least twelve different crafts/occupations may be interdependent in handloom weaving, calling for an appropriate lateral institution.

Box 5.1

Social Ecology in Institution Development

In more recent times, the coevolutionary nature of organizational forms within an institutional system has been captured effectively by the concept of *social ecology*. For instance, the conclusion by scientists and technologists in ASTRA (at Indian Institute of Science, Bangalore) that the design of the traditional bullock cart was optimal, revealed its socio-ecological basis: the logical connections between terrain and wheel, wheel and wood, wood and forest resources, forest resources and occupational patterns, occupational patterns and optimal cartload, and so forth, extended to the interfaces among several rural occupations, such as the village smith, the carpenter, the miller and the cobbler. In contrast, there were other studies that sought to 'modernize' the cart in the sense of increasing its carrying capacity, but ignored the other linkages. Needless to say, these have had limited success, with heavy subsidization at some other point in the larger system.

The organic linkages between an organization and its superordinate institutional system are real and undeniable. From this reality follow the special demands of organization development (OD) in developing countries, especially the creation of new organizations for new forms of social behaviour in new programmes of socio-economic development.

* The goals in organizational effectiveness typically call for a within-organization focus in OD. In many a development programme, the OD task needs to be redefined and extended to the level of institutional effectiveness. Consequently, the task includes the development of an appropriate social institution too, without which the new organization/s cannot be sustained.
* The facilitation of new organizational behaviours (with one set of indicators of 'success') will almost inevitably conflict with other behavioural norms, reinforced through existing institutional systems. As a matter of fact, interventions at lower system levels are often the cause of a dysfunction at the level of the larger system. For instance, the formation and strengthening of small focal groups (of the disadvantaged), emphasized in the currently popular community organization approach in rural development, often impedes intergroup collaborative behaviour in the rural system, so essential for the emergence of truly purposeful politico-economic institutions. This is because the intervention repertoire of tools and techniques is strong on building small groups through increased individual and interpersonal competencies, but is weak on building intergroup/interorganizational/intercommunity competencies.
* Conflict resolution towards institution building objectives calls for sensitivity to the value bases in both the old and the new institutional systems. In the task of institution development, the nurturing of new/alternative behaviour patterns must be seen as parallel to the nurturing of a new/alternative value system.
* Finally, following from the above, it must be recognized that the ethical responsibility in OD in the development context is very high. The change agent must recognize the

fact that we do not know enough about development, that no two development programmes are the same, that there are no tried and tested models of intervention with universal validity and, finally, that every model has its own value premises, and one may be imposing a value system on a community through a development programme without intending it or even being aware of it.

Viable social institutions tend to be those that have emerged from the effective functioning of viable organizational entities, responding to their needs for a higher order of organizational support as explained above. Indeed, it can be said that a social institution is valid only by the criteria of effective behaviours in the constituent organizations and groups.

The task of integration in developmental interventions thus appears to be one of setting up viable institutions, superordinate to the specific socio-technical systems created for specific endeavours in health, education, income generation and so on. However, the 'setting up' of a social institution is a cultural paradox, as we shall see below.

Developing societies are characterized by a race against time, 'running faster and faster to stay where you are'. The luxury of verifying whether new behaviours and organizations stand the test of time appears unaffordable. By observing existing institutions (and their benefits) in the 'model' economies, *institutions are created first* on similar lines. The appropriate organizational forms and the purposeful behaviours in those organizations are expected to follow automatically. Of course they do not—not in societies where people can continue to determine their own destinies. The problems of institutions created out of context, so to speak, are many. For instance:

* Problem of identity: Whose organization is this? What does it mean to the beneficiaries (the constituencies) it is meant to serve?
* Problem of creating/propping up organizations and, further, maintaining behaviours that are not convincing and integral with the societal system.
* Problem of coming to grips with value conflicts: what the institution represents vs. existing needs, values, priorities, traditions, etc.

The problems above are often compounded by a less visible factor. Developing societies are 'aided' by the industrially advanced societies. Inseparable ingredients of the aid package are the organizational and institutional forms considered most appropriate for the endeavour being aided. The appropriate organization and 'management' of the package have evolved in the society where the technology originated, but the problems of transplant into the receiving society are too complex to be visualized readily.

In the receiving society the creators of institutions are often far removed from the users of institutions, and the appearance of parallel, non-formal institutions to fill the need gaps is very common. Not surprisingly, with need gaps filled, the non-formal institutions, (often involving compromised practices from the formal institutions themselves) become the 'real' institutional frames. Hence the dysfunctional character of many 'new' institutions in many developing societies.

In sum, we observe that in many development programmes the imposed institutional structures have had dysfunctional outcomes, retarding or even negating the expected benefits from the programmes. On the other hand, we must accept that the emergence of valid social institutions is crucial if the development process is to be maintained even after the formal closure of the development programme or withdrawal of the development agency.

IV

The task of nurturing viable social institutions demands a strategic view of development. The popular use of the term strategy equates it with 'tactics'. More correctly, strategy involves (*a*) an appreciation of the interaction of all the relevant other systems in the environment with our own system, and (*b*) the future outcomes of those interactions. Institution development may thus be viewed as possibly the most significant, but least understood, strategic task in development interventions. It must combine the techno-economic tasks—namely, providing infrastructure, initiating economic activity, ('economic development')—with the socio-cultural ones—namely, learning, organizing, ('people development')—in a meaningful way. Far from being an abstruse ('soft') concept, institution development makes sense in hard economic terms. Let us see how.

Any development plan (especially in the 'backward areas') must include an employment generation objective at an acceptable wage level. Following from the above, employment has to be in the region where they live. The people concerned need to transform local resources in the most efficient way into useful commodities.

In doing so, we cannot depend either on the market and pricing system or the demand pattern generated by the market *as prevailing in the given larger system*; for these are far removed from the realities of needs in the underprivileged systems. It follows that we must use an alternative economic vehicle. In other words, we must not think in terms of merely financing projects for rural employment, but in terms of *mobilizing local resources to meet local ends*.

From numerous cases of development projects in the Indian experience it seems possible for us to cull out three main lessons as essential conditions for the 'success' of such ventures:

1. Intervention in a region to initiate a productive process must also ensure the marketing process so that the *goods/services produced are actually utilised*.
2. The intervention process must ensure that *the value added in the production process must accrue to the producers* themselves, implying the elimination of (or at least more controlled and reasonable roles for) the middlemen in both inputs to and outputs from the production system.
3. The intervention/change agency must be dispensable. The implication here is that their role is catalytic in the best sense of the term. Concomitantly, it means that it results *in the genuine development of the people concerned* as seen in such things as increased self-confidence, autonomy, participation, group cohesion, self-reliance, etc.

If we examine these three criteria in just a little greater detail, we see how closely they reinforce the concept of institution development.

V

'People development' as an aim is admitted by many a development worker, project and agency. It is visualized in different schemes and expressed in different terms, but we detect a common factor in all such expressions as:

* Self-reliance/managing their own affairs
* Growth in competence and skills
* Shaking off exploitative chains

* Awareness/conscientization
* Empowerment

What is the logical goal of all such individual and social development, in knowledge and competence? Is it possible that different programmes, in spite of their broad recognition of this goal, accomplish it only to different degrees? If so, is it possible that the various levels of people development accomplished (and accomplishable) can be viewed in institution–development terms? The idea may be developed with the help of Figure 5.2.

The schematic representation of a 'central–peripheral' dimension in Figure 5.2 suggests that as we approach the core, the development of individual and social competence gets more and more integrated in nature and becomes a more generalized form of the specific developments at the periphery, such as skill at carpentry, or tractor maintenance, or managing the market or dealing with the bank and so forth. An example of an unintegrated input would be the rote memorization of a lesson in an evening class of an adult education project, with no noticeable bearing on self-sufficiency or autonomy at the core.

What then is at the core? Where do all self-reliance roads lead to? If we examine this desired end state carefully, and without fighting shy of it, we see an abstraction of several specific experiences into an alternative world-view, with a corresponding alternative behavioural state, *the transformation being essentially a political process*. If 'development' has taken place, such an altered state is one of political maturity.

Whenever we conceive of any social group governing its own affairs, we are implying a state of people development in which the people concerned are (*a*) politically mobilized, (*b*) are in a position to 'sense' and 'monitor' their environments for their political parameters, and (*c*) able to control their political environments, at least to the extent of maintaining their productive ends. All this is possible only with the integration of the four task dimensions identified earlier and, of course, the emergence of viable institutions to nurture the alternative behaviour patterns as purposeful to the communities concerned.

Now, it can be argued that the true definition of self-reliance, if we are genuine in our intentions, can only be in these terms. Further, if these development ends are not accomplished in most of our projects, then we must pause and examine the very real possibility of such non-accomplishment being a built-in feature of

Figure 5.2: **MEANS AND ENDS IN DEVELOPMENT PROGRAMMES**

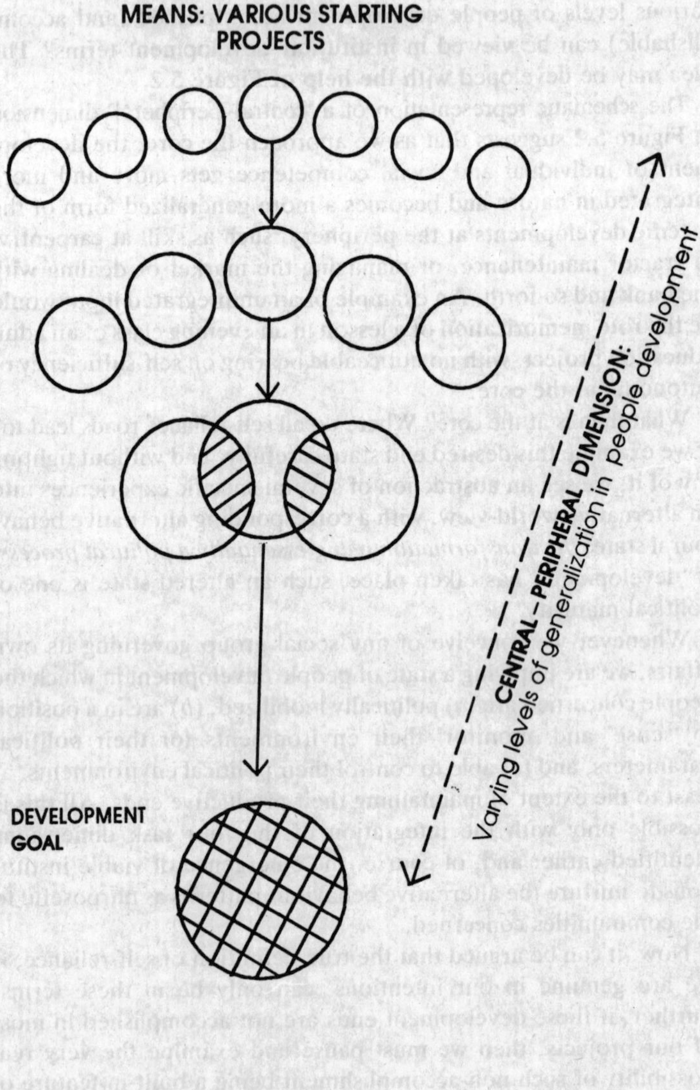

the project; for it would perhaps not be in our interest for development to reach such states of transformation. In the absence of this vital developmental process, by design or accident, any developmental effort will most predictably and inevitably aggravate the same vicious circle of selective development and perpetrated inequalities. Indeed partial or peripheral people development often serves this perpetration rather admirably.

VI

Capsule descriptions of two cases should help illustrate the abstractions so far. The cases pertain to developmental efforts at two quite distinct system levels, one at the microlevel of a single slum in a semi-rural area, and the other at the level of an entire manufacturing sector. More detailed versions of the cases are available separately.

Micro: A Piggery Co-operative (1980)

Susaipalayam is a slum in a semi-rural area of about 300 families. A majority of the men do not work. By long tradition, they resort to petty thieving at night and idling during the day. Most families are engaged in distilling illicit liquor, a livelihood managed almost entirely by the womenfolk. Some additional income comes from the sale of scrap metal, fixtures and fittings stolen. They are forced to accept whatever the pawnbroker offers for the material submitted.

This slum has a long history of church and social work organizations visiting it and dispensing charity. One such Catholic organization embarked on an employment scheme. They chose a group of ten women, consisting mainly of widows or women with invalid husbands, to whom they distributed cows. It was expected that a grant of this nature would ameliorate their lot. Within a span of two months, some had sold the cows, others had pawned them, and still others killed them for meat. Within two years the nun in charge of the project had to leave and asked the pastor of the local Protestant church to take over. Subsequently, this community approached the pastor for his assistance in initiating a new employment scheme.

Since the group was familiar with the raising of country pigs, they chose a piggery for the new employment project. The people themselves found out what they were entitled to according to the government scheme. The pastor's group suggested that employment should be created on a collective basis and that the target group should organize itself into a co-operative. Four or five widows formed the co-operative and gave it a name. The members affiliated themselves to the Association of Unemployed in the area.

The government officials had to be convinced of the utility and viability of a co-operative effort. The co-operative members themselves secured the certificates which made them eligible for the scheme and obtained the pigs collectively, standing guarantee for each other.

The group represented to the municipality for a piece of land to start the piggery project. They paid collective visits to the officials concerned. The latter could not afford to neglect or act bureaucratic with such a large group. The group members also learned to assert themselves from an initial position of diffidence. When the pastor's group first accompanied the co-operative members, the officials accused it of vested interests and asked it to leave, but the co-operative members insisted on its physical presence.

The co-operative finally obtained 1 acre of land near Susaipalayam. The municipality gave it on the condition that the project be started on the land within two years. In about seven months they started construction of the shed for rearing pigs, for which the group gave its free labour. One person was sent for a month's training in pig rearing to a well-known centre. He helped to train the others. The entire group went for a day to an animal husbandry farm, paying their own expenses, where they were exposed to methods of costing and management of a piggery, including fodder, housing and health care.

The total capital expenditure was Rs. 52,000, of which Rs. 25,000 was obtained as a bank loan and Rs. 25,000 was extended as a collateral from an aid organisation. A veterinary surgeon visited the piggery once a month, for which he had to be paid 'travelling expenses'. The co-operative members contributed Rs. 900 each initially and Rs. 100 over a year as their contribution to the project.

Through the experience of the piggery co-operative, the people gradually became confident that they could get their work done with the bank officials independently. The pastor's group only accompanied them occasionally to counter-guarantee their financial need. Additionally it was considered important to be aware of the overall financial picture. Among the co-operative members themselves, there was a change in their dealings. Earlier they had no faith in each other and would make complaints to the pastor's group. But now they confronted each other and sorted out any disagreements that arose.

Such a co-operative venture, which was distasteful to the community earlier, has now been fully accepted. In fact many others have approached the pastor for assistance in securing bank loans for other enterprises.

The pastor's approach has been never to directly advise or 'preach' to the community, not even on their illicit liquor business. Indeed, their experience with the co-operative has made the people aware of the operating market forces, and they are using this newly gained competence to make their liquor business also more profitable.

According to the pastor, their focus is on building values of self-reliance and co-operation, and the dignity of human labour. They want people to experience the success in their jobs. They hope that once people experience these aspects of their existence, they will govern their own lives effectively. Once the piggery brings sizeable returns to the people, they will no longer have to resort to distilling liquor for their subsistence. They plan to start informal group discussions with the co-operative members, hoping to develop a core of people who will initiate the awareness raising and collectivizing in the community. The economic programme is seen as an important means for conscientization.

Macro: The Decentralized Textile Manufacturing System (1985)

The inputs and outputs across a large number of sectors and subsectors in the Indian textile industry can be charted out in economic terms as one large and complex system. In institutional terms, however, we see several separate systems, each with a distinct origin, history and identity. The different sectors of spinning, weaving and composite manufacture (and now processing) have evolved their various federal structures and, through them, their institutional characters. Similarly, in raw material production and trade, whether of natural or synthetic fibre, in yarn and cloth distribution, in machinery, spares and ancillaries, in dyes and chemicals and, indeed, in every subsystem of the whole, there are distinct institutional structures, characterized by a long history and a strong economic basis.

With the existence of institutions of long-standing we might expect purposive, healthy, functioning of the system. Yet, the textile industry in India has been described variously as stagnant, sick, decaying and so on. How do we explain this? What might be the explanation in structural–institutional terms?

The developmental objective for the textile system, through a series of policy pronouncements since the mid-fifties, was the progressive growth of the decentralized sectors of manufacturing, i.e., the diffusion of economic power from the organized (mill) sector. This was achieved through a simultaneous restriction on capacities in the latter and various concessions in taxes and duties to the former. By one reckoning the stated objectives of policy have indeed been achieved. The 75:25 share of production between the organized and decentralized sectors in the fifties has been virtually reversed to 25:75 now. But the manufacturing system is far from healthy on many counts:

* Chronically low operational efficiencies
* Low level of domestic consumption
* Poor export performance
* Continued corrupt and exploitative practices
* Financial losses and low returns

Further, the periodic resuscitations through fiscal concessions and schemes have yielded generally unsatisfactory results. A deeper diagnosis reveals the significance of institutional weaknesses over and above the pat explanations of techno-economic analyses.

The institutional deficiencies in the changes that took place over twenty-five years could be identified as:

* Isolation of the decentralized sectors (vis-à-vis the long evolved federal structures of the organized sectors).
* Absence of apex institutional structures.
* Absence of alternative institutional facilities for changes in the intersectoral structure of the industry.
* Inadequacy of governmental agencies for institutional functions.

* Conflicting demands from multiple governmental agencies.

The rapid structural change taking place in the textile system as a whole, aided primarily by decontrols and the removal of several entry and exit barriers, may be viewed as desirable for the long-term effectiveness of all manufacturing on account of the premises of free and fair competition on which they are based. On the other hand, one serious short-term consequence is not easily perceived or articulated: the dictates of the new textile policy (1985) have the effect of virtually revising the traditional sectoral stratification. The revised strata *can* benefit greatly from the revision in policy, but for that they need to *orchestrate strategy at an institutional level*. However, the institutional frames are weak and inadequate. Further, for genuine long-term strategy, we need a higher order institutional structure over and above the sectoral. If such a superordinate institutional facility was unrealized in the past, it is further set back by the effect of the new policy.

The need for a strong institutional facility for the textile manufacturing system is immediate. However, given the reality of disjointedness among the several sectors, we cannot but revert to the role of government, the makers of policy, in serving the institutional needs. While such an arrangement may not be the ideal one for either the system or the government, it should nevertheless be possible to accept the starting conditions, and yet include *institution development* as a key task objective in the charter of every governmental agency involved. Such an objective demands:

1. Re-examination of every role and function a governmental agency is currently performing that may be better performed by industry itself.
2. Identification of factors compelling the agency to continue with those functions on behalf of the industry.
3. Deliberate assistance for these functions to be 'transferred'.
4. Support to the emerging institutional entities in their early stages of development, both sectoral and inter-sectoral.

The articulation of an institution development objective will throw up a number of specific tasks and targets for individual agencies in the government.

The institution building task we visualize for the industry, at both the sectoral and intersectoral levels, has one component that cannot be supplied by the government, nor can it be generated easily from within the industry: the competence for research and analyses that form the 'coronary' system of the institutional facility. It is here that the existing research institutions can play a very valid and useful role—providing the analyses in the initial stages and transferring the competence to the institution itself in due course.

Likewise, research institutions can provide much useful assistance to governmental agencies in (*a*) providing research based alternatives for policy, and (*b*) providing the action research for institution development in the industry with the support of governmental agencies. Thus, in the institution building tasks ahead, there is a strong case for developing the triangular arrangement across industry, research and government.

Notes

1. For a fuller description of the Indian textile manufacturing system and its intersectoral constitution, see Padaki, V. and V. Shanbhag (eds.), *Industrial Sickness: The challenge in Indian textiles*, ATIRA, 1984.
2. For a more detailed analysis of institutional needs in the Indian textile system, see Padaki, V., On Institutions and System Effectiveness. In proceedings of the national seminar *Indian Textile Futures: An intersectoral perspective*, ATIRA and Gandhi Labour Institute, 1987.
3. The economic dimensions of rural development programmes are explored further in, Padaki, V., and V. Vyasulu, Teaching About Technology. In Ahmad, A., M.A. Qureshi (eds.), *Social Relations of Scientific & Technical Change*, NISTADS, 1984.
4. Vyasulu, V. and V. Padaki, Employment, Rural Development and Social Change. In Radhakrishna, S. (ed.), *Science & Technology for Rural development*, COSTED, 1977.

Bibliography*

Books

ACTION, *Project Evaluation Handbook (vol. I); Project Monitoring Handbook (vol. II)*, Washington: ACTION, 1981.

Andrews, F.M., S.B. Withey, *Social Indicators of Well-Being*, Plenum Press, 1976.

Bardhan, P. (ed.), *Conversations Between Economists and Anthropologists*, Oxford University Press, 1987.

Bennett, Carl A., A.A. Lumsdaine (eds.), *Evaluation and Experiment: some critical issues in assessing social programmes*, Academic Press, 1975.

Breybooke, D., C.E. Lindblom, *A Strategy of Decision: policy evaluation as a social process*, Free Press, 1970.

Bryant, C., L.G. White, *Managing Development in the Third World*, Boulder: Westview, 1982.

Cain, G., R. Hollister, *The Methodology of Evaluating Social Action Programmes*. In Rossi, P., W. Williams (eds.), *Evaluating Social Programs*, Seminar Press, 1979.

Carley, Michael, *Rational Techniques in Policy Analysis*, Heinemann, 1980.

Chambers, R., *Rural Poverty-Orientated Monitoring and Evaluation*, Institute of Development Studies, University of Sussex, 1978.

Cook, T.D., D.T. Campbell, *Quasi-Experimentations: design and analysis for field settings,* Rand McNally, 1979.

Cook, W.D., T.E. Kuhn (eds.), *Planning Processes in Developing Countries: techniques and achievements*, North Holland/TIMS, 1982.

Cooke, T.D., C.S. Reichardt (eds.), *Qualitative and Quantitative Methods in Evaluation Research*. Vol. 1, Sage Research Progress Series in Evaluation, Sage, 1979.

Coombs, P.H., *Meeting the Basic Needs of the Rural Poor: integrated community based approach*, Pergamon, 1980.

* Literature reviewed for the working paper.

Cross, Nigel, et al. (eds.), *Man-Made Futures*, Hutchinson/Open University, 1974.

Feuerstein, M.T., *Partners in Evaluation: evaluating development and community programmes with participants*, Macmillan/TALC, 1986.

Finsterbusch, Kurt, C.P. Wolf, *Methodology of Social Impact Assessment*, Dowden, Hutchinson & Ross, 1977.

Finsterbusch, K., et al. (eds.), *Social Impact Assessment Methods*, Sage, 1983.

Fitz-Gibbon, Carol T., Lynn L. Morris, *How to Design a Program Evaluation, Program Evaluation Kit, Volume 3*, Sage, 1989.

Fox, K.A., *Social Indicators Theory: elements of an operational system*, John Wiley, 1974.

Freeman, D.M., *Technology and Society: issues in assessment, conflict and choice*, Markham, 1974.

Fried, Jacob, Paul Molnar, *Technological and Social Change: a transdisciplinary model*, Petrocelli, 1979.

Ganapathy, R.S., et al. (eds.), *Public Policy and Policy Analysis in India*, Sage, 1985.

Gittus, E. (ed.), *Key Variables in Social Research* (vols. 1 and 2), Heinemann, 1974.

Gonsalez, C.P., *Fallacy of Social Science Research: a critical examination and a new qualitative model*, Pergamon, 1981.

Gronlund, Norman (ed.), *Readings in Measurement and Evaluation*, Macmillan, 1968.

Grumm, John G., S.L. Wasby (eds.), *Analysis of Policy Impact*, Lexington Books, 1981.

Guba, E.G., Y.S. Lincoln, *Effective Evaluation: improving the usefulness of evaluation results through responsive and naturalistic approaches*, Jossey Bass, 1981.

Harris, Chester W. (ed.), *Problems in Measuring Change*, University of Winconsin Press, 1963.

Henderson, D.W., *Social Indicators: a rationale and research framework*, Economic Council of Canada, 1974.

Herman, Joan L. (series ed.), *Program Evaluation Kit* (2nd edition, vols. 1–9), Sage, 1989.

Howes, M., et al., *Assessing Rural Development Projects: an approach to evaluation as if people mattered*, Institute of Development Studies, University of Sussex, 1984.

Jeffers, John N.R., *An Introduction to Systems Analysis with Ecological Applications*, Edward Arnold, 1978.

Kobayashi, H., *Modelling and Analysis: an introduction to system performance evaluation methodology*, Addison Wesley, 1978.

Land, K.C., S. Spilerman (eds.), *Social Indicator Models*, Russel Sage Foundation, 1975.

Laszlo, E., *Introduction to Systems Philosophy: towards a new paradigm of contemporary thought*, Gordon Publishing, 1972.

Lewin, A.Y., M.F. Shakun, *Policy Sciences: methodologies and cases,* Pergamon, 1976.

Lineberry, R., et al., *Community Indicators: improving communities management*, University of Texas Press, 1974.

Little, I.M.D., D.A. Mirrlees, *Project Appraisal and Planning for Developing Countries*, Heinemann Educational, 1974.

Majchrzak, Ann, *Methods for Policy Research*, Sage, 1984.

Mayer, Robert R., *The Design of Social Policy Research*, Prentice Hall, 1980.

McGraw, D., G. Watson, *Political and Social Enquiry*, John Wiley, 1976.

Merton, R.M., et al (eds.), *Qualitative and Quantitative Social Research: papers in honour of Paul F. Lazarsfeld*, Free Press, 1979.

Millar, Annie, et al. (eds.), *Monitoring the Outcomes of Social Services* (vols. 1–3), The Urban Institute, 1977.

Mishra, Madhu S., *Bibliography on Management of Rural Development* (vols. I and II), IIM, Calcutta, 1983–1984.

Morell, J.A., *Programme Evaluation in Social Research*, Pergamon, 1979.

Morris, L.L., C.T. Fitz-Gibbon, *Evaluator's Handbook*, Sage, 1978.

Morris, Morris David, *Measuring the Condition of the World's Poor*, Pergamon, 1979.

Mukherjee, R., *The Quality of Life: valuation in social research*, Sage, 1989.

Mullen, E.J., J.R. Dumpson (eds.), *Evaluation of Social Intervention*, Jossey Bass, 1972.

Nagel, Stuart S., *Interdisciplinary Approaches to Policy Studies*, Policy Studies, 1973.

——— (ed.), *Policy Studies and the Social Sciences*, D.C. Heath & Co., 1975.

———, *Policy Studies Handbook*, Lexington Books, 1980.

———, *Policy Evaluation: making optimum decisions*, Praeger, 1982.

Organization of Economic Co-operation and Development (OECD), *Inventory of Data Sources for Social Indicators*, OECD, 1979.

Panandikar, V.A. Pai, *Governmental Systems and Development*, Popular/Indian Council of Social Science Research, 1976.

Pasmore, W.A., J.J. Sherwood (eds.), *Socio-technical systems: a source book*, University Associates, 1978.

Patton, M.Q., *Utilization-focused Evaluation*, Sage, 1978.

———, *Qualitative Evaluation Methods*, Sage, 1980.

Pearce, D.W., *The Valuation of Social Cost*, George Allen & Unwin, 1978.

Poister, Theodore H., *Public Program Analysis: applied research methods*, University Park Press, 1978.

Posavac, E.J., R.G. Carey, *Program Evaluation: methods and case studies*, Prentice Hall, 1980.

Quade, E.S., *Analysis for Public Decisions*, North Holland, 1982.

Richards, H., *The Evaluation of Cultural Action*, Macmillan, 1985.

Riecken, H.W., R.F. Boruch (eds.), *Social Experimentation: a method for planning and evaluating social intervention*, Academic, 1974.

Rokeach, Milton, *The Nature of Human Values*, Free Press, 1973.

Rossi, Peter H., H.E. Freeman, *Evaluation: a systematic approach*, Sage, 1985.

Rossi, R.J., K.J. Gilmartin, *Handbook of Social Indicators*, Garland Publishing, 1979.

Rutman, Leonard (ed.), *Evaluation Research Methods: a basic guide*, Sage, 1977.

Schonfield, S., S. Shaw (eds.), *Social Indicators and Social Policy*, Heinemann Educational, 1972.

Seidler, L.J., L.L. Seidler (eds.), *Social Accounting: theories, issues, cases*, Melville Publishing, 1975.

Smith, N.L. (ed.), *Field Assessments of Innovative Evaluation Methods. New Directions for Program Evaluation Series, No. 13*, Jossey Bass, 1982.

——— (ed.), *New Techniques for Evaluation. New Perspectives in Evaluation, vol. 2*, Sage, 1981.

Struening, E., Guttentag, M. (eds.), *The Handbook of Evaluation Research* (vols. 1 and 2), Sage, 1978.

Strumpel, B., *Economic Means for Human Needs Social Indicators of Well-Being and Discontent*, University of Michigan/Institute for Social Research, 1976.

Stober, G.J., D. Schumacher (eds.), *Technology Assessment and Quality of Life*, Elsevier, 1973.

Suchman, E.A., *Evaluative Research: principles and practice in public service and social action programs*, Russel Sage Foundation, 1967.

Tribe, L.H., et al. (eds.), *When Values Conflict: essays on environmental analysis, discourse and decision*, Ballinger Publishing, 1976.

Tripodi, T, et al., *Social Programme Evaluation*, University of Michigan Press, 1971.

Trochim, William M.K., *Research Design for Program Evaluation*, Sage, 1984.

United Nations, *Guiding Principles for the Design and Use of M & E in Rural Development Programmes*, United Nations, 1984.

Webb, E.J., et al., *Unobtrusive Measures: nonreactive research in the social sciences*, Rand McNally, 1966.

Weiss, Carol H., *Evaluation Research: methods of assessing program effectiveness*, Prentice Hall, 1972.

Yin, Robert K., *Case Study Research: design and methods*, Sage, 1984.

Zaltman, G., R. Duncan, *Strategies for Planned Change*, Wiley Interscience, 1977.

Articles/Reports

Ackoff, R.L., Does Quality of Life Have to be Quantified?, *Operational Research Quarterly*, vol. 27, 1976.

Anderson, James G., Causal Models and Social Indicators: towards the development of social system models, *American Sociological Review*, vol. 38, 1973.

Angrist, S.S., Evaluation Research: possibilities and limitations, *Journal of Applied Behavioural Science*, vol. 11, 1975.

Bachrach, P., Evaluating Development Programmes: a synthesis of recent experience, Occasional Paper no. 3, OECD, 1977.

Bish, Robert L., The Assumption of Knowledge in Policy Analysis. In Gregg, Philip M. (ed.), *Problems of Theory in Policy Analysis*, D.C. Heath & Co., 1976.

Blalock, H.M., Indirect Measurement in Social Science: some non-additive models. In Blalock, H.M., et al. (eds.), *Quantitative Sociology: international perspectives on mathematical and statistical modelling*, Academic Press, 1975.

Brand, Jack, The Politics of Social Indicators, *British Journal of Sociology*, vol. 26, 1975.

Brunner, Edmund des, Evaluation Research in Adult Education, *International Review of Community Development*, 1967.

Bunge, Mario, What is a Quality of Life Indicator?, *Social Indicators Research*, vol. 7, 1975.

Carley, Michael, Social Theory and Models in Social Indicator Research, *International Journal of Social Economics*, vol. 6, 1979.

Carley, M., A. Walkey, Some Key Elements in Social Impact Assessment, Canadian Conference on Social Impact Assessment, Bauff, 1978.

Caro, Francis G., Approaches to Evaluation Research: a review, *Human Organization*, vol. 28, no. 2, 1969.

———, Issues in the Evaluation of Social Programs, *Review of Educational Research*, 1971.

Churchman, C.W., On the Facility, Felicity and Morality of Measuring Social Change. In Seidler, L.J., L.L. Seidler (eds.), *Social Accounting: theories, issues, cases*, Melville Publishers, 1975.

Cohen, David K., Politics and Research: evaluation of social action programs in education, *Review of Educational Research*, 1970.

Cohen, J.M., Norman T. Uphoff, Rural Development Participation: concepts and measures for project design, implementation and evaluation, *Rural Development Committee Monograph*, Series no. 2, Cornell University, 1977.

de Neufville, J.I., Validating Policy Indicators, *Policy Sciences*, vol. 10, 1979.

Einhorn, H.J., W. McCouch, A Simple Multiattribute Utility Procedure for Evaluation, *Behavioural Science*, vol. 22, 1977.

Enthoven, Alain C., The Systems Analysis Approach. In Gawthorp, L.C. (ed.), *The Administrative Process and Democratic Theory*, Houghton Mifflin, 1970.

Evans, John W., Evaluating Social Action Programs, *Social Science Quarterly*, vol. L, no. 3, 1969.

Fanchette, Serge, Social Indicators: problems of methodology and selection. In *UNESCO Social Indicators: problems of definition and selection*, UNESCO, 1974.

Feuerstein, M.T., Participatory Evaluation: by, with and for the people, *Rural Development Communication Bulletin*, 1982.

Flanagan, John C., Evaluating Educational Outcomes, *Science Education*, vol. L, no. 3, 1966.

Freeman, Howard E., Clarence C. Sherwood, Research in Large Scale Intervention Programs, *Journal of Social Issues*, vol. XXI, no. 1, 1965.

Freeman. Howard E., Ilene N. Bernstein, Evaluation Research and Public Policies. In Nagel, Stuart S. (ed.), *Policy Studies and the Social Sciences*, D.C. Heath & Co., 1975.

Gaikwad, V.R., Measuring Performance of Small Farmers Development Agency (report/mimeo), Indian Institute of Management, Ahmedabad.

Haveman, R.H., B.A. Weisbord, Defining Benefits of Public Programs: some guidance for policy analysts, *Policy Analysis*, vol. 1, 1975.

Heyer, Judith, Special Seminar on Contradictions in the SFDA Programme in Kanur Village, Coimbatore: first impressions (report/mimeo), MIDS, Madras, 1980.

Jones, W.C., E.F. Borgatta, Methodology of Evaluation. In Mullen, E.J., J.R. Dumpson (eds.), *Evaluation of Social Intervention*, Jossey Bass, 1972.

Land, Kenneth C., On the Definition of Social Indicators, *The American Sociologist*, vol. 6, 1971.

———, Theories, Models and Indicators of Social Change, *International Social Science Journal*, vol. 27, 1975.

Kirkpatrick, D.L., Evaluation of Training. In Craig, R.L., L.R. Bittel (eds.), *Training and Development Handbook*, McGraw Hill, 1967.

Leviton, S.A.R., Facts, Fancies and Freeloaders in Evaluation Anti-Poverty Programs, *Poverty and Human Resources Abstracts*, vol. IV, no. 6, 1969.

Luthans, F., T.R.V. Davis, An Idiographic Approach to Organizational Behaviour Research: the use of single case experimental designs and direct measures, *Academy of Management Review*, vol. 7, 1982.

Michalos, Alex C., Social Indicator Research, *Policy Studies Journal*, vol. 6, 1978.

Misra, P.N., T.K. Jayaraman, Performance Evaluation of Sales Tax Administration: a case study of Gujarat, India (report/mimeo), Indian Institute of Management, Ahmedabad.

Moss, L., The Evaluation of Fundamental Education, *International Social Science Bulletin*, vol. VII, no. 3, 1955.

Nash, Christopher, et al., Criteria for Evaluating Project Evaluating Techniques, *Journal of American Institute of Planners*, vol. 41, 1975.

Ott, Jack M., A Classification System for Decision Situations: an aid to educational planning and evaluation, *Educational Technology*, vol. IX, no. 2, 1969.

Owens, Thomas R., Suggested Tasks and Roles of Evaluation Specialists in Education, *Educational Technology*, vol. VIII, no. 22, 1968.

Padaki, V., et al., Health and Sickness in Complex Systems. In Padaki, V., V. Shanbhag (eds.), *Industrial Sickness: the challenge in Indian textiles*, ATIRA, 1984.

Pedersen, Kjeld M., A Proposed Model for Evaluation Studies, *Administrative Science Quarterly*, vol. 22, 1977.

Phillips, D.C., When Evaluators Disagree: perplexities and perspectives, *Policy Sciences*, vol. 8, 1977.

Poland, Orville F., Programme Evaluation and Administrative Theory, *Public Administration Review*, vol. 34, 1974.

Proceedings of Symposium, Evaluating Educational Programs, *Urban Review*, vol. III, no. 4, 1969.

Reisbeck, Gordon, How the Choice of Measures of Effectiveness Constrains Operational Analysis, *Interfaces*, August, 1979.

Rich, R.F., G. Zaltman, Toward a Theory of Planned Social Change: alternative perspectives and ideas, *Evaluation* (special issue), 1978.

Roos, N.P., Proposed Guidelines for Evaluation Research, *Policy Studies Journal*, vol. 3, 1974.

Sen, Amartaya, The Concept of Efficiency. In Parkin, M., A. Nobay (eds.), *Contemporary Issues in Economics*, Manchester University Press, 1975.

Snyder, R.A., et al., A Model for the Systematic Evaluation of Human Resource Development Programs, *Academy of Management Review*, vol. V, no. 3, 1980.

Stufflebeam, Daniel L., Toward a Science of Educational Evaluation, *Educational Technology*, vol. VIII, no. 14, 1968.

Weinberger, Martin, Evaluating Educational Programs: observations by a market researcher, *Urban Review*, vol. III, no. 4, 1969.

Weiss, Robert S., Martin Rein, The Evaluation of Broad-Aim Programs: a cautionary case and a moral, *Administrative Science Quarterly*, vol. XV, no. 1, 1970.

Weiss, Carol H., Alternative Models of Programme Evaluation, *Social Work*, vol. 19, November, 1974.

———, Research for Policy's Sake: the enlightenment function of social research, *Policy Analysis*, vol. 3, 1977.

Wilder, David E., Problems of Evaluation Research. In Brunner, Edmund des, et al. (eds.), *An Overview of Adult Education Research*, Adult Education Association of the USA, 1959.

Zapf, Wolfgang, Systems of Social Indicators: current approaches and problems, *International Social Science Journal*, vol. 27, 1975.

Series

1. Elsevier series on Policy Sciences
2. Pergamon series on Policy Studies
   (Subseries on themes—rural development, energy, etc.)
3. Policy Studies Annual Review series:
   Vols. 1 to 6 by Sage
   Vol. 7 onwards by Transaction Books
4. Sage series on Applied Social Research Methods
5. Sage annual volumes on Evaluation Studies Review Annual
6. UNESCO series on Socio-economic Studies

Postscript

An international conference held at the Centre for Development Studies, University College of Swansea (Wales), explored issues in programme evaluation methodology almost identical to those in the Ahmedabad workshop. The proceedings of the conference are presented in a highly readable form in the book: Marsden, David and Peter Oakley, *Evaluating Social Development Projects*, OXFAM, 1990.

Part II

Case Studies

Introduction

Vijay Padaki

The case-studies presented here have been chosen as much for the diversity of developmental effort portrayed as for the recognizable common features in them. The most notable of these are certain felt concerns:

* The dissatisfaction with commonly available methods in programme evaluation.
* The realization that the given context of perpetuated poverty and inequality calls for radically different approaches and methods, rather than 'adaptations' of standard methods.
* The readiness to critically reflect on one's experiences.
* The realization that a true appreciation of social change comes from a woods-over-trees view of programme parameters.
* The active search for new methods, models, paradigms in actual practice.

The six cases in this collection are, of course, a sampler. They are brought together for the dual objectives of (*a*) illustrating the issues raised in the earlier sections, and (*b*) serving as pointers to innovations possible in the future. The choice of cases was determined entirely by the association of the persons and agencies concerned with the review exercise undertaken. There are surely many more innovations in programme evaluation which have been attempted in this country, with many more insights to be shared. If this publication should stimulate further documentation and greater sharing of the rich experience, all the better.

The first case is on the Tamil Nadu experience in the National Adult Education Programme. It juxtaposes the methodology laid down centrally (for the laudable objectives of comparability and standardization) with the field problems of implementation. The attempts at refinements for greater relevance are described. The reflections on the organizational requirements for effective evaluation research are also interesting.

The second case is on a community health programme that began with the objective of innovating an institutional form that would employ a primary health care organization to promote indigenous forms of health care. The conflicts arising from the politico-economic ramifications underline the systemic consequences of development interventions and, therefore, the implications for evaluative research into them.

The third case describes the Kheda Communications Project, the attempt to deploy the highest orders of technology for development objectives through the programmes of the Development and Educational Communication Unit of the Indian Space Research Organization. The importance of a strong 'boundary' function in the intervention, and the need for a multipronged intervention model are revealed in the narration.

The next case is in the nature of a team stocktaking of the Women's Development Project in Rajasthan. The concurrent evaluation in this project was characterized by a high degree of community participation in several innovative modes of expression. The conflicts in striking balances between subjectivity and objectivity, quality and quantity, parts and wholes are reflected upon.

The fifth case is a more deliberate reworking of material on the already well-known cell for the Application of Science and Technology to Rural Areas (ASTRA) at the Indian Institute of Science, Bangalore. An attempt is made to examine the institutional forces that determine sustained work in generating appropriate technologies and, equally important, their effective dissemination.

The last case is only incidentally about a development programme undertaken in Gujarat, culminating in housing for a long exploited community. The focus shifts to the case writer himself, and the lessons gained through the project—the need to unlearn a lot of what we acquire as unquestioned knowledge, attitude and perspective, before we can become truly useful facilitators in the development process. The implications for 'methodology' in evaluation research are interesting and worthy of serious attention.

Do the cases provide ready alternatives, ready solutions to nagging problems in evaluation research in development interventions? The answer must obviously be in the negative. They cannot be expected to do so. Yet, in raising issues, sharing concerns, and tugging at our blinkers, they might just provide the necessary stimulation for others to innovate even further, and thereby create some momentum in the search for appropriate methodology. The more immediate, and modest, objective of the case collection is probably served better with a simple tip to the reader. Reading each case, one might ask oneself the questions:

* How many of the guidelines suggested by the workshop group for alternatives in evaluation research can I visualize as feasible in this case?
* If I found myself in a similar development programme, how would I go about the concurrent and summative evaluation tasks?

Six

The National Adult Education Programme in Tamil Nadu*

K. Ramakrishnan

In October 1978, for the first time since independence, the Government of India recognised adult illiteracy as a significant problem worthy of a solution, and launched the National Adult Education Programme (NAEP). The need was obvious. According to the Directorate of Adult Education, Government of India, based on the 1971 census data, nearly 66 per cent of the 460 million persons aged five years or more were illiterate. Between 1961 and 1971, although the literacy rate was reported to have improved from 24 to 29 per cent, the number of adult illiterates (age 15 and over) went up to approximately 210 million from the 1961 figure of 190 million. By 1976, the population of illiterate adults in the age group 15–35 (considered the most productive age group) was around 100 million. The Government of India, concerned about the situation, chalked out an adult education programme to be implemented by various state governments and provisionally allocated Rs. 200 crores to be spent during the Sixth Plan period (1978–83). This case is based on the experiences of the author as the chief of the Adult Education Evaluation Unit at MIDS from July 1980 to June 1985.

*** Based on the documentation of the NAEP for Tamil Nadu at the Madras Institute of Development Studies. The interpretations and inferences drawn are of the case writer alone.**

NAEP in Tamil Nadu

Tamil Nadu is among those states to have implemented the programme more extensively. Since the launch of the Adult Education Programme in 1978, the Directorate of Adult Education of the Government of Tamil Nadu has been implementing the programme through the Rural Functional Literacy Project (RFLP) as well as the State Adult Education Programme (SAEP). The former is funded fully by the central government, and the funds for the latter come exclusively from the state budget. As of December 1982, approximately Rs. 6 crores had been spent (in the project alone, not including the administrative expenses at the district, state and national level). A total of 33,501 adult education centres (AECs) had each completed a ten month programme, with a little more than a million learners reportedly having been enrolled. The share of the voluntary agencies, the universities/colleges and a small number of non-student youth clubs called Nehru Yuvak Kendras, together accounted only for about 400 AECs with an enrolment of about 120,000 learners.

The programme in Tamil Nadu had been studied by the Madras Institute of Development Studies (MIDS), an autonomous research institution. The study was commissioned by the Ministry of Education, Government of India, to carry out both quick appraisals (as the ministry termed these studies) and other in-depth studies, as part of a continuing programme of evaluation.

The Development Orientation of NAEP

NAEP was launched in October 1978 by the Government of India. This was the government which had come to power under circumstances unprecedented in Indian politics. It was the first time that the party which had ruled the nation since independence found itself rejected by the electorate. This, in itself, was regarded by many as the harbinger of a major social transformation. The new government, apparently, envisaged the role of adult education in accelerating the social transformation to be crucial, as some pronouncements in the policy document suggest. The document states that the 'government have resolved to wage a clearly conceived, well planned and relentless struggle against illiteracy to enable the masses to play an active role in social and cultural change.' This is further elaborated:

NAEP is visualised as a means to bring about a fundamental change in the process of socio-economic development; from a situation in which the poor remain passive spectators at the fringe of the development activity to being enabled to be at its centre, and as active participants. The learning process involves emphasis on literacy, but not that only; it also stresses the importance of functional upgradation and of raising the level of awareness regarding their predicament among the poor and the illiterate.

Similarly, the formulation of strategies for implementation also reveal the planners' expectations of NAEP as something much more than a programme for basic literacy. It views education on a continuous basis. Although the programme visualized NAEP as a timebound mass movement, on its completion it would create conditions for a different process of socio-economic development. Accordingly it was argued that the NAEP could not be organised by the education ministry alone. The planners insisted that 'every effort must be made to involve other ministries and departments, with a view to sharing the responsibility for organization of adult education programmes.' NAEP was expected to establish mutually supportive linkages with the other developmental activity agencies:

> It is important that the adult education movement should be closely linked with the planning strategy . . . . For this purpose close cooperation should be created with the dominant development activity of the area, whether it goes under the rubric of Integrated Rural Development or Employment Oriented Area Planning or DPAP, or whatever.

The policy planners talked also of the necessity to provide special programmes for special groups based on special needs. Programmes for (*a*) the rural youth, to train them in the scientific methods suited for small-scale production; and (*b*) the urban workers, to prepare them for securing their rightful claims for and participation in management, are some examples to be found in the policy document. Thus we can justifiably conclude that the NAEP formulation at least strongly implied objectives beyond reducing illiteracy, such as a change in the standard of living and the quality of life, albeit in the long run.

Organisation of NAEP

The objectives of NAEP were expected to be achieved through the educational activities to be organized in a number of adult education centres (see Figure 6.1). The adult education centre (AEC) formed the basic administrative unit for the programme. Each AEC was to be organised by an animator (also known as an instructor), who would run the centre for about ten hours per week for a period of ten months. It was expected that each adult learner would spend at the centre between 300–350 hours over this period. The animator was to be a part-time worker receiving an honorarium of Rs. 50 per month for his/her services. A number of AECs together constituted a 'project'.

As far as the responsibility for working the projects was concerned, it was felt that the 'most appropriate body would be the various voluntary organizations engaged in programmes of education or social development.' In addition, it was expected that educational institutions (particularly universities and colleges), local bodies (panchayats and municipalities), and employers could be made responsible for the organization of adult education activities and follow-up programmes. In areas where none of these agencies was available or able to assume the responsibility, it was suggested that the responsibility would have to be shouldered by the state government.

The smallest adult education project was constituted by thirty centres, for every group of which full-time supervisors were appointed. Full-time project officers were also appointed to administer projects comprising 100 AECs or more. The animators were trained for periods ranging from one to three weeks, while the supervisors and project officers were inducted through orientation programmes of a few days.

All the projects in a district were formally under the co-ordination of the district adult education officer (DAEO). According to the NAEP policy guidelines (and the report of a working group on adult education), the role of the DAEO was to assist the district collector to co-ordinate and monitor the programme implementation. However, in practice, the administration of the government programme was entirely by the Directorate of Non-formal and Adult Education, the state level body under the Department of Education, through which the central and the state funds were routed to the programme.

Figure 6.1: **NAEP ORGANIZATION**

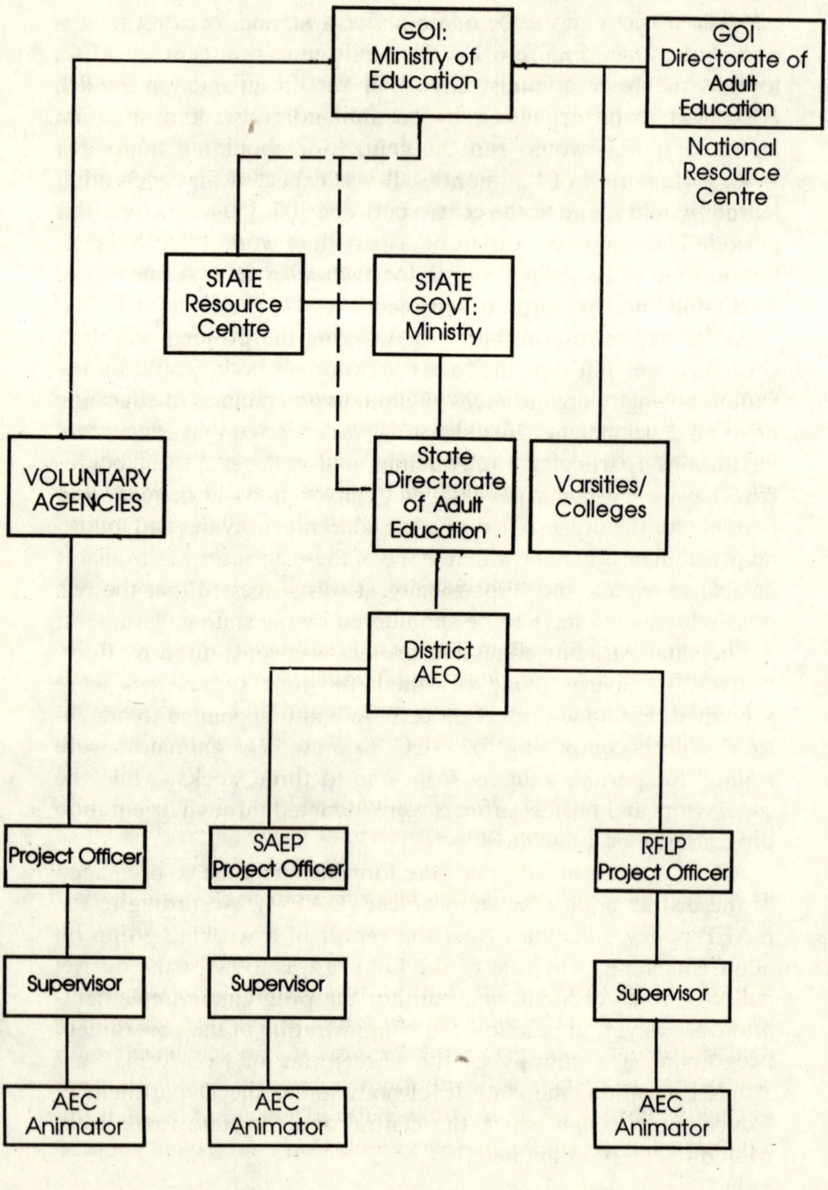

Evaluation of NAEP in Tamil Nadu

Some Background Information

One distinct feature of NAEP was the decision to have the programme evaluated continuously by independent agencies; i.e., agencies other than those implementing the programme. Thus a few quick reviews of programmes in two other states were already completed by late 1979. In Tamil Nadu, however, the programme had a slightly late start. Although some voluntary agencies had been sanctioned financial assistance and had started the programme in 1978 itself, the Rural Functional Literacy Project (RFLP) was not operational till mid-1979. Perhaps on account of this delay in starting the RFLP, and the diffidence to have an evaluation take place before the programme functionaries got a grip over it, the central government's suggestion to get the evaluation of the programme going early enough was not followed in Tamil Nadu. In September 1979 the central government persuaded the state government to have the evaluation initiated and the first steps in this direction were taken by December 1979. Ultimately the evaluation research team of the Madras Institute of Development Studies was in position by July 1980, and the first quick review of the programme by voluntary agencies was started.

The evaluation unit consisted of core personnel of only three: the chief, a research associate and a research assistant. Field studies and the analysis of incoming data were undertaken by temporary investigators as and when necessary. The administrative support was provided by a typist-cum-clerk. The unit was funded by the Ministry of Education, GOI, from year to year based on proposed research and budgetary information provided by the unit in advance. Being part of MIDS, the researchers had the benefit of consultations with some of the faculty of the Institute. During the five years, the unit prepared ten reports on various dimensions of the programme (Appendix 6.1).

Meanwhile, it may be recalled, the mid-term elections in early 1980 led to the Janata Party government, which initiated NAEP, being replaced by a Congress(I) government. This resulted in a considerable amount of uncertainty about the future of the adult education programme, the role of the voluntary sector, and such other policy matters. In fact, most of the senior officials who had been involved in the policy formulation and launching of NAEP were no more on the scene, having been shifted to other assignments. Thus, by the time the evaluation team at MIDS started its work, there was an atmosphere of uncertainty about the programme.

Objectives of Evaluation Policy and Practice

The policy document sets forth the role of evaluation research in the following terms:

> The importance of systematic monitoring and evaluation cannot be exaggerated. It must permeate the entire programme and should provide feedback for introducing necessary correctives from time to time. It is also important to have in-built arrangements for applied and coordinated research so that the experience of NAEP is systematically analyzed and provides guidelines for future action.

Before launching the programme, the Directorate of Adult Education, GOI (DAE), had conducted a couple of seminars with experts to evolve guidelines for monitoring, evaluation and research, and published the proceedings. Autonomous research agencies and institutions of higher education had been identified to accept the responsibility for evaluation research in different regions. Thus, it can be suggested that sincere attempts had been made to build in an evaluation component in the programme.

However, the broad policy outline, it may be suggested, did not get translated into a set of specific operational tasks or terms of reference for the common understanding of the policy planners, implementors and evaluators. Even direct interactions with functionaries in the central government and State Directorate did not lead to any clearly articulated terms of reference. There were only general statements on the need for the evaluation to remain sensitive and sympathetic to the constraints in the field, and the need for some quick feedback. It is not unusual, of course, that programme functionaries are often unable to articulate very clearly the objectives of evaluation research. However, in the case of NAEP, the problem of lack of clarity was compounded by a few more factors.

Any detailed consultative process for evolving the terms of reference was not possible either at the central or the state government level. Consequent to the change of government at the centre, senior officials who had been involved in the programme formulation were no more on the scene. In fact the DAE was without a head, and the head of the Evaluation Division was an ad hoc appointee with the status of a consultant. Consequently, there was nobody to make definite commitments about the details of the evaluation study. At the state level, too, the consultative process was not possible. This was primarily because the functionaries perceived the evaluation as something imposed on them. Their questions were:

1. Why an external evaluation of NAEP at all, when no other government programme of such a magnitude is being subjected to any such process?
2. What is the utility of feedback through evaluation, when the programme procedures have been set down in great detail by the policy-makers?
3. Who will benefit from evaluation, when there is complete confidence in the state machinery to carry out the procedures efficiently?

Consequently, the approach to the evaluation was determined more or less unilaterally by the evaluating team. Of course, the proceedings of the seminars on evaluation and the norms for achievement suggested by the DAE formed the main basis for the evaluation effort. Moreover, by the time the evaluation research by MIDS was initiated, two review studies had already been completed in two other states. The reports pertaining to these studies, as well as personal interactions with the researchers responsible for these efforts, also contributed to the design of the MIDS research effort. But the fact remains that the input by the programme implementors themselves was minimal in the evaluation design.

Divergent Perceptions of Planners and Implementors

The guidelines provided by the DAE had indicated norms for literacy achievement in fairly specific terms. It had been suggested that the learner at the end of the programme should be able to read a simple passage (with five or six sentences) in a minute, with enough comprehension to answer questions relating to it; that s/he should be able to write at a speed of seven words per minute when a passage is dictated; and that s/he should be able to read numbers (up to 100) and do minor calculations involving three digit numbers. These were not unrealistic, given the objective that the literacy skills obtained must be usable, and capable of being further enhanced through self-learning. The norms for assessment of functionality and awareness/conscientization could not be spelt out in a similar manner. However, since the intent of the programme planners had been revealed through the policy statements cited earlier, the evaluation research team designed tools to assess the achievement of these objectives, to be revealed by learners' awareness of some basic issues concerning their lives. (These are described in Appendix 6.2.)

However, the functionaries at the field level did not, apparently, perceive the need for such a systematic evaluation. The State Directorate dismissed the task of the evaluation unit with just one statement: 'It has already been established that the Government of India norms are too high to be achieved.' (Of course, no such conclusion had been reached. Views had been expressed questioning the validity of the norms, and a continuous review of the norms had been indicated.) Rejecting the norms suggested by GOI, the State Directorate graded the learners' performance in literacy skills (based on scores awarded by the animators in an internal evaluation process at the end of the ten month duration of the centre) according to three categories: second standard level of formal school, third standard level and fourth standard level. This classification, according to the evaluation researchers, did not lead to any meaningful understanding of the achievement through the programme, because it was not clear as to what 'second standard level' really was. The assessment of the researchers (as a result of their study) was that the programme had equipped only a small proportion of the participants with adequate literacy skills. This observation was unacceptable to the State Directorate of Adult Education. It may be recalled that this agency was the dominant participant in implementing the programme. Soon, officials of the Directorate became totally indifferent to all evaluation research. This continued for a considerable period.

It was not merely differences of opinion regarding assessment that divided the implementors and the researchers, but differing perceptions regarding the concept of development education itself. We had already mentioned the approach we followed, based on our interpretation of policy statements. Attempts were made to 'measure' the awareness of the existence of legislations on minimum wages, maximum landholdings and marriageable age, as well as the perceptions on fighting injustices (e.g., untouchability). However the State Directorate of Adult Education considered such questions as 'controversial' and unsuitable for judging awareness. In fact, they were of the opinion that 'we should be very cautious in dealing with such topics in a welfare scheme like the Adult Education Programme.' (In other words, these topics should not be raised.) The DAEOs, project officers, as well as supervisors were mostly categorical that discussions on such 'sensitive' issues would lead to conflicts in the community, and the programme being closed down. This lack of concurrence between the perceptions of policy planners and programme implementors regarding the objectives of the programme led to a basic misunderstanding of the role of the evaluators as fault-finders.

It is difficult not to raise the question about the extent to which the programme formulators were responsible for this wrong perception about evaluation. It is, of course, not an unusual phenomenon. Evaluators all over the world are perceived as fault-finders by the programme functionaries, especially when the culture of critical self-assessment has not been developed. But it may be fruitful to examine whether the programme planners, namely, the functionaries at the central government (Ministry of Education and the Directorate of Adult Education, New Delhi), had not inadvertently contributed to the apprehensions of the programme implementors. For example, in a letter from the centre to the Tamil Nadu government, it was indicated that the continuation of grants to the voluntary agencies would depend on the evaluation findings. Although, at an abstract level, such a stand cannot be faulted, the practical implications of such a communication seem to be detrimental to the evaluation process. The casualty was the frankness and candour in self-assessment that is essential in any development intervention—that is probably possible in the absence of a threat of loss of financial support. The evaluation reports mention the adverse consequences of an 'inspection atmosphere' that prevailed during the researchers' visits to the AECs.

The effects of misperceptions are revealed, typically, in the nature of participation in official forums.

Response to Evaluation Findings

Nine reports assessing various dimensions of programme implementation in Tamil Nadu were submitted to the central government, the state government and other relevant agencies such as the State Resource Centre and Department of Adult and Continuing Education. The State Directorate commented, on its own, only on one of the reports. On two other reports, they provided comments only when a follow-up meeting was organised at the initiative of the central government.

Summaries of the reports from various states, along with some comparison of their methodologies, were provided twice by the Directorate of Adult Education. Two meetings were held to discuss them. In one of them, the evaluators and state officials participated. Discussions were confined to (*a*) the strengths and weaknesses and (*b*) possible future studies. There was hardly any discussion on the appropriateness/feasibility (or otherwise) of some of the policy level recommendations made by the evaluators.

Evaluating the Evaluation

What did the evaluation achieve? This, indeed, is the most difficult question to answer. Let us look at what some of those concerned with programme planning had to say:

> While these studies have helped to enhance the credibility of the programme in many ways, they have also provided an opportunity to the social science research community to develop better sensitivity and understanding of the programme that is designed to bring about social change. For those associated with the policy, planning and management of the adult education programme, these studies have provided the first authoritative data-base for assessing the strengths and weaknesses of the conceptual, operational and technical aspects of the programme.

These comments were based only on the first round of quick reviews. Subsequently, it must be recalled, several reports on different aspects of the programme were prepared.

The most significant outcome of the evaluation research, in our opinion, has been that pertaining to the organizational process. Although the evaluation research team began by looking at the programme as an objective 'outsider', over time the dynamics of the evaluation process led to a far greater involvement. The advantage derived from the ability to move across the different hierarchies of the programme administration—from the animators at the lowest rung right up to the top echelons of policy-making—without the encumbrances of a typical hierarchial structure, aided the researchers to serve as an unseen link among the functionaries at different levels, as well as between the functionaries and the beneficiaries. An illustration would be in order.

We have noted earlier that the functionaries were diffident in official forums to candidly voice the problems (of the programme) arising from the existing policies. However, the functionaries did not feel as diffident with the researchers. Consequently, the researchers were able to glean a lot more of the field problems which otherwise would have escaped notice. For instance, while the animators would dutifully report to the supervisors, the project officers and other officials that the sessions were very well-attended, and would put on a show of strength for the benefit of these 'inspections', they were more candid with us and reported that learners had to be literally dragged to the sessions every day—a chore they found increasingly difficult to keep up. Thus, the lack of motivation of the learners, for whatever reasons, would not have been brought to the attention of policy planners and the higher level programme implementors, but for the objective findings of an 'outside' evaluation team.

Similarly, the evaluation research brought out the unrealistic expectation about establishing any significant linkage between AEP and other governmental departments. Besides pointing out the difficulties of the departmental officials in contributing to the AEP, the research also highlighted the inadequacy of resources that were available for many development and poverty eradication programmes. In the course of this research, many functionaries in the concerned departments were made aware of the size and significance of AEP, and the potential it had to become an effective intervention programme. Thus, in a variety of ways, the evaluation process was also a learning experience for all those associated with it.

The process of evaluation and the outcomes in the form of appraisal studies, disseminated widely among programme functionaries and others, have created considerable awareness about the magnitude and nature of the problem of illiteracy and its nexus with underdevelopment. The issues raised by the evaluation research, if systematically followed up, will lead to an appreciable expansion of knowledge, not only in the field of adult education, but also regarding many programmes of social intervention. The process of evaluation facilitated interactions between evaluation researchers and programme functionaries that led to some soul-searching on both sides.

Appendix 6.1

National Adult Education Programme: Summaries of Evaluation Reports

An Appraisal of the Role of Voluntary Agencies in Tamil Nadu*

This report presents the findings of a study of programme implementation by voluntary agencies. The findings indicate that even the voluntary agencies run the programme in a bureaucratic and inflexible manner. A majority of the adult learners had not gained anything in the three dimensions of literacy, functionality and awareness. Animators reported lack of motivation on the part of the learners, and learners complained of lack of facilities at the centre, inability to attend classes at a particular time every day, and a sense of frustration at the irrelevance of literacy. Programme officers reported the difficulties arising out of rigid guidelines for expenditure and inordinate delays in receiving funds from the government. The state government was preoccupied with its own literacy programmes, and hardly played any supportive role in the voluntary agencies' programmes. The programme fell far short of the expected quantitative as well as qualitative targets.

An Appraisal of the Role of the State Government

This report presents the findings of a study on programme implementation by the Directorate of Non-formal and Adult Education, Tamil Nadu. It reveals that the programme was more extensive than those by the voluntary agencies. But in terms of the final outcomes, there was no significant difference. Most of the district adult education officers (who considered their shift from school education to adult education a punishment), and

* Editor's Note: The term appraisal appears in several titles here, referring to assessments during or after programme inputs. The more appropriate use of the term is for assessments of potential/prediction before a programme.

the supervisors (who were on temporary appointments), were unable to put their hearts into the programme. Consequently, the programme was run ritualistically, and the emphasis on quantitative targets alone mattered. Lack of community support and adequate preparatory time before starting the adult education centres led to many a centre being wound up, informally, if not officially, at various stages of the ten month phase of a project. On an average only about four to six learners out of an expected thirty per centre attained sustainable levels of literacy skills.

An Appraisal of the Programme for Training Functionaries

The training programmes were observed and the participants' knowledge and attitudes were assessed before and after the training programme. The findings suggest that the training programmes were not designed with any specific objectives in view. As a result, a set of disparate activities, largely in the form of talks by different government officials, took place. In many instances, the desirable world-views of the animators, before their training, were distorted, and some undesirable values were inculcated as a consequence of the training. The animator trainees were generally talked down to, rather than being involved in the discovery of adult education methods.

An Assessment of the Internal Evaluation Practices

An assessment of the internal evaluation practices in on-going projects suggests that the practice was more of a ritual than for any purpose of feedback to the participants. The evaluation exercise had been thoroughly bureaucratized, with the result that only the 'quantitative' information was of concern for everybody.

An Appraisal of the Programme Implementation by Universities and Colleges

The study of the programme carried out by the universities and colleges reveals that the programme was considerably more flexible compared to the programme by voluntary agencies and the state government. However, the centres functioned rather spasmodically, on account of the students' preoccupation with their examinations, extra-curricular activities, etc. The discussions with faculty co-ordinators and student animators indicated that involvement in the programme was largely without commitment and enthusiasm.

A Longitudinal Study of the Programme and its Outcome

This study conducted over a span of two years looked at the adult learners' competencies before, during and after the programme. The findings indicate that about 20 per cent of the learners who were motivated and were regular in attending the programme gained sustainable literacy skills within a period of six months and retained these skills. Others either did not gain anything, or lost whatever little was gained.

A Study of the Linkages with Development Programmes

The objectives of integrating the programme into the development process could not be achieved partly because of lack of linkages with other development agencies. Many of these agencies were not aware of the order of magnitude of the NAEP extant, and had their own reasons for non-involvement in the programme. These were to a large extent related to the politicization of government administration.

A Study of the Effects of Concentration of Adult Education Centres

The programme officers' apprehension that locating a large number of centres in one village would be less effective than having only one or two centres was not valid as revealed by this study. An implication is that it may be desirable to saturate a given community, rather than to spread the efforts over a wider area.

An Examination of the Problems of Special Target Groups

This study revealed that although the NAEP policy document emphasized the need to concentrate on the disadvantaged sections of the society (e.g., SC/ST groups and women), the programme implementation did not adopt any special strategies for these sections.

The Role of Evaluation Research

This publication is in the nature of a postscript. It is a reflection on the evaluation research experience of the preceding five years, and the outcome of the conviction that the reflections should be shared with all parties involved in such development interventions.

Appendix 6.2

Approaching Functionality

Functionality Topics

The investigators were given a set of examples with which to steer the conversation on each issue listed below to assess the level of knowledge, and ability to functionally use the knowledge. Only the items are given below, and not the guiding queries.

1. Transactions through the post office
2. Starting and operating a savings account in the post office
3. Getting the children immunized against certain diseases
4. Knowledge and adoption of prenatal and postnatal care for mothers
5. Getting essential commodities through ration shops
6. Knowledge and utilization of bus routes relevant to the community
7. Concessions available for poor school children
8. Functions of a gram sevak
9. Loan schemes applicable to the poor
10. Benefit schemes applicable to individuals or households of the economically weaker sections
11. Obtaining a ration-card
12. Minimum wages for agricultural labour

Assessment of Functional Knowledge: A Categorization

Levels of Knowledge Regarding the Chosen Issues

Note: In addition to the three levels A, B, C, shown below, level D indicated 'No Knowledge' and X indicated that the information could not be collected.

Transactions in Post Office

A. Knowledge of all common postal stationery and their prices; other transactions possible through the post office (e.g., telegram).
B. Knowledge as above but partial or incorrect with respect to details.
C. Only the knowledge about postal stationery, without any details about their prices, etc.

Post Office Savings Account

A. Adequate knowledge about opening and operating an account.
B. Partial knowledge as above.
C. Only the knowledge about the existence of the facility.

Immunizing Children Against Common Epidemics

A. Adequate knowledge about when the child should be given shots and for what diseases.
B. Partial knowledge.
C. Only the knowledge that immunization can be done.

Prenatal and Postnatal Care for Mothers

A. Adequate knowledge of how, when and for what purpose pregnant/lactating women should seek medical care periodically.
B. Partial knowledge.
C. Only the knowledge that such care is needed.

Availability of Essential Commodities through Ration Shops

A. Adequate knowledge about commodities available through ration shops and quantities available; knowledge about who operates ration shops.
B. Partial knowledge.
C. Only knowledge regarding the existence of ration shops.

Transport Facilities Relevant to the Community

A. Complete details of bus routes operating through the community.
B. Partial knowledge.
C. Knowledge confined only to the existence of such facilities.

Concessions Applicable to Poor Schoolgoing Children

A. Knowledge about concessions (free books, meals, uniforms, etc., for poor children); eligibility criteria.
B. Partial knowledge.
C. Knowledge limited to the existence of some concessions.

Role of a Gram Sevak

A. Knowledge regarding who the *gram sevak* is; what he is expected to do; how frequently he visits the village, etc.
B. Partial knowledge.
C. Only the existence of a *gram sevak* is known.

Loan Facilities from Banks and Other Agencies

A. Knows about the different loan schemes applicable to the poor and the sources of assistance in detail.
B. Partial knowledge.
C. Knows that some relief schemes exist.

Relief Schemes for the Poor

A. Knowledge about relief schemes (old-age pension, assistance to destitute widows, free legal aid, etc.).
B. Partial knowledge.
C. Knowledge that some relief schemes exist.

Getting a Ration-card

A. Knows the procedure to get a new ration-card (or replacement) in detail.
B. Partial knowledge.
C. Only knows that a ration-card is needed for getting some essential commodities.

Legal Minimum Wages

A. Knows the correct legal minimum wages applicable for different operations in their area.
B. Partial or incorrect knowledge.
C. Knowledge confined to the existence of a legal minimum wage.

Awareness and Attitudes Assessment

Guidelines to Investigators

People have different opinions about the poor in our country, and the programmes to benefit them. Given below are pairs of certain such perceptions about the poor. Ascertain, through informal conversation, which *one* of the themes in each pair is more acceptable to the respondent and mark it. Please also note down the important excerpts of the conversation to aid analysis.

1. Reasons for poverty:

   a. Lifestyle of the poor and their laziness.
   b. Accident of birth and lack of opportunity.

2. Reasons for people's diffidence to adopt family planning:

   a. Ignorance and superstition.
   b. Expectation that children will be an additional source of income for the present and provide support during old age.

3. Poor can progress only:

   a. If the government and the rich voluntarily help them.
   b. If poor collectively struggle for their rights.

4. Most of those who are rich are in that position:

   a. Because of their hard labour and education.
   b. Because they were born in affluence.

5. Most important reasons for the rising prices are:

   a. Population increases and lack of production.
   b. Increased taxes; hoarding by merchants; mismanagement by the authorities, etc.

6. Opening liquor shops leads to:

   a. Benefits for the poor since the revenue earned by the government through licensing the shops can be utilized to help the poor.

b. The misery of the poor since only they spend in these shops, while the revenue earned by the government gets utilized for schemes to benefit the rich.

7. Lying, cheating, fighting, etc., are activities largely resorted to by:

   a. Poor illiterates.
   b. Those with power, but they are never accused.

8. Many illiterates do not join the AEP because:

   a. They do not realize the importance of education.
   b. They do not find any use for the education.

9. The more important activities at the adult education centre should be:

   a. Literacy teaching.
   b. Understanding the approaches for solving the community's problems besides literacy teaching.

10. The decision regarding the centre's activities must be:

    a. Made by the animator.
    b. Made by the learners collectively.

11. The benefits of the development schemes do not reach the poor because:

    a. The poor are not aware of them.
    b. The more powerful manage to divert them for their own benefit.

12. The SC/ST groups have not progressed in spite of concessions provided for them because:

    a. There are not many among these groups who are adequately knowledgeable and hardworking to take advantage of the concessions.
    b. There are very few among them with enough resources to avail of the facilities.

13. Individual ownership of land is:

    a. Not subject to any ceiling.
    b. Subject to a ceiling by law.

14. The status of women in our society is:

    a. Largely equal to that of men.
    b. That of the oppressed.

15. The effort needed for the welfare of the family is:

    a. Largely contributed by men.
    b. Probably contributed equally by both men and women.

16. The responsibility of bringing up the child must:

    a. Rest largely with the wife.
    b. Rest with both husband and wife.

Note: In all the cases we consider the choice of statement (*b*) 'desirable' from the point of view of an awareness for realizing the role of the oppressed in the society (or in the family) and getting conscientized for action to change the existing conditions.

Seven

Crossroads on the Way to People's Health Care*

C.R. Bijoy

The case is an offshoot of an innovative, long-term, participatory process among three parties: (*a*) the Comprehensive Rural Health Project (CRHP), (*b*) Solidarity Action Research and Information Network International (SARINI), and (*c*) the communities for whom the rural health project was undertaken. There has been an on-going dialogue right from the planning stage of CRHP, through its implementation, up to the selection of research methodology, the assessment of data, as well as the analyses and reporting.

Episode: The Visit

The monitoring and evaluation team arrived from New Delhi to look into the finance and programme aspects of the project. The team cursed the airlines for the unholy departure timings. We moved them to the comfortable hotel and enquired when they would be refreshed enough to start work. 'Oh, half an hour at the most, and we can begin', was the reply.

To put us at ease, the team reiterated that it was the voluntary agencies who delivered the goods, far better than the government,

* Reflections on the experiences in a large project. Positions or viewpoints implied in the narrative are those of the case writer only.

which was now reflected in the government's policy towards the voluntary agencies. A little more system and professionalism in approach and the voluntary agencies can do even better. The job of the monitoring team was only to help, they said. A visit to the rural health centre for a preliminary discussion, followed by visits to any two of the health units, and discussion with their staff would be in order on the first day. A second round of discussions to tie up things, and a meeting with the management on the second day, and they would be ready to take off on the third day. The schedule was set.

The long drive to the rural health centre was uneventful. The auditor from the team sat with our accountant, labouring through the ledger and vouchers. The others produced a checklist. It contained such items as staff recruited and in position, their qualifications, training conducted, establishment of facilities and services, etc. The information we provided was compared with the project appraisal document. Eyebrows were raised. Why, we were very much behind schedule. We talked of our difficulties in the field, the rationale for midstream changes, the acts of omission and commission necessitated by compulsions at the ground level. Hence, the flexibilities needed. After all, in certain respects the project appraisal report had drastically changed what we had originally planned. For example, the role of the village level health workers. There was no 'model' to fall back on. The project proposal envisaged an exploratory time period for the content of their roles to evolve naturally. But the appraisal denied the Project this time. The workers had to be shown their work from the start of the project. This was quite impractical.

We adhered to the steps in our project proposal, in accordance with our understanding of the project needs. By our schedule we had not done badly. The response was firm and final. The project should be implemented according to the appraisal report. If we had done that, we would have been caught up with the 'delivery' of services, and killed the emerging creativity. We appealed to their reasoning. We challenged the dominant notions which were only proving to be fallacies. We insisted that past lessons should be incorporated to reduce mistakes. Tempers slipped. How dare we question the authorities on health care approaches? They had come to help us out, to ensure that the project was implemented as per the appraisal report. We, on the other hand, were creating barriers, questioning well-accepted methods.

We knew we were at crossroads, and we withdrew. The day was getting over and much time had been wasted on unwarranted arguments. The plan to visit two health units had to be altered. Only one unit on the way back to the city was visited. Back at the hotel, tensions eased. A good night's rest and we should all be ready for the next day. We cursed ourselves for not keeping a check on our impulses. It did not help to share concerns and field experiences. We decided to change tack for the next day.

The exercise was resumed with the visit to the second health unit. There was further confirmation of the weaknesses spotted the previous day. Further questions were accompanied with further comparisons. Our answers were brief, to the point, controlled. The task over, we returned to the hotel. After a few hours' rest the team revealed their satisfaction. They were happy with the work they had done over two long days. They concluded that by and large the project was OK, but needed to be speeded up. Certain changes were suggested. They reassured us that there was no cause for worry, as they were there to help us out. At the evening courtesy call on the project authorities (the 'management'), they declared their overall satisfaction with the project. Except for certain things. They had already discussed these and sorted them out with the project leadership. The management requested the team to provide continued guidance for the success of the project. The team responded that the project leadership was dynamic and receptive to their advice. Pleasantries over, we drove back to the hotel.

With tensions eased, we decided to try again. For we were not ready for the full co-option yet. Anecdotes from the leaves of our diaries, the grassroots experiences in the work areas, were placed before them. They surprised us with a patient hearing. Encouraged, we pushed further. They heard us out, with the gently interspersed 'I see' or 'Is it?'. There were things to do, getting ready for the early morning departure. Last minute checks and things. We excused ourselves. The questions in our mind remained with us. The community? Who were they? The *project* had to succeed.

The Project

Starting Objectives

The Comprehensive Rural Health Project (CRHP), aided by the Ministry of Health and Family Welfare, Government of India, is financially assisted by USAID (United States Agency for International Development) under the scheme, Private Voluntary Organizations in Health. It was launched in April 1984 with a workshop that provided guidelines for its implementation. The Project seeks to develop and implement a primary health care programme through the community health approach, utilizing essentially the traditional systems of medicine (Ayurveda and Siddha); along with this the national health programmes are also implemented, in co-ordination with and in support of the government health structure. The main objective of the Project is to develop Ayurveda and Siddha as a culturally acceptable and appropriate promotive, preventive and curative health care programme, and to improve the health services through an innovative, alternative and endogenous health care approach. While the Project started essentially on the existing primary health care model, the main difference was the incorporation of Ayurveda and Siddha, seeking to enquire what Ayurveda and Siddha can do at the primary health care level. The Project also adopted the aim to develop the sensitivity and health culture of the people. This was to be accomplished by orienting itself away from the standard preoccupation with coverage and targets, and towards initiating such processes in villages that would view health in totality, that is, a socio-political and ecological perspective that regards health as a matter of the community's right.

Project Coverage

The Project is operational in Perianaickenpalayam Union block and part of Karamadai block in Coimbatore taluk in Coimbatore district, Tamil Nadu. The main highway and railway line connecting Coimbatore to Ootacamund in Nilgiri district pass through the eastern edge of the project area, while the mountain ranges of the Western Ghats flank the western and north-western side, bordering Palghat district in Kerala. Developmental activities are concentrated alongside this main highway. Farther to the northern, southern and western sides of the project area, an underdeveloped economy and maldevelopment have compounded the problems of the majority of the people living there. The area is predominantly rural in the plains and tribal in the hills.

The Project initially operated in four village panchayats, namely Veerapandi, Nanjundapuram and Narasimmanaickenpalayam, in

Perianaickenpalayam block, and Thekkampatti in Karamadai block, with a population of around 23,000. This was extended in the latter half of 1987, attempting to cover a population of about 2 lakhs in seventeen village panchayats. The project area is divided into four, each area having a health unit which is the peripheral unit, while the headquarters of the Project is designed as the rural health centre containing the project office, out-patient and in-patient departments, laboratory, drug unit, herbal garden and documentation unit. The rural health centre also maintains links with the district government hospital, the district health office, and with the neighbouring primary health centres. Each health unit is under the charge of a physician from the traditional systems of medicine, Ayurveda and Siddha, assisted by an ANM (auxiliary nurse and midwife), a compounder and a team of health promoters. The health promoters act as the link between the community (especially those in special focus: eligible couples, children, pregnant women, the sick, women in general, as well as the local health practitioners, dais (midwife), etc.), on the one hand, and the project personnel as well as the subcentre level staff of the concerned primary health centres, on the other side.

Background and Institution Links

The AVR Educational Foundation of Ayurveda (AVREFA) is sponsored jointly by the Arya Vaidya Pharmacy (Coimbatore) Ltd., a pharmaceutical enterprise, with well-established marketing outlets, and the Ayurvedic Trust, an offshoot of this industry with its 100 bed hospital. It was established as a registered society in 1978. Development of Ayurveda and Siddha, through the establishment of such activities as education, research and development, training, extension work and services, publication, etc., are its stated major activities. Having established a regular Bachelor's programme in Ayurveda, it embarked on R & D work with modern facilities. The foundation has persevered in the application of modern scientific approaches for the systematic development of Ayurveda, especially in the various aspects of medicinal plants, standardization of Ayurvedic medicines, computer applications, etc. As mentioned elsewhere, the isolated but strong 'noises' (in the seventies and early eighties) on the questions of utilization of indigenous systems of medicine, not only for the advancement of

Figure 7.1: **CRHP ORGANIZATION**

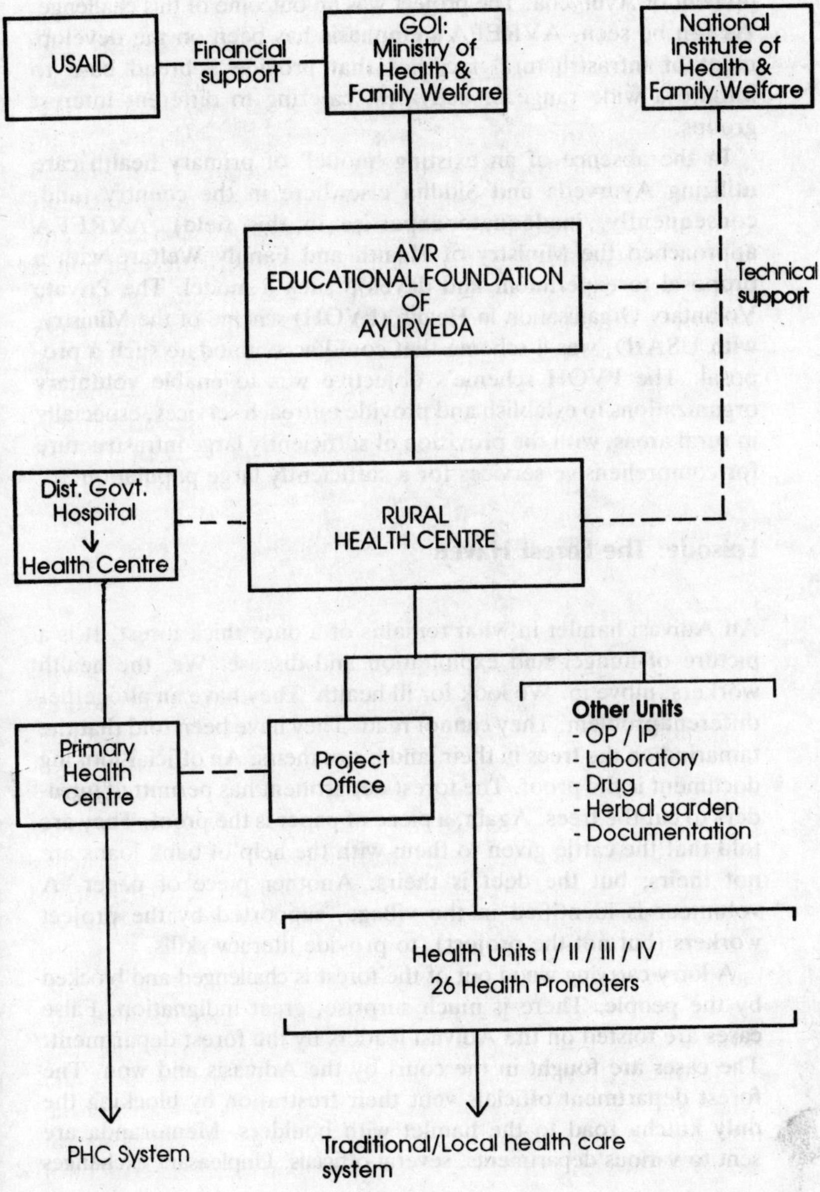

the indigenous systems themselves, but in primary health care, was regarded by AVREFA as another challenging area in the development of Ayurveda. The project was an outcome of this challenge. As can be seen, AVREFA's emphasis has been on the development of infrastructural facilities that provide a broad base to initiate a wide range of activities, catering to different interest groups.

In the absence of an existing 'model' of primary health care utilizing Ayurveda and Siddha elsewhere in the country (and, consequently, inadequate expertise in this field), AVREFA approached the Ministry of Health and Family Welfare with a proposal to experiment and develop such a model. The Private Voluntary Organisation in Health (PVOH) scheme of the Ministry, with USAID, was a scheme that could accommodate such a proposal. The PVOH scheme's objective was to enable voluntary organizations to establish and provide outreach services, especially in rural areas, with the provision of sufficiently large infrastructure for comprehensive services for a sufficiently large population.

Episode: The Forest Haven

An Adivasi hamlet in what remains of a once thick forest. It is a picture of hunger and exploitation and disease. We, the health workers, move in. We look for ill health. They have an altogether different problem. They cannot read. They have been told that the tamarind on the trees in their land is not theirs. An official-looking document is the proof. The forest department has permitted intruders to cut the trees. Again, a piece of paper is the proof. They are told that the cattle given to them with the help of bank loans are not theirs; but the debt is theirs. Another piece of paper. A volunteer is identified in the village, supported by the project workers (but not the project), to provide literacy skills.

A lorry carrying wood out of the forest is challenged and blocked by the people. There is much surprise, great indignation. False cases are foisted on the Adivasi leaders by the forest department. The cases are fought in the court by the Adivasis and won. The forest department officials vent their frustration by blocking the only kutcha road to the hamlet with boulders. Memoranda are sent to various departments, several officials. Unpleasant exchanges between the collectorate and forest department yield no result. The boulders are removed . . . by the minor forest produce contractor. We, the health workers, move on with them, with 'health work' tucked away somewhere.

Land is sold away for as little as Rs. 200 an acre. There is hunger. There is no work, even from those who smuggle the wood out. They no longer come here, as the people in the area have become hostile to deforestation. Just across is the border of Kerala state, where free rations are given to Adivasis. The land does not bear fruit. The labour is wasted. So why not sell the land and migrate to Kerala? The health care workers panic; for very soon there will not be people here whose health they can care. There is much discussion and debate. Sericulture is seen as a hope. The health workers drag the sericulture department into the hamlet, cajole them, pressurize them. A nursery is developed on the river-bed, the site which provides a little dampness. The sale of land is stopped. They decide to stay.

Project Boundaries

The project team recognized one anomaly in the intervention 'model' at the very start. The prevailing primary health care structure had evolved as a centre-to-periphery model to provide newer knowledge and practices to alleviate the suffering of the 'ignorant' masses. Indigenous systems of medicine, on the other hand, had evolved endogenously. The structure required to systematize and organize the practices should be devised in a bottom-up manner. This constituted a major contradiction. While on the one hand a genuine understanding of the problems, experimentation, and development of alternative services will need to be given sufficient time, on the other hand the compulsion of the Ministry was to establish services right from the start of the project with preset schedules of activities and targets.

The project team, with an emphasis on facilitating community processes, adopted an approach of experiential learning. Through an on-going participatory learning process with the community, they opted to base decisions entirely on this learning. Towards this it was absolutely necessary to ensure that the project personnel did not undergo the standard training and adopt the routine approaches and methods established in community health practices.

In an early phase of the project, since the project operational headquarters was established close to the hills adjacent to where the Adivasis dwelt, and the staff recruited was small in number, a dynamic learning process led to a participatory involvement in such issues as atrocities on the Adivasis, land issues, deforestation, etc. This involvement led to gradual mobilization of the Adivasis through critical awareness. Not unexpectedly, such an involvement was viewed as a direct threat by the vested interest groups, the oppressors. Conflicts that arose in this process also posed a threat to the (then) project staff and to the implementing institution. The first major conflict that emerged was between the compulsions of involvement at the grassroots and the formal requirements of the project. With further recruitment of staff, especially the sizeable number of health professionals, two lines of conviction polarized. One group (in minority), who had by now become associated with the issues of the most oppressed sections, adopted the *political economy* approach to health as the valid process in the project. They had also become the more vocal group, exercising informal leadership over the project. They increasingly disliked the pressure to focus a major part of their energies on the achievement of formal project targets, given the time constraints. The other (majority) group, dominated by health professionals, intensely disliked the process and the situations in which they had got themselves involved, as these demanded far more from them. Appeasements and compromises were inevitable, as was the fall-out. There was a tendency towards mediocrity. Gradually the articulation and assertion of the minority group (and, consequently, the use of participatory processes) was further suppressed, especially with the interventions of the monitoring and evaluation agency. The implementing agency, too, when it perceived the conflict as the dominant trend in the project, preferred to go by the counsel of the monitoring and evaluation agency. A staff turnover had commenced.

The initiatives and experiences in 'non-health' areas were rejected as irrelevant, as they fell outside the scope of the project, and project implementation alone was defined as the task.

Episode: Teachers Learning

Sri. Dongre, a pseudonym of course, drops in on us. He has heard about our work in utilizing indigenous systems of medicine in community health. He wants us to train his animators. We ask the purpose, and the type of training he has in mind. Why, of course, the animators are to be trained in the use of medicinal plants, home remedies, etc, and they in turn can pass on this newly acquired knowledge and skills to the community. We state that we are ourselves learning from the ordinary rural people, and that our 'experts' might contribute very little to his needs in turn. Taken aback, he requests that we elaborate further.

Our experience shows that the process is far more important than the technical content, and that in fact the process determines the technical content. In a typical rural situation, if we begin by asking ourselves what people know, we might be surprised by the reality that they do know quite a lot. In health care, a majority of the people, especially the women, are a storehouse of practical knowledge on indigenous methods. Some have a broad range, while others are quite specialized, just as among our own doctors. We discover this only when we talk of what they know rather than what they do not know—when we pay attention to practices that have been transmitted through oral traditions from generation to generation, rather than the practices that are to be introduced from elsewhere through 'modern' systems. The first step, and the most important is . . . sitting. We must sit down and get to know each other. They talk. They share their experience in the health care known traditionally. An expert need not sit in judgement on their knowledge. The process of sitting and talking continues. Humility and respect are essential prerequisites. Knowledge is shared and experiences expanded. Activities to learn new knowledge and skills from them are charted out. The animator is an active participant and organizer. He notes down the experiences accepted by the participants as common to all of them. Learning from each other is facilitated. Constant evaluation of newly identified experiences increases the area of common knowledge. Experimentation, using parameters developed by them, creates further knowledge in a clearly empowering process.

What about scientific validity? Are institutionally trained experts not needed to validate these bits of information?

When we talk of knowledge evolved by the people, evolved empirically all along, the task is to encourage this process conscientiously, in a systematic manner. So why not extend this process fully? Why cannot they be the ones to validate the information generated, using parameters that they develop experientially in the practical laboratory of the community? Why should people not be encouraged to grow from within, especially when we can see the knowledge they possess? We realize that the sensitive point is their control over the production of knowledge, the potential in their skills, and their possible growth in putting that knowledge to use. The animators need to be sensitive to this and sustain the process. They also need to facilitate the spread of knowledge. The trainers and communicators should emerge from within their own people, especially women. This appears sensible as an approach if we truly believe in an endogenous development process.

Sri Dongre rises to leave, and enquires if professionals and experts have any role at all in a community health programme—indeed, in any development programme.

Looking at Outcome

In the process of project implementation, we had to recognize:

* Local health traditions existed, encompassing aspects of primary health care.
* These health traditions formed local 'streams' and had their origins in Ayurveda and Siddha, the main streams.
* The local streams had weakened considerably, at places getting substituted and distorted.
* The local streams could be strengthened by a deliberate plan of interaction and exchange among the functionaries of the stream, as well as with the main stream in a meaningful manner and through a confidence-building and restorative process.
* The local stream was represented by local health practitioners, *dais*, housewives, etc., and was mostly based on locally available resources, knowledge and skills and was generally non-commercial.

A plan of work was set into motion accordingly. Home remedies for promotive, preventive and curative aspects based on locally available resources were promoted. The process entailed collection of local practices and their assessment; exchange of experiences, information and skills in the preparation and use of home remedies; and demonstrations. *Documentation* of such practices by people formed the basis of strengthening the tradition, supplemented by additional useful practices provided by the project personnel. Such remedies and practices were promoted at various points: the out-patient contacts, during field visits of ANMs and health promoters, during village level meetings of traditional practitioners, *dais*, women and others, at field demonstrations, training programmes, etc. Various audio-visual materials were developed and employed in the process.

The locally available medicinal plants and their various uses were documented. Horizontal communication of knowledge and skills on availability and use of medicinal plants was promoted at the village level with a view to sharing experiences and enhancing mutual understanding. The cultivation of useful medicinal plants, especially for common ailments at the household level, was encouraged through exchange of seeds and seedlings. Health promoters prepared herbarium sheets on locally available medicinal plants. Self-reliance and control at the level of the village health practitioner and the household was the primary focus in all these activities.

Currently there are twenty-six health promoters, of which twenty-three are women. Besides being involved in the activities mentioned above, they act as facilitators for grassroots level health work, including registration of ANCs, newborns, PNC (prenatal care), treatment of common ailments, organizing immunization and other MCH (maternal and child health) services, referrals and health education through training, discussions, production of audiovisual materials, songs, street plays, etc. Along with ANMs of the respective health units and subcentre staff of the primary health centres, they carry out family welfare programmes. As an outcome of their collective experience, and in an attempt to reach out further, the health promoters have commenced a bimonthly publication in Tamil with financial support from the people and subscribers, providing information on health and home remedies, problems at the village level, community experiences, and other social concerns. A few of them have organised women in an attempt to understand their problems and help them solve them. Some are attempting to revitalize village level youth forums and sangams, while a few others are mobilizing the community in general. All these experiences are shared in an attempt to restore control over their own lives.

How, then, do we view outcomes from the project? How do we read the balance-sheet, and what colours do we employ to ink the bottom line?

What 'comes out of' the project represents, inevitably, a spectrum. Yet, invariably, in viewing the spectrum we resort to a dichotomy—the palpable, the discrete, and the countable on the one hand, and the longitudinal and the organic on the other. The former are 'visible' to the outsider. The latter are experienced from within, and can be documented only by a truly participatory approach. The differences in the two sets of observation can be stark, inexplicable, although supposedly made on the same endeavour.

A Participatory Effort

SARINI (Solidarity-Action-Research and Information Network International) is an informal network of like-minded people. It has been engaged in a dialogue with the project from an early stage. More specifically, the involvement of SARINI was to facilitate a participatory process among all concerned with the project. Excerpts from their essay on the project, titled 'Traditional Medicine, Primary Health Care and Health Care For All By 2000 AD—An Experience', follow:

> The participation of the local communities as an ongoing process is . . . the most important aspect of CRHP, which also lays the ground for future developments. Less evident, but most important, as a result . . . is the local people's identification and prioritization of their problems. In some areas under CRHP, in fact, 'health' turned out to be of less priority. In such situations the community itself took action, whereas the CRHP-team played only a supportive role, and at times even had to withdraw from the area. Such was the case in Health Unit II area which has a fairly large population of tribal people . . . .
>
> Health Promoters, who are considered the most important group of agents for change, have been identified from and through the local communities. A very visible result of community participation is found in the fact that the locations of all the peripheral service units (Health Units) were suggested . . . by the respective communities. After the establishment . . . there has been an ever increasing demand on further extension of services . . . .

The participatory orientation... has been carried forward in terms of an ongoing dialogue, focused towards rapport building and community contact, orientation to the project, data collection, survey of people's opinion on location of Health Units, organizing the community, identifying health problems, establishing Health Units and services, records and reports, compounding and dispensing drugs, establishing curative services, preventive services . . . coordination with existing services . . . promotion of local health traditions, identification of locally available resources, knowledge, skills and their utilization, herbal garden development, development of targets and evaluation methods, etc. In addition, 'intensive' programmes are being launched that are aimed at planning, monitoring and evaluating community programmes with a view to further decentralize the health services.

Promotion of local health traditions is one of the important issues taken up by CRHP. Traditional methods of medical care and health care are practised by:

* ordinary people (housewives), in the form of home remedies;
* traditional birth attendants/*daïs;*
* traditional medical practitioners . . . .

CRHP has been increasingly involving these three groups with the perspective of developing an 'Endogenous Model of Health Care'. Regular meetings . . . organized through the Health Unit staff . . . have resulted in a process of learning and understanding on both sides, also (among) the Ayurvedic and Siddha physicians. An indication of the potential of this horizontal learning process is a listing of more than 300 simple treatments as home remedies . . . around 26 locally available medicinal plants . . . . In pursuit of the same 'Endogenous Model of Health Care', herbal gardens have been established, initially at the Rural Health Centre and at the Health Units, and increasingly also in the villages and even in the hamlets. They display some of the medicinal plants that are locally available and also in local use, and plants that are used in Ayurveda for preparing medicines by simple techniques. A consolidated list of the plants grown in these herbal gardens has recently been prepared, which also gives details about the use of these plants.

Health promotion activities under CRHP are focused on health education, nutrition education and environmental sanitation, and are being carried out through:

* group and mass meetings;
* Balwadi (Under Five) Programmes;
* School Health Programmes;
* Youth Groups;
* exhibitions, puppet shows, street theatre;
* involvement of TBAs and TMPs;
* individual contacts at the occasion of curative services and antenatal care.

All such activities are also closely linked up with the promotion of local health traditions . . . . School Health Programmes have been carried out in several cycles with the close collaboration of local volunteers and TMPs, focusing on issues like nutrition, personal hygiene, medicinal herbs and their use in simple home remedies, explanation and dressing of wounds, etc.

Documentation and data collection of the pilot area under CRHP have been completed in a 100 per cent baseline survey through a Family Survey Schedule . . . . Photographic documentation has been carried out from the inception of CRHP. In addition to that, a number of case studies are also available.

The Maternal and Child Health (MCH) programme has been a major focus of interest of CRHP as it was to be expected that the traditional systems of medicine would prove especially valid in this respect . . . the majority of deliveries is still being conducted without the assistance of (modern) medical personnel. MCH under CRHP comprises antenatal care services and registration, deliveries, post natal care services, child registration and child care services during home visits, in the Health Units and at the RHC, through Health Promoters, ANMs and physicians.

Much of the acceptance of CRHP's approach by local people is, of course, (because of) the responsibility shouldered by the project staff, right from the Health Promoter to the Ayurvedic or Siddha physician based at the Health Units. Health Promoters . . . have recently even formed their own research and communication network, and are thus laying the ground for a successful extension of CRHP as an 'Endogenous Model of Health Care' . . . From the records of the Health Units and the Rural Health Centre, an enormous amount of data on the morbidity pattern of the region is now available. They remain to be studied in detail and to be matched with the available medicines from Ayurvedic and folk practices. Medicinal preparations are made predominantly at local and Health Unit levels, and to some extent they are supplied by the pharmacy at the Rural Health Centre. 30–40 items of medicines are prepared in this pharmacy as per demand. The referral system under CRHP extends to the District Government Hospital in Coimbatore city.

The Blueprint Orientation

Many of the observations of SARINI were in fact in terms of numbers—the out-patient attendance, the beneficiaries reached, the schools, the *balwadis*, the births, the immunization, and so on. Notwithstanding their pertinence, we could also see the far greater significance in interpreting what those figures might actually reflect—or fail to—as organic processes. On the other hand, a mechanical adherence to indices put into a project document at the start could only elicit the observation that there was much diversion into 'non-health activities' and, consequently, the inference that the project was 'not on course' as recommended and implied by the project appraisal report.

On surface the conflict might appear to be the common qualitative vs. quantitative one. That is deceptive, and the project experience reveals that the seat of the problem might be elsewhere. The real dichotomies that appear to need examination have to do with presuppositions about 'delivering development'; for example:

* Unilateral vs. bilateral learning
* Rigidity vs. flexibility
* Top-down vs. bottom-up
* Status quo vs. change

In our own project experience we had to recognize that there were many agencies or groups involved with direct or indirect links to its evaluation: those providing the funds, the government agency funnelling it, the institution designated to implement the project, the group selected to lead it, the agency asked to monitor, and lest we forget, the people themselves for whom it was all intended. If we were not all quite in consonance, was the problem one of differing vocabularies, or were there differences in our orientations as well?

Appendix 7.1

The Modern and Traditional Health Systems

Modern

The rise of industrialism and worldwide colonialism, followed by the uncritical adoption of models of development from the Western industrialized nations by the erstwhile colonies, came about through tremendous strides in science and technology. The adoption of these modern technologies as inevitable, desirable, logical and progressive was the larger whole, of which the appearance of modern medicine was an essential component. The dismissal of non-Western cultures and traditions as primitive and unviable was an inevitable consequence. It led to the dominance by modern medicine of the health system of our country. The state (and the market) organized health care with a well-established network, consisting of educational institutions, pharmaceutical companies, medical equipment manufacturers, distribution channels, and the medical establishment—the hospitals, nursing homes, clinics and private practices. This *system* continues to develop further adopting the advances made in the developed nations, both in terms of science and technology, as well as the institutional forms in which health care services are organized.

The state, whose function is to mediate between the people and the market, clearly recognized its responsibility for the health of all the people, and expressed it in the constitution of our country. The state health care service has been primarily built around the principles of modern medicine. The development of national institutions at the apex to develop and guide the establishment of the state health care services, the development of a primary health centre structure since 1952, the national programmes for communicable diseases, the programmes in maternal and child health and nutrition and family welfare, the training of an army of multipurpose health workers and public health teams, the orientations given to medical and nursing education, the establishment of research and specialized institutions—these have all been steps in the direction of fulfilling the responsibility of the state. The huge structure of the state health system has now penetrated into the most remote areas. The continued growth of this health delivery system is considered legitimate and logical to meet the health needs and growing aspirations of our people.

The existence of organized systems of indigenous medicine (SIM), including homoeopathy, was also acknowledged, as can be seen by the state patronage extended to them in the later period as well as by the attempts of the state to regulate these systems of medicine. As early as 1948, the Chopra Committee recommended the use of indigenous systems at the 'lower' level and synthesized medicine at the 'higher' levels of medical care. An official committee also recommended a national system of medicine and health services, in keeping with our lifestyles, needs and aspirations (GOI, 1975).

The WHO (World Health Organization) Assembly's resolutions in 1976 and 1977 urged member states to give adequate importance to traditional systems of medicine, with appropriate regulations suited to their national contexts. The study group of ICSSR–ICMR (Indian Council of Social Science Research–Indian Council of Medical Research) recommended that there should be a national system of medicine with a 'synthesis' and not 'integration' of different systems; practitioners of indigenous systems should be utilized in the national system; each system should be allowed to retain its own identity and grow according to its genius; in institutions of medical care, patients should be offered a choice of systems; in course of time all training institutions of medical and health personnel should teach the same system of medical care, with individual systems being offered as specializations at the postgraduate level; and in due course medical graduates from any medical college should be able to provide such multisystem care (ICSSR–ICMR, 1981). The National Health Policy (1983), recognizing the large stock of health manpower in the indigenous systems of medicine (see Table 7.1), emphasized the need to integrate their services in the overall health delivery system, especially since they enjoyed local acceptance and respect, a rich heritage, glorious achievements and cultural compatibility (GOI, 1982).

The inability of modern medicine by itself to provide a safe and satisfactory solution to all health problems, and the past experience of indigenous systems of medicine in doing just that for various health problems, should ensure the co-existence of these two systems. The inability of the modern health system to meet the needs of a vast majority of people, and their continuing to resort to self-care and indigenous systems of medicine, has further led to the tacit acceptance of the existence of a vast health manpower outside the modern system. The services of this vast manpower are to be integrated at appropriate levels, within specified areas of the system (GOI, 1981 and 1982). This has been further elaborated in the *Manual for Practitioners of Indian Systems of Medicine and Homoeopathy*

(Ministry of Health and Family Welfare, 1985), wherein the task assigned to them is to refer the patient to the health worker or the primary health centre for proper investigation and diagnosis. This manual, however, does not contain a single instance where the ISM practitioner is required to use or draw upon his/her training. Implicit in this is the further strengthening of the modern health system, to be made more acceptable to the vast majority. Moreover, the continued entrenchment of the Western development model dominates the state decision-making process. Over time, this modern health system has led to an increase in disparities, with a privileged minority enjoying its benefits and the deprived majority having little access to it. On the other hand, the majority is fast losing whatever benefits it enjoyed previously from the indigenous systems because of its steady erosion. While the rich minority avail of the best of modern medicine as well as the indigenous systems of medicine, the poor majority lose their hold on the indigenous systems, even as they fail to get benefits from modern medicine.

The medicalization of health has led to the hospital–doctor–disease–drug approach to health care. The commercialization of health has led health care to focus on 'cost effectiveness' (an euphemism for profit), rather than the health of people. The commodification of health has led to the notion that health is a package of interventions available at a cost. Consequently, the modern health system has become highly exclusivist, expensive, promoting overuse of drugs, and creating a dependency on a class of medical/health care practitioners through the invocation of scientific mystification. With this, the importance of primary health care supposedly increases. Yet, the majority continue to be beyond the reach of the state structure. Even the official view has to admit that the state health services have been unable to meet the actual health needs and priorities of the people; they have been hospital based and cure-oriented, neglecting the preventive, promotive, public health and rehabilitative aspects of health care. They have benefitted only the upper strata of the urban population (GOI, 1982).

Traditional

The term 'traditional medicine' has been frequently used in the wider sense of 'traditional systems of medicine'. This is convenient, but at the same time rather vague and confusing; and at times it also irritates the protagonists of certain sections of the traditional systems of medicine, e.g., Ayurvedic practioners, who do not like being subsumed under this category. It is convenient because it sets off the concept of 'modern medicine'. We propose the following differentiation within the fold of traditional medicine:

Table 7.1A: **Health Systems and Capacities**

	Total No. of Registered Practitioners	*Admission Capacity*	*Hospital Beds*	*Dispensaries*
Ayurveda	2,32,247	3,306	9,783	12,027
Unani	22,756	535	627	986
Siddha	18,190	75	—	426
Homoeopathy	1,09,493	7,513	2,249	1,782
Modern Medicine	2,68,712	10,934	4,86,805	17,455

- Folk medical practices.
- Theorizing systems of Indian origin (Ayurveda, Siddha, yoga).
- Pre-'modern' theorizing systems of alien origin (Unani, homoeopathy).

For the purpose of this note, only folk medical practices and Ayurveda/ Siddha shall be examined.

Folk medical practices (and folk health culture) have been evolving from time immemorial in close relation to the environmental, economic and social conditions of localized groups of people, with as many variations. Such practices have formed the 'raw material' for the more elaborate systems of medicine which have evolved historically in a comprehensive process of cultural development. Parallel to the growth of the theorizing systems of medicine (Ayurveda, etc.), folk medical practices have continued to exist and develop, and there has also been a steady mutual exchange between them. In the later stages of this process, the more elaborate systems have been increasingly alienating themselves from the folk practices. This has been reinforced by the advent of Western modern medicine in India, when even the elaborate systems like Ayurveda found themselves in the process of becoming marginalized. An inferiority feeling may also have played a major role in the trend of 'modernizing' Ayurveda. The result of this modernization has been further neglect of folk practices at local levels. Folk medical practices are presently subject to a process of further marginalization under the impact of modern medicine; it is being forcefully and literally 'injected' in even the remotest areas under the primary health care strategy of achieving 'Health for all by 2000 A.D.', not without the commercialization of medicine and the furthering of business interests of national and multinational drug companies. Presently, folk practices survive mostly among tribal groups, and in the form of simple home remedies, predominantly practised by the women. Until recently, folk medical practices and local health culture have not been studied systematically, and least of all with regard to their material contents and validity, their rationale, their relations with the elaborate systems, their social contexts, and their potential role in a comprehensive health care system that is based on and derives its sustenance from the participation of local people.

Ayurveda is defined here in the narrower sense of a system of medicine which has evolved from various local traditions, and developed a systematic and analytic approach to the phenomena of health and ill health in close rapport with experiences gathered at local levels. Ayurveda appears to provide a valid alternative in the context of comprehensive health care, on the following counts:

* Its being rooted in the culture of the people.
* Its scientific content which relates closer to the local culture than the alien Western culture and science.
* Its major emphasis on health education.
* Its patient orientation rather than disease orientation.
* Its use of locally available raw materials for the preparation of medicines.
* Its wide range of medicines, including single drug preparations and simple home remedies.
* The efficiency of its treatments in many diseases.

It should be of interest to note that what have been termed as folk medical practices, in the form of simple home remedies and other health care traditions, are predominantly in the hands of women, whereas the practice of elaborate systems of medicine, like Ayurveda, is mostly the domain of men. This fact may also be another indicator of the progressive influence of the patriarchal system at a comparatively early stage of Indian history. The new focus on the role of women in community based systems of health care may therefore be analyzed not only in terms of a traditional responsibility for the welfare of their families; it may also be analyzed as a potential for restructuring society in the widest sense of an alternative mode of production, which would be ecologically sound, based on renewable resources, and have a low capital input but a high labour content.

In viewing primary health care and 'Health For All by 2000 AD' it should be understood that simply 'injecting' traditional medicine (most often equated with Ayurveda) into the PHC set-up cannot be a solution. It should equally be understood that the PHC strategy as such (as it is found in practice today) will not attain health for all by 2000 AD. It should as well be understood that 'health for all' will remain an empty rhetoric, unless fundamental changes are effected in environmental, economic and social conditions, and in decision-making, planning and implementation processes. Under such conditions alone, 'health for all' may emerge as a reality. And it will have the correct meaning that any individual, anywhere, has developed an understanding of her/his health in the context of her/his physical, economic, social and political environment such that it ensures:

* That s/he has a right to adequate health care.
* That s/he has access to health care facilities, whenever and wherever the need may be.
* That the health care delivery system is such as to ensure this, because it is made, maintained and further developed by and for the people, through their resources in terms of material and personnel, and through their political will.
* That s/he has a responsibility towards the totality of these aspects.

Notes

1. *Health Services and Medical Education: a programme for immediate action*, Government of India, Ministry of Health and Family Welfare, 1975.
2. *Health for All: an alternative strategy*, ICSSR–ICMR and Indian Institute of Education, Pune, 1981.
3. *National Health Policy*, Ministry of Health and Family Welfare, Government of India, 1983.
4. *Health Statistics of India*, CBHI, Ministry of Health and Family Welfare, Government of India, 1983.
5. *Statement on National Health Policy*, Ministry of Health and Family Welfare, Government of India, 1982.
6. *Report of the Working Group on Health for All*, Planning Commission, Government of India, 1981.
7. *Manual for Practitioners of Indian Systems of Medicine and Homeopathy*, Ministry of Health and Family Welfare, Government of India, 1985.

Eight

The Kheda Communications Project

Subhash R. Joshi* and B.S. Bhatia†

What did it mean, reflected Shubha Jacob, a student of social work, during her summer project at DECU, driving back from a field visit to one of the villages served by the development programmes in the Kheda Communications Project. The community television set in the village had been malfunctioning for some time. It was an old set, installed at least five to six years ago. It was now dead and needed to be taken away to Ahmedabad. The group she had just met in the village was, however, vociferous in its resentment. They did not want the set removed. Had they come to regard it as 'theirs'? Had television been so 'internalized'? Was there a fear that the passage to 'development' that the set provided was being closed?

One question led to another, and the journey back was full of reflection. After all, it was an easily observable fact that within the space of two years the number of privately owned TV sets had gone up substantially in the villages served by the project. It had meant, among other things, that more and more people there had more choice in the programmes they would see, receiving the Ahmedabad and New Delhi national network programmes directly,

---

* Manager, Kheda Communications Project.

† Co-ordinator, Social Applications Research. The case is prepared with the assistance of K.S. Karnik, Director, Development and Educational Communication Unit, ISRO, Ahmedabad.

rather than the fixed time Pij transmission only. Were people in the village insisting on the retention of the Pij transmission through the community set? Was there some sort of polarization of audiences taking place between the private set viewers and community set viewers? If so, who was seeing what kind of programme? Or were all seeing both? What might be the consequences of the steady increase in privately owned TVs? Was it in line with the objectives of development communication as understood back at the office? What did it all mean, reflected Shubha Jacob.

* * *

Development and Educational Communication Unit (DECU) is an outgrowth of the 'software' activities in TV programme production and social research initiated for the Satellite Instructional Television Experiment (SITE). DECU was spun off from the Space Applications Centre (SAC), the Ahmedabad based unit of ISRO, in December 1983, with a mandate that included programme production, development and adaptation of video hardware, communications research, training, consultancy and studies in fields of interest to space applications. Its major tasks on hand include: (*a*) the Kheda Communications Project; (*b*) training, especially of Doordarshan staff; and (*c*) communication studies and research. Production of TV programmes for the Kheda area is the major activity of DECU, undertaken as part of the Kheda Communications Project (KCP). Programmes on agriculture, animal husbandry, health, nutrition and family planning are broadcast, along with a number of programmed serials on socio-economic issues specifically for women and children. School education programmes have also been produced by KCP. Recently, social marketing spots on the minimum age of marriage and other aspects related to women's health (and indirectly to the population problem) have been produced. Similarly, programmes in the areas of adult education, wasteland development and water conservation were produced for transmission in the national programme.

The Kheda Communications Project

KCP was conceived around 1970 as a part of the Satellite Instructional Television Experiment. The major initiative came from Dr. Vikram Sarabhai—often referred to as the father of India's space programme. It was a part of his deep concern to ensure that space technology (and indeed all technology) is used to tackle the real problems of the people of India. The idea was to create a 'field laboratory' to see how television could be used to accelerate development and social change. At the same time, the Kheda project was an attempt to provide a technological alternative to the centralization inherent in satellite broadcasting. As we know, with a satellite one can have a single originating point and 'shower' the country with this signal. Kheda was an attempt to introduce an element of decentralization through local programme production and transmission that covers only a limited area. At the same time the satellite provides a wider exposure, a 'window onto the world', and thereby avoids the dangers of parochialism. We might thus have a system that could be called 'integrated decentralization'.

The most important objective of the Kheda Communications Project has been to take communication to those who need it the most: the poor, the illiterate, women and children, those who are 'information poor'. In short, the deprived or the disadvantaged. Given the economic situation in India, the disadvantaged can be reached through television only if there are community reception facilities that provide access to the media to all sections of the target population. Accordingly, a vital feature of the KCP is the infrastructure of community reception sets. These community sets—about 600 of them in approximately 400 villages—were financed partly by the villagers themselves and partly by the state government or the local milk co-operative. (Kheda district is well known for its milk co-operatives.) To reach the disadvantaged, there seems to be no alternative to community sets, despite the very serious problems involved. These include: problems of maintenance and of non-availability of power; the need for a 'caretaker' to switch on the set; overcoming the socio-cultural realities in a village, especially problems in bypassing the 'information gate-keepers', the unquestioned sources of power and influence through whom information traditionally flows.

Some other key elements of the Kheda system (see Appendix 8.1) are:

1. A clearly enunciated philosophy that is spelt out in operational terms and defines the specific target audience (basically, the disadvantaged).
2. Audience involvement, with the intention of making the programme participatory or a people's medium.

3. Considerable stress on research, both as a means of determining audience needs and getting feedback from the audience. Researchers are involved in all stages—from pre-production planning to post-transmission impact evaluation and feedback, with the programmes also being made in the 'team mode', including research inputs.
4. An attempt to reverse the traditional flow of broadcasting and to use the media for communicating from the people to the decision-makers; also to provide horizontal communication between different groups in the audience.
5. An organisation committed to development, and structures to promote and channel individual creativity.

A unique feature of the KCP is its organization. It is operated on the basis of a memorandum of understanding between the Ministry of Information and Broadcasting/Doordarshan organization and ISRO, which had initiated this experiment a decade ago. According to the MOU there is time reserved for KCP exclusively, although the transmission is by Doordarshan. Further, there is complete autonomy for programme content and structure in the KCP.

Social issues account for a substantial proportion of the transmission, and the focus here is on those aspects that are a barrier to development, like superstitions and wasteful rituals or caste divisions. A lot of effort has also been devoted to programmes that tackle women's issues and aim to improve the status of women in society.

Children are the largest and most dedicated part of the daily audience, and efforts have been made to make programmes of special interest to them. These include programmes related to the school curriculum, but they are a part of the general evening transmission, so that drop-outs may also benefit.

In these efforts, DECU has had the help and co-operation of a number of different agencies and individuals, including especially the Ministry of Information and Broadcasting. But the biggest source of inspiration has been the audience, the villagers of Kheda. DECU considers as the measure of 'success' the extent to which the villagers themselves can accelerate development, bring about social change, and feel that this is 'their medium'.

There is a need to recognize that communication is a societal resource. Often it can substitute for capital, a resource that is scarce in developing countries. But it can also help in terms of another resource that is even scarcer in developing countries: time. We are in a race against time on all fronts—illiteracy, malnutrition, poverty—and communication can be of vital importance in this context.

In keeping with the overall philosophy of KCP, the focus of all production effort is on the *development process* to be initiated, and sustained, and not on production per se. This focus is reflected in the production process too. The following sequence of events is somewhat typical.

Programme ideas emerge from formative research. The assessment is generally on the basis of studies by KCP/DECU social scientists, or the observations of the concerned field agencies. Programme proposals (generally originated jointly by a producer and a researcher) are discussed in a large group that examines objectives, relevance, target audience, approach, format, extent of utilization/field support required, etc. The script is then prepared by a scriptwriter, working with the producer, researcher and, where necessary, with a content expert who would, in most cases, have supplied the writer with a 'brief'. A script committee examines and approves the script. Pretesting is done when it is considered necessary, and the script is modified or even discarded, depending upon the reaction of the sample audience. If a series is being produced, the first couple of programmes are often pretested in one or more villages. This results in the incorporation of minor changes for future programmes in most cases, but occasionally there is a major surprise, requiring drastic revision or even scrapping of the programme.

A regular system of feedback is part of the total process. This feedback from the village audience is given to all the producers, so that their programmes can be tuned in to audience needs, tastes and reactions. In addition, occasional summative evaluations are done to determine the impact of specific series or programmes.

Right from the stage of programme conception, attempts are made to involve the field agencies concerned. These include not only the governmental and voluntary agencies concerned with extension (e.g., health or agriculture extension organizations), but also banks (for loans), marketing co-operatives (for marketing the suggested households' production), employment exchanges (for employment problems), etc. In many cases, the content expert, who is a part of the production team, is from the field agency concerned. There have been efforts to go further and encourage the user agencies to themselves take up programme production. In a few cases, these efforts have already borne fruit, based on the training provided by KCP/DECU to personnel of the user agencies, especially in the use of 'portapacks' (see Appendix 8.2) for programme production. Among the agencies involved was AMUL. Initially, DECU worked with them, using their veterinarians as subject specialists for animal husbandry programmes. This went on for more than a year. Once in a while, when DECU brought up the subject of their taking on the programme production themselves, there would be great reluctance expressed. They felt that TV was an expensive and difficult medium to handle. Finally, about a year ago, they decided to take the plunge. This is what Dr. Gupta of AMUL had to say about their experience:

> First of all, our subject matter specialists, being in constant and close touch with the rural producers, know precisely what know-how the milk producers already have, and what is required to further advance that knowledge and the rate of progress.
>
> Secondly, the subject matter specialists have also been trained by DECU/SAC in all the component aspects of the VTR system, such as theory of production in extension programmes, subject selection, motivation, scriptwriting, analysis of scripts, composition, framing and editing of shots and transfer techniques. The specialists have thus been able to advocate the essential scientific principles to the milk producers by mass contact in simple and popular language, which helps them to appreciate and understand the programmes. If these programmes are generated by those who are not quite aware of the clientele's current state of technical knowhow (and 'do-how'), or the extent of finances, material resources and other facilities available within their actual reach, things may lead to confusion, and may even retard the rate of progress.
>
> Thirdly, our extension staff has won the full confidence and faith of the milk producers, since its recommendations have already produced fruitful results for them. Hence these programmes can be generated by our staff at a faster rate and made

quite realistic to the rural situations, in close collaboration with the village leadership.

Programme ideas emerge from field observations and a general concern for the 'development process'. The idea may occur to any member of the team: producer, researcher, writer, anybody. Depending on the issue, the amount of effort involved, the number of programmes made, etc., the processing of this idea may follow different routes as shown in Figure 8.1.

Ideally, the process begins with formative research, but occasionally, if only one or two programmes have to be produced, a proposal may even be sanctioned directly.

It was earlier thought that programmes aimed at improving economic conditions in the target villages were of prime importance. Concurrent research indicated otherwise. It was found that more programmes were required for special audiences, such as landless labour. Most important, we realized that economic improvement was often stymied by social and structural problems in village society. Accordingly, in the last few years, the focus of programming has shifted from the purely economic to socio-economic and social–structural issues, even as the earlier programmes on agriculture and animal husbandry have continued. Programmes have also been made on cottage industries (things that can be made by the villager in the house with little investment, e.g., chalk, soap, handloom products, etc.), self-employment, and on outside employment opportunities.

Programmes on social problems have been the most difficult, but also the most challenging. They now account for about a third of all production. In these, the villagers have themselves been involved to the maximum extent possible, not only as actors, but also as writers and even visualizers of the programme. The topics have had a wide range; among others, exploitation, caste discrimination, minimum wages, alcoholism, co-operatives, and elections (both local and national). All possible formats, from interviews, documentaries and plays, to folk forms, songs and ballet have been used. Often, the portrayal of reality as such (through documentaries and interviews) is not considered desirable, since it might expose the disadvantaged to further oppression. To overcome this difficulty, a unique genre has been created, involving the fictional portrayal of reality. In most cases, social issues are dealt with in episodic serials with each part complete in

Figure 8.1: **THE PRODUCTION PROCESS**

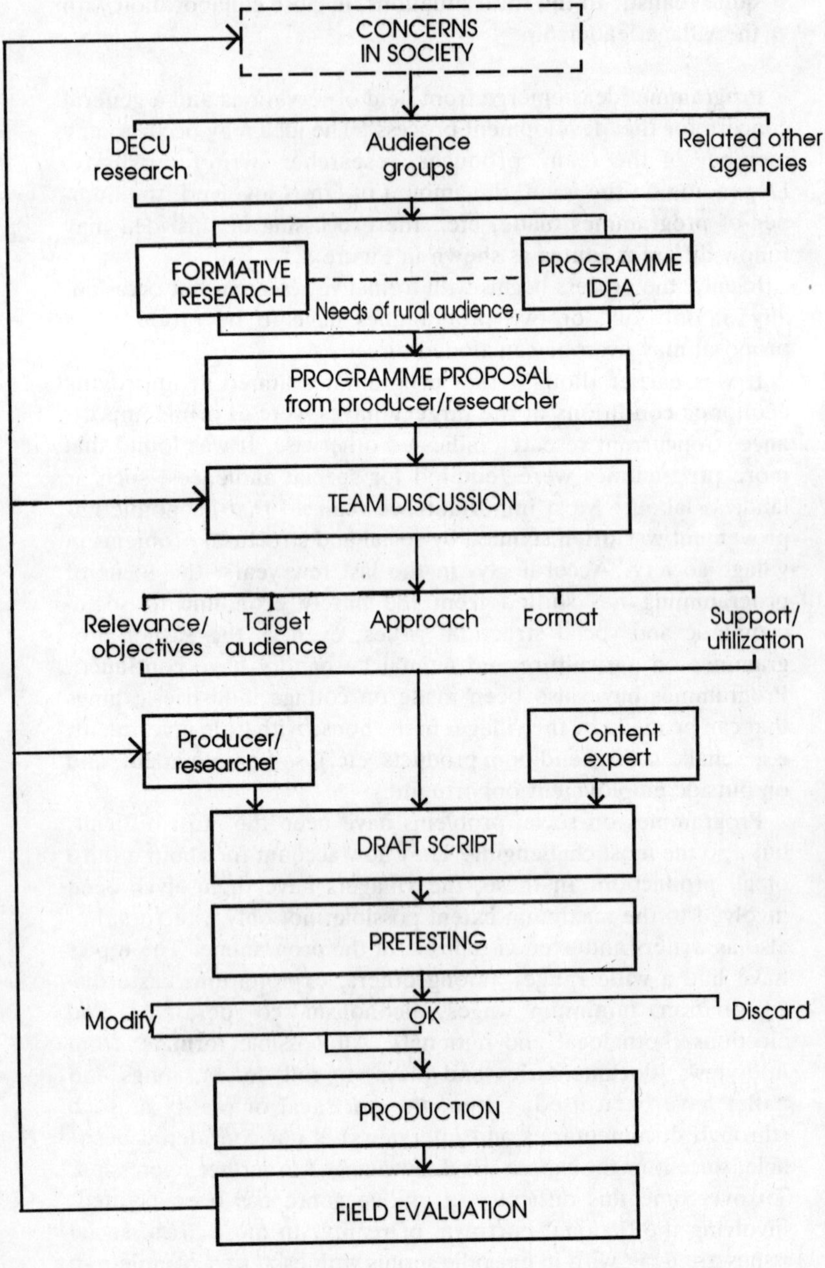

itself, but with the same anchor characters reappearing in separate 'stories'.

An example might be in order. The production team came across an incident of great concern in a village. The sarpanch of the village had taken about Rs. 100 each from a large number of people under a house building scheme for the poor. No receipt was asked for and none was given. Weeks and months passed by, but no house was built, nor any money refunded. A large number of interviews were recorded. Person after person gave exactly the same account and sought our intervention through the Kheda TV programme. The sarpanch too was interviewed. He denied the whole story. He said that no such money was ever taken, and alleged that this was part of a political game against him.

All this was put together in the form of a programme. It was indeed a big 'scoop', with very interesting programme content. It was set for transmission, and there was a lot of excitement at KCP. However, before it could be transmitted, some of the villagers who had given the interviews came to KCP, and pleaded that the programme should not be transmitted. It seems after the production team had left, the sarpanch had threatened them that if the programme was transmitted he would make sure that all those interviewed were beaten up, thrown out of jobs, or even thrown out of the village. They were mortally afraid that if their identities were revealed they would be in serious trouble.

It was a dilemma—loss of a 'good' programme or the suffering inflicted on someone else. KCP decided not to transmit the programme at the risk of the villagers' lives. The story was therefore fictionalized in the form of a play. The identities were not revealed and yet the message got across. Feedback on the programme indicated great interest, indentification and effect. This technique has proved to be tremendously successful with the audience, and the more popular of these programmes draw huge crowds, rain or cold notwithstanding. One such serial has crossed 100 parts (broadcast once a week) and is still going strong.

Women have been an important focus of programming, and one or the other serial dealing with women's issues has been more or less continuously on for the last ten years. The general objective is to improve the economic and social status of women. While this is obviously important in itself, research shows that it has also contributed to family planning (especially by reducing the importance of having a male child), and promoted the education of girls.

Research from the field has established that children not only form almost half of the TV audience in a community viewing situation, but that they are also the most regular and dedicated segment. Accordingly, a great deal of importance is given to programmes for children.

Over time, KCP has arrived at a 'model' of intervention for social change, although not explicitly articulated as such. Figure 8.2 depicts the main features of the model and their interlinkages.

Over several cycles of events there is probably the reinforcement of a behavioural pattern of arousal and goal directed acts: in both the client group and the change agents! Repetition of the cycle (and experience of success) has the effect, hopefully, of stabilizing the organizations created. This process is strikingly close to the awareness–competence cycle of events attempted in variants of the conscientization approach.

It will be seen in Figure 8.2 that while the production process operates on one front in the intervention, two other fronts of activity are necessary complements to the programme effort:

1. The involvement of external agencies in the issues being discussed in the programme.
2. The creation of local organizations to deal with the external agencies formally, on behalf of the community concerned.

The three pronged intervention in rural areas has made demands on the KCP personnel far beyond the domains of their individual disciplines. One is no more a cameraman or a scriptwriter, but an *activist* who only happens to be proficient in a vocational skill. It has also meant acquiring the ability, the social skills, to work in teams, constantly visualizing the interfaces among the various components in the intervention. One important effect of these modes of working appears to be the emergence of a working principle of great significance: *Flexibility*. This is manifest in such things as adapting/adjusting along the way, benefitting from feedback, a 'loose-light' administrative structure and so on, all within a governmental organizational set-up. Over time, these behaviour patterns have got stabilized as organizational norms. This is important, because it is likely that any viable 'model' for intervention will demand a series of *balances* across several dimensions of conduct. For example:

Figure 8.2: **TOWARDS AN INTERVENTION MODEL**

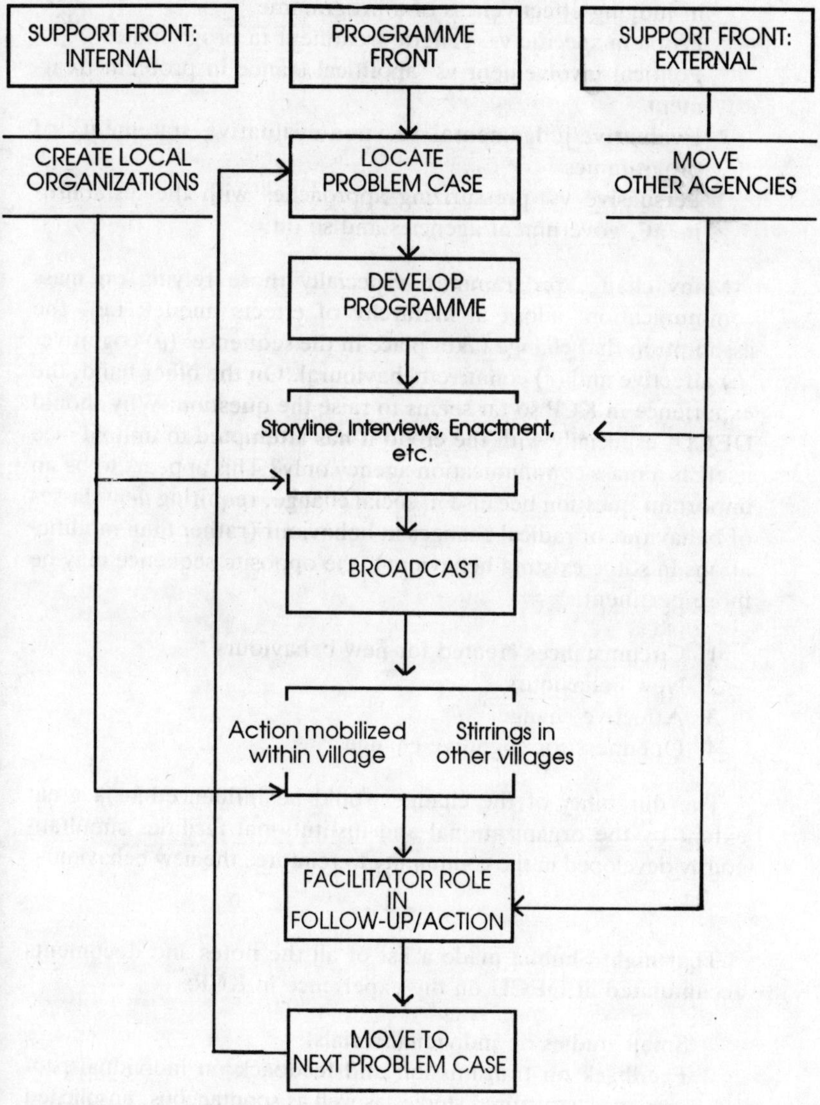

* Individual creativity/expression of a producer vs. need for-conformity
* Aesthetic criteria vs. practical criteria (e.g., change indicators) in judging effectiveness of a programme
* Problem specific vs. generic treatment in programmes
* Political involvement vs. apolitical stance in problem treatment
* Evaluative/judgemental vs. non-evaluative statements of programmes
* Persuasive vs. pressurizing approaches with the 'establishment', government agencies and so on.

Many change programmes, especially those relying on mass communication, adopt a 'hierarchy of effects' model; i.e., the assumption that change takes place in the sequence: (*a*) cognitive, (*b*) affective and (*c*) conative/behavioural. On the other hand, the experience in KCP so far seems to raise the question: Why should DECU, especially with the credo it has attempted to uphold, see itself as a mass communication agency only? This appears to be an important question because in social change, requiring *new* classes of behaviour or radical changes in behaviour (rather than modifications in some existing behaviour), the opposite sequence may be more pertinent:

1. Circumstances created for new behaviours
2. New behaviours
3. Affective change
4. Openness for cognitive change

The durability of the change would be influenced to a great extent by the organizational and institutional facilities simultaneously developed in the community to reinforce the new behaviours.

* * *

That night Shubha made a list of all the notes and documents accumulated at DECU on the experience in KCP:

* Small studies on individual serials.
* Feedback on transmission and feedback on individual programmes; structured studies as well as spontaneous, unsolicited mail.
* Programme pretesting reports.

* Case notes, diary and anecdotal material from producers and other team members.
* Unrehearsed dialogues and interviews in the programme contents.

There were, of course, the impressions that she herself had gathered too, both at DECU, from the numerous meetings and discussions with the KCP staff, and in the project villages. The Kheda Communications Project started programme production activity in 1973–74. Most of the production team members were young, just out of college or technical institutes. They were charged with ideas and energy, and were out to change the world with their various talents lined up. Had they remained unchanged? What were the effects of so many years of field experience, of changes in personal circumstances or in contexts? How did they view their professional lives? Did the narrow focus of rural communication programmes give them sufficient opportunity to grow and gain due recognition in professional circles?

She proceeded to draw a line down the middle of the page in her notebook. On the one side she put down impressions of social change in the villages served by KCP. On the other side she put down impressions of the KCP staff and organization itself:

KCP Villages	*KCP Organization*
* Knowledge levels raised in specific areas: health, animal husbandry, agriculture.	* Development 'credo' internalized by staff—beliefs and convictions, rather than ritual.
* Awareness increased—rights, public services, programmes.	* 'Process awareness' in production teams—sensitivity to factors of rural reality aiding/hampering development process.
* Confidence raised—something can be done for age-old problems, solutions do exist.	* Autonomy—steadfast adherence to convictions in approach/ends/means in spite of pressures from the environment.

* New concepts introduced—scientific explanations, principles/objectives in development programmes. * New attitudes formed—co-operation, self-reliance, horizontal communications.	* Team mode of functioning—effectively interdisciplinary.

The stocktaking and the abstraction took much effort and time, but it appeared worthwhile. For it helped her to pose the main research questions for her project:

1. How to find out if the various, and separate, indicators of achievement in the KCP were interrelated or mutually supportive? In other words, is there a systemic development process underway, or do we have a set of discrete, target specific, achievements before us?
2. How are the observations in the KCP villages related to the observations about the KCP organization? In other words, are there some (prerequisite) characteristics in the change agency for the development process visualized? Must these also be assessed systematically in evaluating a programme?
3. Will the appearance of privately owned TV sets in the project villages significantly affect the change processes initiated by KCP? If so, how is this to be assessed? In other words, how does a programme, or the change agency, cope with larger socio-economic trends that might have a bearing on the development process initiated?

Appendix 8.1

The Kheda Credo

(*A philosophy that should be the basis of all our productions.*)

Development—economic, social, cultural or ideological—implies a break from the status quo, from inertia; it implies movement, change. Change requires a certain attitude, motivation, information and, of course, appropriate physical and social infrastructures. It also requires an objective understanding of one's predicament, the family and social constraints one works within. This necessitates the development of a rational outlook, a scientific attitude towards life.

Development implies social change, education, awareness and, of course, economic development. However, economic development cannot take place in isolation, it requires changes in the social systems and in the attitude of the individual; it implies breaking away from bondages and oppression; and most importantly, it necessitates an 'awakening' of the individual and his self-confidence.

In trying to accelerate development, communication can play a very major role. Television, in particular, can be a powerful tool in creating a 'climate' for development.

Our attempt in Kheda will be to use TV—and also supplement it by other means—for development in the broadest meaning of the term. Concretely, the attempt will be to:

1. Focus on the oppression and bondages in the present social and economic system in such a way as to heighten understanding.
2. Mobilize the community and the individual himself to break away from these bondages.
3. Promote self-reliance among the individuals and the community

   * involving a reduction in apathy, in dependence on a god or others;
   * implying improvising with and optimal use of local resources;
   * necessitating a co-operative spirit and a willingness to take risks.

4. Educate the community—particularly the deprived—about their duties and rights, e.g., minimum wages, etc.
5. Provide utility programmes in areas like agriculture, animal husbandry, health, family planning, crafts and skills, functional literacy, etc., so as to improve the social and economic condition of the masses.
6. Broaden the horizon of the viewers by showing them persons, places and events outside their immediate environment.
7. Improve horizontal communication between the village communities and vertical communication between the masses and decision-makers.
8. Inculcate a scientific temper among the younger generation by improving the educational level of children, particularly in the areas of science and mathematics.

The prime target audience will invariably be the classes/castes who are the most oppressed and who need the catalytic input that will help them to help themselves. Accordingly, programme content, presentation, etc., will be designed keeping this audience in mind.

Appendix 8.2

Explanation of Terms Used

Portable Equipment

This usually refers to video recording or playback units which can be easily taken from one place to another—in the DECU context, usually to a village for shooting or playback purposes.

The shooting portable unit comprises a small, hand-held camera, a lightweight VCR, microphones. The playback unit consists of a TV monitor and a lightweight VCR, popularly known as 'video'. Portapack refers to the 1/2 inch video using a spool tape system in the 1975–80 period.

Video Cassette

The video tape is a magnetic tape in plastic housing. It comes in different widths. Professionals generally use tapes of width 3/4 inch (or more), while the ones used by amateurs are normally less than 3/4 inch in width.

Source and Destination

Source refers to the origin of the message, e.g., the producer of television programmes, the agency that sends information. Destination is the target group for whom the communication is intended. In other words, the terms refer to the sender and the receiver. Bringing them closer would mean the source would know the kind of audience, its needs, aspirations, problems, etc., as also the reactions of the audience to the communication. It means the destination has access to the source; it can communicate its feelings, thinking, desires to the source. This can happen in several ways: physical proximity, communication research, viewers' letters, field based programme production, participation of the audience in programmes, field visits by the source, etc.

Transmission Mode

This refers to the television broadcast mode wherein the transmitting authority decides to show a programme and the audience has no control over it. In contrast, if you have a video, you can decide when to see, how often to see, rewind, fast forward, etc.

INSAT System

Refers to the system wherein the Indian satellite INSAT is used for national networking for TV broadcasting. The National Programme, for example, is broadcast through this system.

Participation Mode of Programme Production

The basic principle in this mode is the direct, active involvement or participation of the community. This participation of the community may happen with them as planners, performers, writers or producers. It provides a means of expression of the people rather than for the people. It facilitates exchange of views and news, and not mere transmission from one source to another. (Based on Berrigan's definition of community communication).

HPT

High Power Transmitter; coverage area 80 km radius, 10 KW.

LPT

Low Power Transmitter; coverage area 30 km radius, 1 KW.

Appendix 8.3

Different Phases in DECU Organization

Phase I: KCP started in 1975–76 along with Satellite Instructional Television Experiment (SITE), though it was not a part of SITE. Kheda was served by a terrestrial transmitter located in Pij and it received some national programmes from the SITE chunk.

Phase II: After SITE ended, i.e., from mid-1976, KCP became an entirely local project. There was no national or regional networking. This pattern continued until 1982 when INSAT came into operation.

Phase III: In the year 1982 with the operationalization of INSAT, KCP got linked to the national network. Side by side, the nearby city of Ahmedabad got a 10 KW transmitter and, for a few months, the people in Kheda had the option of two channels: Pij for local programmes, Ahmedabad for city-oriented programmes.

Phase IV: In the year 1985 the Pij transmitter was shut down. KCP produced programmes for Kheda, but these were transmitted as a small chunk from the Ahmedabad transmitter. The Ahmedabad transmitter being a high power transmitter, the coverage was larger—it covered about seven other districts, including Kheda.

Phase V: The Pij transmitter was restarted in the year 1988, and continues to be operational till today. KCP makes programmes only for Pij transmission in the local language (Gujarati) for one hour from 7 pm to 8 pm.

Apart from the phases mentioned above, many changes have also taken place in the television scenario. In Kheda there were previously only community television sets; now there are a large number of private television sets even in the villages, though access to them is limited to the more affluent. Earlier, there was only black-and-white transmission; now, most of the programmes are transmitted in colour. Because of the regional and national networking, the kind of programmes to which the people are exposed has also undergone several changes. There is a great deal of emphasis on entertainment, soap operas, cricket test matches, or live transmission of events and hapenings, etc. The use of video also is on the rise, and it is not unusual to find people watching films on locally hired video sets. All this means that the kind of competition faced by Kheda TV and the kind of clientele that Kheda Communications Project has today are quite different from the earlier days.

Nine

Distancing in Empathy*

Sharada Jain

The keyword, it seems, is intervention. Here is a system—the human body for the physician, the cluster of villages for the social scientist. As we see it, the system calls for an intervention. There is something happening there that we do not like, which we regard as wrong or dysfunctional. If the available knowledge of the system is less than perfect—that is, what exactly the different components of the system are, how exactly are they interconnected, what happens to other components when something is done to one of them, and so on—then we are not sure of the exact outcome of any intervention. But we do not wish to remain passive spectators. We must do something. The only recourse then is to intervene first, keep track of system consequences of the intervention, control them if possible, and guide the resultant process towards the ends we desire. And hope for the best. It is the same for a physician dealing with a troublesome ailment as well as the development worker tackling bonded labour in a village. Is that any different from trial-and-error muddling through? Yes, indeed, in a couple of important

* Based on a juxtaposition of notes from *Exploring Possibilities*, a report on the Women's Development Programme, Rajasthan, December 1986, and notings in a Workshop on Concurrent Evaluation Methodology, 28–30 January 1989, held at Institute of Development Studies, Jaipur. The report was the joint endeavour of the WDP team, as is the on-going search for alternatives in PE methodology.

ways. In action research, the learning is not incidental. There is a deliberate search for knowledge from the consequences of intervention, and therefore it is a disciplined act of research. Secondly, perhaps more important, the knowledge of outcome (which might interest the intervention agent, or others in the world around) is accompanied by an increase in competence in the system itself—to cope with and overcome the dysfunction, and to be proactive to processes that might precipitate similar dysfunctions. As a matter of fact, if the intervention does not explicitly aim at this increased internal competence in the system, it can hardly be called action research.

Clippings: One*

We have come to view concurrent evaluation as a necessary part of action research. This workshop is therefore intended not only to review the experiences in the Women's Development Programme, but to review the review process itself. At this Institute one of the important research activities is the search for alternatives in research methods.

I have heard three or four people here using the term action research. I am afraid you will have to educate me on this matter.

There is the famous quote. It says: there is no action without research, and there is no research without action.

I can't think of any human activity in which there isn't some learning or the other from the task on hand. Isn't that a basic feature of the brain? Part of nature's design?

Action research begins by recognizing the limitations of theoretical propositions about social behaviours. You simply can't say how things actually work out there.

From concepts to application. Isn't that the same as applied research?

That's the trouble with so much of our research. We can't get out of the given categories and labels. Applied research is fine

* This and the other three 'Clippings' sections in this chapter reproduce the voices of the participants at the IDS, Jaipur, Workshop on Concurrent Evaluation Methodology, 1989.

as a label when you are thinking of 'applying' some known scientific laws to produce some goods, like some pills or powders or a cigarette lighter, or something like that . . . .

But action research is different.

It is quite different. It has to do with complex phenomena—the unknown, the unprecedented, with other things not being equal.

All sciences have encounters with the complex, the unknown, the unprecedented.

And yet action research is different. Because research in human social behaviours is different. Because the very act of research is different.

The Programme Conceived

The Women's Development Programme of the Government of Rajasthan was launched in mid-1984 by the Department of Rural Development and Panchayati Raj. 'The principal aim of WDP', it was announced, 'is to empower women through communication of information, education and training, and to enable them to recognise and improve their social and economic status.' The first activity in WDP was a *sathin* (village level worker) training programme conducted in August/September 1984 in Padampura, a small village in Jaipur district. It was followed by *pracheta* (block level worker) training conducted at Jobner (Jaipur district) and Manaklav (Jodhpur district).

This training was innovative and experimental in nature. It marked a low profile, soft beginning intervention for the rural women of Rajasthan. There was no formal inauguration, none of the fanfare which marks the launching of a new government programme. Despite their 'smallness', the positions taken in this training were fairly clear. Conceptually, development was understood as 'internalized growth' and, therefore, was not a matter of handing down schemes. This growth demanded, as its precondition, a climate of hope and confidence, generating self-respect and group effort. The main thrust of the programme for rural women, therefore, was to facilitate the creation of these 'conditions' through diverse processes. What these processes would be was something which had to be discovered continually through experiments. Evaluation had to be an integral component of every stage of activity, providing for revivability in attitude and action. The programme, in a very real sense, had to be an on-going exercise in learning organically by doing, based on the premise that a development programme had to *develop* rather than be *implemented*.

Obviously this was a very unusual approach to developmental intervention initiated by a government department. It implied activity which was extremely difficult. It meant a daring attempt to go to the very roots of the problems of deprivation and subordination. This needed various kinds of strengths, a joining of hands, in the hope of creating an alternative structure. A structure which would have the inner strength and grassroots linkages of voluntarism, the security and stability of government, and a continuous incorporation of critical reflection from research bodies. Theoretically, these three groups were recognized as the pivots of developmental activity in the planned programme. Would this precarious mix work?

The following organizational structure was envisaged for WDP in early 1984. This continues to be the formal pattern around which WDP weaves its activities.

Village Level

Each selected gram panchayat has a trained village level worker called a *sathin* who belongs to one of the villages of the gram panchayat. She is responsible for the formation of women's forums at the village level. She works in close link with nine other *sathins* of neighbouring gram panchayats. The cluster of ten gram panchayats with ten *sathins* is co-ordinated by one *pracheta*.

Block Level

The *pracheta*, a block level government functionary, provides support and guidance to the *sathin*. She also provides the communication link with the district level.

District Level

1: At the district level is the district women's development agency (DWDA), under the chairmanship of the district collector. Each DWDA has a project director who is assisted by a project officer.

2: Technical resource support is provided at the district level by the Information Development and Resource Agency (IDARA). This is a voluntary agency working in the field of adult education and rural development.

State Level

At the state level:

1. District IDARAs are co-ordinated by the state IDARA.
2. Director of WDP is the overall in charge of the programme.
3. Monitoring and evaluation of the programme is facilitated by the Institute of Development Studies, Jaipur.

Some important features expected of such an organizational structure were:

* A co-operative networking among *sathins*, no matter where they belonged, highlighting the crucial role of the *sathin*.
* A continuously expanding horizon, providing greater reach to communities.
* A good communication culture—timely, reliable and open both ways.
* Strong support functions, readily available, from IDARA and DWDA.
* Strong administrative momentum, with governmental authority strengthening village level activity.

Clippings: Two

Evaluation implies many things. It means assessment, stock-taking, comparison, inference. It means, finally, judgement. More precisely, a value judgement. In whatever words and phrases it might be couched, an evaluation must imply conformity or deviation from some state considered desirable.

If evaluation is by design, rather than by accident, then it must be with a motive. The act of evaluation, to serve the design, must be motivated.

What if the premises are wrong? If what is considered desirable is actually not so? The norms against which one makes judgements are then quite useless, perhaps even harmful.

You cannot ignore the politics of evaluation. All evaluation represents a political reality. It says something about who is calling the tune.

If the information sought is to serve the purpose of the outsider, information seeking is clearly an exploitative practice.

If the Government has invested eight thousand crores in IRDP, does it not have the right to find out if things have improved after all? If a programme is for something good, the evaluation too, is for the good.

Worse, what if there are two or more quite different ideas of what is a desirable state? If the receiver disagrees, but does not say so? Can evaluation not perpetuate and aggravate differences?

That is not information seeking at all. That is information-making. The preoccupation with discrete, itemized, data collection too easily turns into a production routine. The means becomes ends in themselves.

You also have the problem of layers and layers of invalid interpretation. From events to observation, from observation to data, from data to analysis, from analysis to reporting. Data are never neutral. When subjected to distortion, consciously or unconsciously, they are not harmless. When there is no recognition of the systematic distortion, let alone any mechanism to check the distortion, the information system might actually be perpetrating underdevelopment.

Participatory evaluation can easily be nothing more than a mere catch-phrase. It can be a jargonistic escape, just so much empty rhetoric. It would also be a naive, wishful, belief that it provides the magical solution to all problems of scientific validity. These are all the abuses of a participative methodology. On the other hand, if you empower the people themselves to keep track of what is happening in their own lives, and help them develop valid tools and techniques to keep track, that is not only good participation, it is good evaluation as well. In essence it cannot be too different from good medical practice relying on the patient's own report of his bodily states, and helping the patient to do the job more systematically.

Empowerment is just another romanticized notion. You can't really believe that you will empower the powerless, can you? Not as long as you sign the cheques.

The real problem seems to be the confusion around intentions—the implied difference between *programme* objectives and programme *evaluation* objectives.

The Observation Cornerstone

Evaluating an innovative on-going programme calls for improvizing sensitive and adequate tools for observation and judgement. In the Women's Development Programme, this challenge becomes more complex because there is a simultaneous demand for 'understanding' as well as 'distancing'. The authenticity of a description rests on its capacity to reach out to diverse levels of perception. On issues like women's suffering and subordination, this sensitivity to delicate nuances is possible when one relates to the situation not merely in a cerebral manner, but also at an emotional level. However, 'judgement' is valid only when this involvement is suspended, a distance created and a balanced reference is made to the 'values' which these processes are meant to actualize.

The central principles adhered to in this process are:

1. Diverse levels of perception deserve to be respected and taken seriously before any judgement can be made.
2. These perceptions can be elicited only if there is no strict demand made through a specific format or for a specific idiom.
3. Validations for the authenticity and adequacy of information are best made when observations are subjected to group sharing and reflection.
4. The process of recording, analyzing and reporting observations is an integral part of developmental intervention in that it reinforces what is worth doing and how it should be done.
5. Participation in the activity of evaluation is itself a mode of development for the individual. This implies that the more people are involved in the process, the greater is the consolidation of the developmental activity.

6. To facilitate this process, it is important to involve at least one outsider to the activity who shares the objectives of the programme, but is not part of the process which is evaluated.

This report, therefore, relies essentially on perceptions at different levels, recorded over a period of two years in the form of letters and reports of *sathin* and *pracheta* meetings, observations from project director/officers and reflections from IDARAs. It also incorporates experiences of informal meetings which are a regular feature of the programme. The reports of these meetings take the form of reliving the situation. The choice and weightage given by the writer of these reports are taken as important indicators. Though this kind of information is neither formally systematized nor computable, it clearly records the mood, level of enthusiasm, perception of priority, anger, disgust, hope, fear and, above all, the horizon of action in the specific context of the village reality.

For a consensus on 'what is the overall picture', a series of evaluation meetings and workshops have again been conducted at the district and state level. The groups have critically looked at their own processes, and occasionally it has meant the spending of enormous energies over issues which might appear trivial to an 'outsider'. However, the assumption underlying this process has been to simultaneously correct the drifts and not just observe, record and report them. If rural women really need assistance to shake off their subordination and suffering, the processes of evaluation have to be simultaneously seen as processes for strengthening the activity. Again, if it is correct to assume that improvements in the human situation are possible not by ordering change, but only through an internalization of change, the evaluation activity acquires an added responsibility for sharing of information and consolidated knowledge. Both these points have been taken as serious principles of direction in this evaluation study.

Clippings: Three

The quantitative–qualitative dichotomy is really a non-issue. The two are neither exclusive, nor in conflict. The concern for truth in observation and inference is far more important than the quibbling about numbers.

There is no need to regard the concern for scientific rigour as being misplaced. It does not become anti-people or anti-development or anything like that just because it asks questions of the development worker.

We say there were five schools. What does this quantity mean? Surely it means nothing at all without a minimum definition of the attribute *school*. Do the generators of the numbers have any shared appreciation of the attribute, or are we really talking of two different things?

When in pain, action first, theory later. There is a story of Rajaji who once admonished his civil servants for their bureaucratic attitude to social programmes. He asked them: if the room was buzzing aloud with mosquitoes and you were bitten all over and in pain, would you get rid of them first, or would you wait till you had the exact count of mosquitoes in the room? Is the job on hand counting mosquitoes or relieving pain?

Measurement and definition are inseparable. One depends upon and yet gives to the other. Putting them into a happy spiral is what scientific enquiry is all about. You cannot go on describing some phenomenon without wondering at some point of its extent. You cannot help asking the question: How much?

There is no need to equate the quantitative–qualitative dichotomy with objectivity–subjectivity. There is a lot of objective qualitative assessment, just as there surely is a great deal of subjective quantification. And, of course, even with objectivity and quantification you can still be barking up the wrong tree, and therefore quite wrong in your inferences.

To be scientific is to learn, first and foremost, to describe things clearly and fully.

An Evolving Methodology

Training, in a significant sense, can be seen as the backbone of the programme. Chronologically, the central processes, revised approaches and evaluation procedures have all been initiated through the training programmes. However, an equally important aspect of this training is the fact that its pattern has evolved out of the feedback from the fieldwork. Each subsequent training represents a deeper response to the 'reality' as perceived by the growing number of participants.

The realization that 'development' is a notion which demands a qualitative shift in the attitudes of the people involved has had major implications for WDP training. The exercises have primarily been to generate experiences which facilitate altered perceptions of the self-image, as well as the shared social image, of women. Far from being lectures on 'cleanliness', 'nutrition' and 'child development', the training programmes experiment with the possibility of creating a climate of questioning, reflecting, sharing, choosing, seeking and discovering—through listening and talking. These core concepts, the guiding principles, provide the basic texture to all the training programmes, notwithstanding the different patterns into which they are woven.

In a way each training programme has been a unique story created by each specific group. When the tribal groups assembled they began with the issues related to forests; the Marwari *sathins* started with the issue of water. The Bhilwara group focussed a good deal on mines and labour. Training in Ajmer concentrated on famine works and the harassment of women. The take-off has always depended on how the priorities are seen by the specific group. And yet, they are the same at a very basic level. Each training has as its central feature an assumption that the trainers are not outside 'controllers' of the situation, but go through the same processes themselves. The training is in effect a learning through camp experience.

The first step, almost always, is an exercise in coming out of oneself, i.e., looking at one's own being and actions as an 'outsider', asking oneself, 'What is it that I do?', 'What is it that I think?' In a climate of togetherness, these questions slowly melt into a deeper perception of 'What are the things that *we* do?' and 'What are the kinds of experiences that we go through?' An experience of being part of a larger group emerges imperceptibly. It is a move from the personal to the collective ethos.

At another level, this move from the 'private' world to a 'shared' world generates an experience of strength. Suffering in privacy, recognizing one's lot as God-given or 'destined', is always an experience of powerlessness. Sharing, listening and reflecting lend a distance from oneself and facilitate a balanced perspective. There is an understanding of solidarity from living it.

This jotting from a participant's diary gives a feel for the current understanding of training in WDP:

Why do we call these training?
It sounds a misnomer
for an experience where
each one's turmoil and trepidations
are transfused
and transformed.
A transition takes place
with new experiences
changed attitudes
and revised stands.
With so much going into
these experiences
how can we call it
a mere training? (IDARA Diary)

Given these broad features, it is obvious why WDP training programmes have not had a set of common teaching aids. It was discovered in the first few training programmes that the process of composing songs or creating charts was probably far more significant than the finally prepared material. However, two significant features have emerged throughout these training programmes. Firstly, with each new training, it is being realized that there is no dearth of trainers. From amongst the *prachetas*, almost 80 per cent have developed skills for training. So also the *sathins*. Beginning with its own concept of a 'highly skilled trainer', WDP has now moved to a decentralization of this very important activity. Secondly, the notion of training is increasingly being seen as one long process in which the camp experience has to be linked with the existing structures of action at the field level. Hence there has been a growing stress on more frequent field visits, analysis, involvement of associated groups, and visualization of long-term linkages.

Precisely because of this—the uncertainty of things—training programmes also became forums for evolving the pattern of WDP activity. It led, perhaps, to an overemphasis on 'training' and trainers. Training was sought as a panacea, a magic cure for all field situations. One recognized that this, again, needed a balance. All this reaffirmed the need to think over the training programmes. Training within the confines of a particular period of time had to be stopped and it had to be understood as the initiation of a process. The field situation had to be accepted as presenting another facet of the training task, and not be seen in isolation. A conscious recognition of training and fieldwork as a *continuous exercise* was made. What is the core convergent point of all training schemes? The answer must be: *the effort to evolve a different perspective,* to rediscover the lost faith and confidence in ourselves, in our collective strength. It was never an easy task. All those archaic values that had been dinned into our heads decrying and rejecting the positive qualities of womanhood: all those stereotyped images had been so absorbed into the system that questioning had almost become sacrilegious. But it emerged, slowly and steadily—faith in solidarity and sisterhood born of sharing all those moments of personal pain, humiliation, the years of silent suffering and the moments of happiness. It was a pooling of experiences and recollections, so remote that even thinking about them seemed forbidden, let alone talking of them. Many had almost forgotten them in the course of coping with everyday life.

From all these, a pattern began to emerge. From the ruins of old images rose the new roles, the unguessed, uncharted capabilities. The training programmes now initiated a revised, positive perception of a woman's own identity in a larger social process. Later, training began evolving its own characteristic features.

Each district's character—climatic, geographic, socio-economic and others—started to feature in the training. Constant feedback from the field brought about the realisation that WDP's work cannot take place in isolation. This meant tackling many issues—hand-pumps, famine works and minimum wages, ration-card and grazing land problems, other village level workers and their functioning, health and birth control, and many others. To effectively start dealing with all these issues, relevant information (with constant feedback) had to be collected and disseminated.

Clippings: Four

> Somebody provides the money. Somebody implements the programme. It receives academic help from another party. The programme identifies some beneficiaries. But who is the evaluation for?

The agency is told that the programme is for the people, but the agency is accountable to the funder, the Government. Is that correct?

If evaluation is an integral part of the programme, the main beneficiaries of the evaluation must also be the beneficiaries from the programme—the people.

You cannot wish away the Government. Whoever puts up the money for a venture has the right to seek information about progress and outcome. If you don't wish to answer these questions, you shouldn't take the money in the first place.

The direction and nature of accountability determines the content of evaluation. We must try and visualise the content of the evaluation exercise with all agencies accountable to the people.

The purpose of the sponsor, the purpose of the programme, and the purpose of the beneficiary call for different types of information. But need they be in conflict? At cross purposes? If so, the agencies have not done their homework before launching the programme.

The main issue is not the content of evaluation at all. Nor the end use. Nor even its non-use. It is really a question of the power over methodology. If one party has the power and another has not, it cannot be conducive to any development process. The methodology itself must promote open examination, open analysis.

The group has rejected the orthodoxy. By all means celebrate the rejection. But let the celebration not be so heady that we neglect the responsibility of providing a viable alternative.

Forms of Communication

Having dispensed with the conventional, narrow and quite unhelpful concept of training, and replaced it with something far more comprehensive, encompassing diverse facets—such as communicating, sharing, co-operating, mobilizing, organizing, planning, initiating, reinforcing and so on—we might reflect on some of the forms of communication employed in the *sathin* meetings. We cannot make an exhaustive list of all the forms used, nor can we make an evenly detailed analysis of each form mentioned. Quite often the most effective developments were products of the events—the purposes chosen and the atmosphere set.

Alice, (in Wonderland), on being admonished to think carefully before she spoke, indignantly exclaimed: 'How can I know what I think till I can see what I say?'

Drama

'Putting up a play'—the phrase implies distance, deliberation and effort. However, the *sathins* constantly freewheeled into impromptu plays, making drama an extension of speech, a continuation of narrative. A play was not 'a performance'. Rather, it seemed to be an animated situation, a discussion in action. The ease with which this spillover into a play was effected was like switching from one language to seek the particular strength of another. This recourse to another language, drama, could be for any one of numerous reasons. Some examples:

* Analysis
  (The milk cooperative play)
* Elucidation, recapitulation, consolidation
  (Chipko and others)
* Reflecting existing values
  (Good woman/bad woman play)
* Approaching an issue
  (Minimum wages, drinking, ration shop plays)
* Planning and anticipating
  ('When I go back to the village' play)
* Learning and teaching
  (Roles of *sathin* and *pracheta* play)

Some plays aimed to give information about government schemes (IRDP, NREP, NAEP, etc.), while many dramatized the events and stories narrated by the *sathins* about their lives and villages. In a single month-long training, there would be as many as ten to fifteen plays. The thirty odd plays one has seen, have certain common characteristics, whatever the subject matter, whosoever the participants:

* All the *sathins* willingly and eagerly participate in plays. Acting is not seen as a special skill in the hands of a few.
* The plays include songs and ceremonies. For instance, weddings, visits, partings, are shown along with the traditional songs and rituals.
* If two or three groups are doing different plays by turn, the *sathins* who are watching as audience also join in the play, interpose, comment. The distance between audience and actors is easily and unconsciously crossed.
* The plays are panoramic, showing two or three settings at the same time, with simultaneous action. Usually, this simultaneity of scenes entails a bare minimum of overlap and confusion.
* Very often, the plays go on and on. The actors and audience get so involved in it that the play continues. The separation between reality and play-acting is dissolved, one merging with the other.
* Often actual time is shown; for instance, if a character is making rotis, then the time taken to make a sufficient number of rotis is also taken in the act.
* Linked to this is the approach to repetition. Sometimes, instead of showing an action as representative of a regular routine, the action itself would be shown several times. Or again, if a certain scene is enjoyable, it is repeated.
* The play, thus, is not geared to an audience, it is an expression.
* It features an unwritten script, no sets, a flexible stage/floor space size, and a kind of collective direction.

Acted Narrative

This is not a defined, particular form, but a name one has given to a style of narration observed innumerable times. While recounting a story or event, a *sathin* would suddenly get up and accompany her speech with action. (This was a style adopted mainly by the illiterate *sathins*.) For instance, while saying, 'So I went to the moneylender', she would walk up to one of the group, assign the character of moneylender to her, address the character, but at the same time speak the lines of the moneylender herself!

Narration: Stories, Events, Anecdotes

Assertion of a stand, a point of disagreement, a clarification, a tangential approach—the very same lines which form the grid of a discussion, but each in the form of a 'story'. The end of one narration was usually followed by some murmurs, comments, preceded by 'look how it happened that . . . .' These comments abstracted the essential elements of the episode.

Doha, Paheli, Chutkula (Couplet, Riddle, Joke)

To get something across effectively and in essence, the *sathins* use a few quick lines, an impressionistic sketch—the *doha*. Often, summing up a discussion with the major ideas and arguments was not as effective as a *doha* recited by a *sathin*, which beautifully captured the spirit of it all. They had a fund of riddles, too, which they kept exchanging in night-long sessions. While the narrations and plays are rooted in concrete, physical details, the *dohas* involve abstractions and essences. The *sathins* are comfortable in both.

Songs

Nearly 150 rural women of Rajasthan (the *sathins* during their training), have together created over sixty songs in the last year and a half. Like drama, the composition and singing of songs was not the preserve of a talented few. All joined in the making of the songs.

The *sathin-geet* were composed by the *sathins*. Such a song could open an entirely new phase in the training. When the *sathins* of one district heard a song about drinking (during their training), which had been composed by the *sathins* of another district, they suddenly started narrating their own experiences. Till then, personal experiences had not been shared. A song was often resorted to as a method of documentation, and an easy-to-handle, readily accessible information-retrieval system.

Dance

Dancing together meant several things—relaxation, abandon, solidarity, joy and pride in the body's expression of physical vigour and wellbeing. Dance had an engulfing quality. And a gut appeal. It was one form of communication which continued unabated throughout the night.

Games

Many complex concepts could be discussed with ease, because they had already been played in a game. Not all these games were designed to lead up to such discussions. Many were familiar childhood games seen anew. And some of the games with built-in concepts were just played, with no discussions afterwards. Games played the important roles which nonsense and fantasy play in life, that of balancing, providing an outlet, stimulating the imagination, putting a perspective 'on its head', offsetting and keeping in proportion the sometimes overwhelming sense of seriousness and reality.

Writing

In the first training, writing not only occupied a place of ease, but made positive contributions. The removal of two tacit fears—of being grammatically incorrect and of not writing in a certain 'style'—liberated the act of writing from its schoolroom confines. In the reorientation programme six months later, writing was used for making forceful stands, for critical comments and synopses. The major issues which came up during the reorientation have been written by the *sathin* groups and included verbatim in the reorientation report.

Drawing

In a group where only one or two were fully literate, writing had to be abandoned after a few attempts. Instead, drawing was used extensively for documentation and expression. Just as writing, to be complete, had to be coupled with listening, drawing had to be coupled with commentary.

Visuals

Several sets of flash cards, dealing mainly with health, provided insights into visual literacy, as well as the possibilities of this medium. The *sathins* decided to make their own sets of flash cards in one of the training programmes. They made one on menstruation and another on XY chromosomes. A 'new' form, that of flash cards, became theirs—it held no secret and authority. They, too, could make and show picture stories.

Puppets

Puppet-making stretched over several days—pounding, pasting, kneading, stitching, all areas of strength. The tape, mike, camera, formed a fractional part of the training (they were hardly there, really), so not much can be said about them. Or, then again, perhaps their very absence speaks?

The distinctive feature underpinning these communication forms is *the kind of relationship* between (*a*) the *sathins* and the forms of communication, (*b*) the forms themselves, and (*c*) the *sathins* themselves. What has to be seen in the use of all these forms, is the possibility of dialogue, accessibility and control. The questions one would ask before the choice of a form would centre around these three parameters, firmly located in the specific cultural context of the women in rural Rajasthan.

Ten

Generating Appropriate Rural Technologies: The ASTRA Experience*

K.S. Jagadish

It was in the year 1974 that a few professors in the Indian Institute of Science, Bangalore, led by Prof. A.K.N. Reddy, were convinced of the need to form a transdepartmental cell to look at the scientific and technological problems related to rural development. Prof. Reddy was supported by Prof. K. Krishna Prasad, Prof. R. Narasimha and Dr. Madhav Gadgil. The basic arguments in support of this move stemmed from a recognition of some of the features of the socio-economic context in which science and technology activity had been pursued (see Appendix 10.2).

Following from these arguments, this faculty group felt that a new policy for rural development should be based not on the wholesale transfer of Western technologies, but on alternative technologies which would require less capital and utilize more labour. It was also felt that these alternatives should mobilize local resources and skills, save energy, and flourish in small-scale production systems. In short, self-reliant rural advancement was to be the new approach to development. The group then argued for a

* Several accounts of ASTRA exist in various publications connected with appropriate technology, science and technology policy and development studies. The case study presented here is in the nature of a reflection, fifteen years after the Centre's inception, on the institutional prerequisites for successful dissemination of alternative technologies in rural areas. The interpretations and inferences drawn are of the case writer alone.

new role for scientific institutions in the country in tune with this philosophy. It was felt that alternative technologies could only be developed by committed groups with a high degree of multi-disciplined competence. Such conditions were generally expected to exist in the advanced institutions. The sophisticated scientific and engineering expertise available in such institutions needed to be harnessed for the development of alternative technologies. The need for a 'cell' in the Indian Institute of Science, dedicated to alternative technologies for rural development, was thus clearly visualized.

The Formation of ASTRA

The cell for the Application of Science and Technology to Rural Areas (now designated a Centre) was formally started in August 1974 with Prof. A.K.N. Reddy as the Convenor. The Council of the Indian Institute of Science commended the decision to form ASTRA. It must be emphasized that this programme for developing rural technologies had the support and encouragement of the then Director, Prof. S. Dhawan. The Institute provided a small annual budget and some supporting staff to get the programme quickly off the ground.

The formation of ASTRA was accompanied by a great deal of discussion in various departments. Prof. Reddy formally met the faculty of several departments to forcefully present the case for ASTRA. Prof. Narasimha and Prof. Krishna Prasad went about enthusing the aeronautical and mechanical engineers to work for ASTRA.

The broad objectives of ASTRA were stated as follows*:

1. ASTRA should serve as the agency for increasing the Institute's awareness of the rural situation.
2. It should play a key role in correcting the present urban bias in the educational, research and development programmes of the Institute so that a significant fraction of these programmes may acquire a rural orientation.

---

* Extracted from the first ASTRA document prepared by Prof. A.K.N. Reddy. See Appendix 10.2.

The specific programmes of ASTRA, in tune with these objectives, were stated to be:

1. The development/testing of village-oriented technologies on the Institute campus.
2. Establishment of an extension centre in a village near Bangalore.
3. Transfer of developed/tested technologies either to the village through the extension centre or to other rural development agencies.

It was also fairly clear that in the initial stages the Institute faculty had to educate themselves about the rural reality. The standard approach of the elite institutions is to 'meet rural needs' through cheaper and cruder versions of imported urban technologies. The first ASTRA document made it clear that such an approach would not be appropriate. A proper study of rural lifestyles and traditional technologies would lead to an in-depth understanding of the rural situation. Such an understanding was an essential prerequisite for the satisfactory generation of appropriate rural technologies.

Several faculty members of the Institute were quite excited about the prospect of working on rural problems. Yet, it must be admitted that there were quite a few problems and uncertainties. While the ASTRA objectives looked askance at the careless import of Western technologies, the Institute of Science did, indeed, have a strong Western bias in its research programmes. Most of the research problems of the Institute were selected from Western journals, if not based on direct contact with academics from the West. The publication of papers in refereed journals abroad was the sine qua non of academic excellence. The prestige and status of an academic was directly proportional to the number of trips he made abroad. Experimental research, when not based on sophisticated imported equipment, was automatically considered to be of poor quality. The philosophy of applied scientific research with a bias towards local needs propounded by ASTRA was almost heretical in the value system obtaining in the Institute.

The Extension Centre

The establishment of an extension centre was an important feature of the ASTRA programme. About 55 acres of government land in Ungra village (Kunigal taluk, Tumkur district) was formally transferred to the Indian Institute of Science in 1976 on a 20 year lease. (Prof. Krishna Prasad was the Convenor of ASTRA at that time. Prof. A.K.N. Reddy was away at Nairobi with UNEP, on sabbatical leave, and returned towards the end of 1976.) The Ungra extension centre started functioning in July 1977.

The year 1977 saw the start of several activities in Ungra. The project on Rural Energy Consumption Patterns was funded by the ICSSR. The programme on low-cost building construction was started as part of the DST (Department of Science and Technology) project, Village and Agricultural Ecosystems Study. A new windmill design (vertical axis savonius rotor) was fabricated and erected as part of a project with Tata Energy Research Institute.

The Early Years

The first five years of ASTRA saw the launching of a diverse number of projects on rural technologies. For instance:

* Biogas plants
* Bullock carts
* Windmills
* Sisal plant utilization
* Hand-pumps
* Building technologies

Several of these were undertaken as sponsored projects. There were many innovations attempted.

For biogas plants an optimization exercise was carried out to minimize the plant costs per unit of biogas produced. The use of solar heating to increase gas yield was also attempted. In the case of bullock carts, a force analysis was made to understand the stresses developed in different parts of the bullock cart. Traditional bullock carts were also studied to understand the selection of timbers for various parts of the cart. (One interesting finding was that existing designs, evolved over countless generations, were sound on many counts!) In the study on hand-pumps an analysis of the failure modes of the various components was carried out. This provided avenues for improving the design of several parts for better performance. A laboratory study was also made to study the failure characteristics of modified designs. The work in these three areas followed a methodical and analytical approach, on the premise that better designs will emerge when the performance of the various systems is more correctly understood.

The work on windmills, however, followed a different approach. The available knowledge on the aerodynamics of windmills was applied straightaway to come up with an innovative design of a savonius rotor windmill, coupled to an equally innovative scooter tyre pump. In this approach one detected the earnestness to get on with design, fabrication and field trials, rather than to wait for the results of an elaborate analysis. There was no conscious effort to produce 'scientific' results. The main emphasis was to quickly arrive at a working model. Improvements through the development of the science (which in general are slower) could come later.

Looking back on the early attempts, a few observations might not be out of place. It is clear that ASTRA was both enthusiastic and defensive in its approach. The enthusiasm stemmed from the sense of a mission-oriented programme. The defensive stance was in response to the latent criticism that ASTRA's work was not 'scientific' enough. Accordingly, the work on biogas plants, bullock carts and hand-pumps indicated a sincere but hurried attempt to produce science with a rural bias.[1] This approach, by failing to recognize the possibility of technological improvements preceding developments in science, appears rather simplistic today, as indeed revealed very often in the history of science and technology. This is evident from the fact that although these studies did produce useful information, the excitement generated was inadequate to produce technological improvements in their wake. The approaches required for scientific research and technological development are distinct and different. While science and technology are very closely related, the methodologies of development in both can be different and need to be recognized as such.

Later Years: Building Technologies, Energy Systems and Technology Dissemination

ASTRA has now generated a large number of technological options in building construction. Stabilized mud-blocks, rice husk

[1] See for instance, Reddy, A.K.N. (ed.), *Rural Technology*, Indian Academy of Sciences, 1980.

ash based cement, brick panel roofs and ferrocement are some of the alternatives. These technologies have been widely demonstrated in several rural and urban locations. Stabilized mud-blocks have started spreading commercially in Bangalore.

The community biogas plant at Pura, a project commenced in 1979 but implemented in 1988 after overcoming some initial set-backs, is another example of a successful rural technology. This plant now provides energy for water pumping and lighting in Pura village. This pilot plant is one of the very few successful community biogas projects in India.

ASTRA has also carried out extensive R & D in wood gasifiers. A 3.7 KW wood gasifier has been set up in the village of Hosahalli to provide lighting to the forty homes in the village. A captive forest provides the wood on a renewable basis.

In recent years, ASTRA has started its activities in mixed species forestry, leaf biomass gasifiers and environmental education for rural schools.

It has become increasingly clear that the proof of the appropriate technology pudding is in its actual use in the field, and not in the neatness of the recipe or the prototype in the lab. ASTRA's experience with the improved wood stove illustrates the many-sided nature of the dissemination problem and the issues confronting R & D professionals in an institutional setting.

The ASTRA Stove

Dr. M.S. Hegde (of the Solid State and Structural Chemistry Unit of the Institute) posed a problem from Uttara Kannada district to Prof. R. Kumar. The process of making liquid jaggery was normally carried out with firewood as the fuel rather than bagasse. Prof. Kumar was requested to design a liquid jaggery unit using bagasse. This project, funded by the Karnataka State Council for Science and Technology (KSCST), was successfully implemented in 1981. The interest in smokeless and fuel-efficient stoves for cooking was also alive in ASTRA. Mr. Howard Geller, a visiting scientist from Princeton, spent a year making measurements on rural stoves and conducting some experiments on alternative designs. His studies showed that traditional stoves had an average water boiling efficiency of about 15 per cent. However, his studies did not succeed in developing the concept of an improved stove. At this juncture, a new idea emerged during discussions with Prof. Kumar. The jaggery stove could, perhaps, be scaled down to produce a domestic cooking-stove. The work on the domestic stove was started immediately by Profs. Kumar, Lokras and Jagadish. Later on, the group was assisted by Mr. D.S. Sudhakar Babu and Ms. Swati Bhogle. After a few months of sustained effort, the three pan ASTRA stove was ready. It gave an average water boiling efficiency of 45 per cent.

Preliminary field trials of the stove were carried out at Unchagi (Uttara Kannada district), Anekal (Bangalore district) and Ungra (Tumkur district). The response of the villagers in these places was overwhelmingly favourable in view of its advantages of fuel saving and smokelessness. The Government of Karnataka was very enthusiastic about the new device, and a programme of stove dissemination was launched in 1984 through a KSCST project. ASTRA trained about twenty diploma holders in engineering in the technique of stove construction. These persons became stove instructors and conducted stove training camps in all taluks, training sixteen persons in each taluk in stove construction.

Each taluk administration was then given a stove target under various central and state schemes. The BDO was expected to get the stoves constructed using the trained stove builders. Scheduled Caste households were to get the stove completely free of charge. The others had to provide bricks and mud, and pay Rs. 25 for the stove (subsidized cost).

According to government records, about 2 lakh stoves were built by 1987–88. It was publicized as a very successful programme in the upper echelons of the government. ASTRA and KSCST carried out a random sample survey in several villages in 1987–88 and obtained the following information:

A. Stoves in government records	: 3,648
B. Stoves built in the field	: 2,752(75.4 per cent of A)
C. Stoves in use	: 1,598(38.1 per cent of B)
D. Stoves rejected	: 1,088(39.5 per cent of B)

It was found that the government promptly undertook block construction of stoves in SC/ST homes to complete the targets, since sporadic construction in other households was more time-consuming. The quality of construction was often rather poor.

Even when the stove quality was good there were other problems. The cooking practices were not always in line with the basic concepts in stove design that called for three openings and tightly fitting vessels. Also, no communication was given to the housewife (mostly illiterate) on the best way of using the stove. The new stove was invariably introduced in a swift one-time intervention in the household, with no follow-up whatsoever. Little wonder, then, that stove installation failed in a variety of ways.

The ASTRA stove could also perhaps be faulted on another ground. Out of the total expenditure of Rs. 125 for each stove, nearly Rs. 76 was spent on the purchase of metallic and cement asbestos components. About two or three suppliers, situated in urban Karnataka, monopolized the supply of these components. This expenditure, which went straight from the government coffers to the suppliers, could hardly stimulate the rural economy. If the stove design relies on locally produced components and better local participation, one can expect improved economic activity in villages due to the stove programme.

ASTRA and the Institute

There are contradictions between the mission-oriented objectives of ASTRA and the broad (albeit unwritten) goals of the Institute. ASTRA was formed specifically to generate and test technologies appropriate to rural development. The Indian Institute of Science was supposed to carry out scientific/engineering research of the highest order in the country, comparable to the best in the (Western) world. A large number of the faculty tended to believe that research in rural problems would lead to poor quality of scientific research. The initial ASTRA reaction to this hidden attitude was to emphasize the importance of sophisticated science and engineering skills in solving rural technological problems; that it was not enough to merely provide solutions to 'alleviate' rural problems; and that the generation of appropriate technologies should be done in a manner worthy of the Institute, by employing all the competence and skills available there. Inadvertently, this in-house re-education task became the primary goal of ASTRA, and solving rural problems was of secondary importance. The various areas of research described earlier reveal, in a sense, this feature of ASTRA. The ASTRA stove and the mud-block technology represent sufficiently sophisticated approaches, which would meet the Institute criteria of excellence in R & D. However, the success of the ASTRA stove in rural areas is no longer an absolute certainty. Most of the 'sophisticated' features of the ASTRA stove were absent in the rural versions. It was probably an unimplementable dissemination programme, since the problems of dissemination were not envisaged in the stove design. Again, the mud-block technology turned out to be much more successful in metropolitan Bangalore than in rural Karnataka, in spite of twelve years of rural demonstration. Here, again, the design of the technology did not take the rural situation fully into account. The biogas programme in Pura, on the other hand, can be regarded as more successful. But the programme itself was not a demonstration of the ultimate engineering skills expected of the Institute. Problems tackled in the biogas programme were of the routine variety, with little challenge to the best minds at the Institute.

The above contradiction is perhaps neatly resolved in the views of Prof. R. Kumar. He generally regards the solution of rural problems as a piece of useful work requiring the immediate application of a known science. It might or might not lead to scientific problems of a challenging nature. A scientist in the Institute could spend a fraction of his time on this kind of research without prejudicing his professional advancement in conventional research areas. It appears a pragmatic resolution of the dilemma so typical in an institution of higher learning in a poor country. On the other hand, such an approach also carries with it the distinct probability of relegating a centre like ASTRA to a peripheral role in the Institute.

Some other contradictions in the work of ASTRA in the context of the Institute also need to be recognized. It was quite clearly envisaged in the beginning that an understanding of the rural situation could only emerge through a process of interaction with communities in rural areas. It was understood that the faculty would have to spend a reasonable amount of time in the extension centre or in other rural areas for this purpose. This has remained, by and large, unrealized—with of course some exceptions. All the understanding of the rural situation was obtained, apparently, from Bangalore city. It is likely that this has lent an air of superficiality to the work of ASTRA. The faculty members are more likely to end up undertaking (and solving!) problems which, in their own opinion, have a rural relevance, thus ignoring the basic tenets of appropriate technology, articulated in great detail at the inception of ASTRA. It is difficult for the faculty not to be influenced by the predominant culture of the Institute with its strong Western bias, and the yet inchoate ideas of what should be done to help India's villages. Each member of ASTRA only followed diligently whatever appealed to him in rural technology. The various members were not closely bound by any well-orchestrated grand design. It was a loosely knit, disparate set of actions of the faculty, sometimes pulling in several directions.

There is a need for a balanced and pragmatic approach to resolve the issue of relevance of ASTRA to the Institute. It is also necessary to recognize the fact that ASTRA is a minuscule part of the Institute. If such a small part of the Institute focusses exclusively on rural technological problems, it need not be considered as a lowering of the scientific level obtaining in the Institute as a whole. On the other hand, a technology generation programme can often throw up problems challenging to the scientist in the conventional department. This might be said to have happened in the projects on building technology and sisal leaf processing, and in ecosystem studies. In this manner ASTRA can be seen to be adding to the Institute's strength and increasing its versatility, rather than diluting its quality.

Appendix 10.1

Aspects of the ASTRA Stove Dissemination Programme*

Implications of Caste Categories

The Scheduled Castes and Tribes represent the economically and socially backward groups of Indian society. Very often, they do not own land, their educational levels are low, and they are generally engaged as seasonal labourers. The settlements of such communities are generally segregated from those of the upper castes. The government, hence, attempts to correct the social and economic backwardness by devising special programmes for them. Accordingly, they are offered special privileges in education and employment. They also receive food and clothing subsidies from the government. The ASTRA stoves are provided completely free of charge to these groups.

Production and Dissemination Strategy

The ASTRA stove has a variety of components, usually made of metal and cement–asbestos, which are centrally manufactured/supplied by private agencies. (There are only three agencies supplying parts all over Karnataka.) The district administration also fixes the stove construction targets of the various block development offices. These, in turn, organize the stove construction through the village level worker (*gram sevak*), who delegates the task to a stove builder. The latter is paid his labour charges only after the stove is constructed. In the case of Scheduled Caste/Tribe households, the *gram sevak* identifies the groups which will receive the stove (completely free of charge). It is not uncommon for a village level worker to pressurize these households to accept the stove in order to complete the target assigned to him. In such cases, the Scheduled Caste

---

* From *ASTRA, Evaluation of the ASTRA Stove Programme*, Indian Institute of Science, 1987.

households are relatively unprepared to accept the somewhat different stove concept. Relatively higher rejection rates are noticed in such households.

Typical Problems of Dissemination

There are two categories of problems associated with the stove dissemination programme. The first category concerns the training programme for the stove builders. In the other category, one may consider the actual process of dissemination.

The Training Programme

A: The first rather important step lies in the selection of the stove builder for training. This is not carried out with care. Many of them lack the motivation and the ability to absorb new skills. There is, at present, a very great desire among village youth to secure salaried employment in an urban centre. The prospect of staying in a village, waiting for the uncertain stove construction activity to pick up momentum, is not very attractive to most of them. Again, a stove builder with a mediocre stove building ability, is rejected either by the stove customer or by the officials at the BDO.

B: There are many instances where women stove builders have been imparted training. A majority of them are reluctant to build stoves far away from their villages. The concept of a woman stove builder travelling to far off villages, building stoves in unfamiliar environs, is not readily accepted. However, the authors have come across a couple of upper-caste women who have become motivated and skilled stove builders. But such instances appear to be exceptional.

C: The stove builder is trained over a period of twelve days in construction. The stove operation is also demonstrated during the training. However, the builder has inadequate exposure to situations where the stove or its operation can go wrong. If a stove is not performing satisfactorily, he is generally not clear about the reasons. It may hence be surmised that the twelve day training period, involving only stove construction, is rather inadequate. Very often, it also happens that the stove construction programmes do not get started immediately after a training camp. It is likely that the trainees would have forgotten stove building by the time the construction programmes are started.

The Dissemination Process

A: The stove construction process and the mechanism of payment of money to the stove builder are fairly tortuous. It has also been found that the stove construction operation is rather tardy in the first nine months of the financial year. The administration wakes up in January and tries to force the pace of construction, with disastrous consequences for the quality of construction. There have been complaints that in some blocks a builder is paid only Rs. 10.00 per stove and he goes around building three stoves per day. There have also been instances of the stove builders collecting additional money from the beneficiaries to cover their travel and other overhead costs.

B: If the stove builder has to travel to a far off village for stove construction, he would like to ensure that there are sufficient customers in that village. It is rare that he travels some distance to build only one or two stoves. Organization of the stove construction by keeping all materials ready and informing the stove builder about the suitable days of construction pose problems of logistics and communications.

C: The block development office often pressurizes the village level worker to complete the stove target. The worker sometimes dumps the stove components in a village and reports completion of the stove construction target. Accordingly, several districts show a disparity between government figures of stoves constructed and the actual number of stoves in rural homes. Sample surveys are now in progress to ascertain the extent of this disparity.

Reasons for Stove Rejection

Systematic statistical information on reasons behind the rejection of a stove is yet to be collected. However, a number of field visits have revealed some typical reasons, voiced by the stove users, for the rejection of the stoves. They may be listed as under:

1. Water leaks through the chimney–roof junction and damages the stove
2. Stove top gets damaged easily
3. Consumes more fuel than the traditional stove
4. Cooking of the jowar pancake is not satisfactory
5. Cannot be used to dry wet clothes during the rainy season (in heavy rainfall areas)
6. Long pieces of wood cannot be used
7. Fire hazard for thatched roofs
8. The smoke does not go through the chimney easily
9. Cannot use the three pans effectively

Appendix 10.2

Extract: Original Proposal for ASTRA

It is becoming increasingly clear from the experience in India and other developing countries that the benefits of urban industrialization, intensive agriculture and medical progress have not trickled down to the rural poor to the extent hoped for and expected. One major reason for this situation is the uncritical import and adoption of the technologies of the advanced countries.

The development policy followed in India since independence has led to the growth of industries in urban regions leaving the majority in rural areas largely untouched. One major reason for this situation was the uncritical import and adoption of western technologies. These technologies catered only to the needs of the elite, while depending critically on raw materials, energy and skills not sustainable in the Indian context. Above all, by emphasising the saving of labour, they aggravated the already acute problem of unemployment.

By becoming more and more intensive with respect to capital, energy and skills, imported industrial technologies gravitate away from the countryside and towards urban centres. By emphasising an agriculture which requires massive investments on machinery, irrigation and expensive inputs (seeds, fertilizers, pesticides, etc.), the benefits of the green revolution accrue almost wholly to the rural rich. By diverting attention, firstly to the curative rather than the preventive aspects of medicine, and secondly, to diseases arising from affluence rather than poverty, the exploitation of medical advances does not help the rural poor in any significant measure. By concentrating on luxury goods and services which have a higher import content than goods and services for mass consumption, the technologies of the advanced countries increase the import bill of the country and cater only to an elite. By demanding raw materials which are not available locally, they increase imports and/or load the struggling transport system and thereby necessitate dependence on fossil fuels. By originating largely from the interests of private enterprise, these foreign technologies are inimical to the rational utilization of public resources such as soils, waters, grasslands and forests; the result is a steady loss and degradation of these resources. By consuming non-renewable materials, they squander precious natural resources. By pursuing an ever-increasing scale of production, these imported technologies become critically dependent on a supply of raw materials, energy and skills too large to sustain with ease under Indian conditions—the result is long gestation times and under-utilization of industrial capacity. Above all, by emphasising the saving of labour, they accentuate the already acute problem of unemployment. Thus, given *this* country's resources (including manpower), an indiscriminate adoption of the technology of advanced countries results in rural impoverishment, balance-of-payments difficulties, crises of raw materials, energy and skills, under-utilization of industrial capacity, growing income inequalities, large-scale migration to cities and mass unemployment.

It is imperative therefore to consider a totally different approach to development in which the starting point is the following set of facts:

(1) four-fifths of India's population lives in the villages;
(2) three-fifths of the population has a per capita expenditure of less than one rupee per day;
(3) about 20 millions are unemployed and 100 millions are under-employed.

This starting point suggests that a valid development strategy should be based not on the technologies of the advanced countries, but on alternative technologies that facilitate low capital investment (Rs. 100–500 per work-place instead of Rs. 5000–10000), employment generation in rural areas, dispersal of miniproduction units to the villages and production of inexpensive goods and services of the mass consumption variety. Only such alternative technologies can lead to reduced inequalities through the poorest sections of society having more to spend by virtue of greater employment and at the same time having access to inexpensive essential goods and services which can be bought with the greater earnings. Thus, alternative technologies are technologies that are directly in the interests of the unemployed or under-employed rural poor.

It is not proposed that alternative technologies be chosen irrespective of cost considerations. In each case where a choice of technologies is available, it is essential to carry out a social cost benefit analysis of the options. Some of the obvious preferences to be exercised in this choice of technologies are listed below:

(1) a preference for capital-saving and employment-generating rather than capital-intensive and labour-saving, technologies;

(2) a preference for cottage-scale and village-scale, rather than large-scale technologies;
(3) a preference for the technologies of goods and services appropriate for mass consumption, rather than for individual luxuries;
(4) a preference for technologies requiring little skill, or small modifications in the skills of traditional craftsmen like potters, weavers, blacksmiths, carpenters, cobblers, tanners, oil millers, midwives, and medicine men;
(5) a preference for technologies using local materials, rather than materials which have to be imported from abroad or transported from distant parts of the country;
(6) a preference for energy-saving, rather than energy-intensive, technologies;
(7) a preference for locally available sources of energy such as the sun, wind and bio-gas;
(8) a preference, in the machine-building and machine-tool sector, for the technology of scaled-down, dispersable, miniaturized factories, rather than the technology of mass producing consumer goods in gigantic city-based enterprises;
(9) a preference for technologies which promote a symbiotic and mutually reinforcing, rather than parasitic and destructive, dependence of metropolitan industry upon the rural population;
(10) a preference for technologies based on rational sustained use, rather than indiscriminate rapid devastation, of the environment.

In short, what is needed is a preference for technologies which put the poor before the rich, "men before machines, people before governments . . . the country before the city, smallness before bigness, wholeness before reductionism, organic materials before synthetic ones . . . craftsmanship before expertise, and quality before quantity."*

Despite the vital necessity of developing these alternative technologies, it is unfortunate that the challenge has not been taken up by more than a few institutions. These few institutions may be committed, and commitment is, of course, a necessary condition, but it is not sufficient. Competence too is required, particularly because alternative technologies cannot be, as they often are, confused with primitive technologies. In fact, alternative technologies are quite advanced in that they require sophisticated scientific and engineering thinking. This point becomes obvious when one considers any specific alternative technology, e.g., the development of biogas plants which requires microbiologists, chemical engineers,

* Robin Clarke, 'Technology for An Alternative Society', *New Scientist*, 57, 66 (1973).

materials scientists, mechanical engineers and economists; the development of windmills which requires aerodynamicists, structural engineers and materials scientists; or water conservation in drought-prone areas which requires civil engineers, soil scientists, fluid dynamicists and ecologists.

Only major scientific institutions possess the multi-disciplinary competence to tackle the task of developing alternative technologies. Unfortunately, however, not a single institute of advanced study has interested itself in the challenge, perhaps because their criteria of excellence are derived from alien soils or because alternative technologies are not viewed as glamorous enough to merit attention. At the same time, these institutions have been engaged in a desperate quest for relevance, but this relevance has been almost universally interpreted to mean relevance to large-scale industry and urban problems. The possibility of relevance to rural problems has been scarcely considered.

Faced with this unconscious boycott of the rural scene by established institutions of science and technology, attempts are being made in the country to set up institutes of appropriate technology and rural development. This is hardly a solution to the problem because the number of disciplines required to make such institutes function effectively is so large that the inevitable result will be additional institutes of science and technology with a whole paraphernalia of extra staff and services. Further, once particular projects are completed, it may turn out that some of the expertise assembled for those projects will become redundant.

A far more effective approach is for functioning institutes of advanced study and research to initiate and promote work in alternative technology, particularly as applied to village development. Such a redeployment of efforts with existing infrastructures is a more economical measure from the point of view of the country.

Creation of ASTRA: An Institute Cell for the Application of Science/Technology to Rural Areas

It is amidst the above background that the Indian Institute of Science has created in August 1974, ASTRA, a cell for the application of science and technology to rural areas. This step is in keeping with the pioneering role which the Institute has played in many educational, scientific and technological movements in the country. It is also quite consistent with the objects of the Institute as envisaged by its far-seeing and enlightened founder, Jamsetji Nusserwanji Tata:

(1) To provide for advanced instruction and to conduct original investigations in all branches of knowledge and, in particular, in such branches of knowledge as are likely to promote the material and industrial welfare of India.

(2) To co-operate as far as possible with such recognized institutions as exist or are founded in future for cognate objects in India.

What is being attempted is not a change in the techniques, methodologies and quality of the current programmes of the Institute, but the definition of a new vista with regard to the ultimate endproducts of these efforts. (Thus, the techniques used for the design of aeroplane wings can equally well serve the development of low-cost windmills, and researches in bacterial fermentation and in the chemical engineering of reactors can be used for the scientific design of bio-gas plants.) The new perspective is such that the present total neglect of rural problems will be transformed into a partial emphasis on work relevant to the needs of the rural poor.

The objectives of ASTRA are that it should:

(*i*) serve as the agency for increasing the Institute's awareness of the rural situation; and
(*ii*) play a key role in correcting the present urban bias in the educational, research and development programmes of the Institute so that a significant fraction of these programmes acquire a rural orientation.

In order to achieve these objectives, it is envisaged that ASTRA will in the first phase of activity: (1) catalyse the development/testing of village-oriented technologies on the Institute campus; (2) establish an Extension Centre in a village near Bangalore; (3) transfer developed/tested technologies either to the village through the Extension Centre or to other rural development agencies.

The main emphasis in this initial phase is on the Institute educating itself about rural reality, particularly about age-old techniques, empirical knowledge, the problems of those below the poverty line and their response to technologies developed in urban settings.

The necessity for this educational phase cannot be overstressed. The standard approach of western-oriented elite institutions is to assume that the needs of villages and of the rural poor can be met with cheaper and cruder versions of imported or urban technologies. Not only does such an approach inevitably end up with capital-intensive and labour-saving technologies, but it accentuates the debilitating dependence of the villages upon the cities and does damage to the fabric of village life. A more appropriate approach is to start with a scientific study of traditional life and technologies and generate qualitative changes with minor alterations and improvements. This presumes however a depth of understanding of villages and their poorer sections that can only be acquired by a process of education in the countryside.

As experience of the rural environment grows and as expertise develops in the technical component of solutions to rural problems, the Institute may well consider organizing educational programmes to produce rural technologists, i.e., engineers with a wide range of competence who can build low-cost houses, erect windmills and gobar-gas plants, design water conservation and management systems, set up small-scale chemical industries, etc. Such a long range perspective would be in keeping with the Institute's historical mission.

Types of Projects to be Undertaken

The tentative thinking is in terms of seven main classes of projects:

(1) application of civil engineering to the rural environment, for example, development of low-cost building technology based on local materials;
(2) development and exploitation of locally available energy sources, such as the wind, the sun and bio-gas, and the rational management of fuel sources such as forests;
(3) application of mechanical engineering design for the improvement of agricultural implements and operations, and of rural transport facilities;
(4) development of small-scale industries to exploit local raw materials and agricultural products and wastes;
(5) development of small-scale industries to produce consumer goods for urban markets;
(6) development of techniques, books and low-cost learning materials for education in rural schools;
(7) application of the environmental and ecological approach to rural resources such as soil, water, grassland, forests, livestock, wildlife and fish.

This thinking has emerged from reading, suggestions and discussions in an urban environment. It is obvious that contact with other institutions and agencies for rural development will increase the number of projects; but it is only a direct study of the rural environment which will result in a critical assessment of the list of projects and the definition of priorities.

Eleven

Role of the Facilitator*

Sandeep Virmani

This case is based on the documentation of a housing project in Golana village near Khambat (Cambay) in Gujarat. The documentation itself was not the need of the voluntary agencies working there, nor of any official body. It was the felt need of the people themselves. To the community concerned, the housing represented a monument to a long and tortuous struggle over many years. In the process there was much awakening, many insights gained. One important awareness, it appeared, was that their continued exploitation in the past, and the misery and hopelessness that enveloped it, was due in great measure to a distorted history that was thrust upon them. A history that served the interests of some others, but had been accepted by them uncritically over generations. If their own children were to grow up with their heads held straight, the history of the struggle over the last decade had to be written afresh. It had to be written as a record of collective triumph.

The first person narration in the case is as it occurs in the documentation, highlighting the crucial changes in perspective necessary in the outsider to do any justice to the task of recording a people's history.

---

* Incorporating excerpts from the document *A Struggle for Housing: A Statement by the Vankars of Golana*, facilitated by Sandeep Virmani. Sponsored by Janvikas and Vikas Centre for Development, Ahmedabad, 1989.

The Vankars of Golana village are a Scheduled Caste community of about a 100 families. Largely bonded labourers, about fifteen years ago they intensified their struggle against oppression. Their struggle for change was a threat to the upper-caste Darbars. In January 1986, 150 Darbars attacked and killed four of the Vankar leaders and left seventeen badly wounded. The immediate issue was a dispute over the land for a housing colony that the Vankars wanted to build for themselves.

I was to work with the Vankars on the documentation of their housing programme. The documentation evolved slowly. The first step was for me to go and live with the people in Golana.

I was to stay with Lala Mahetar, one of the nine headmen of the community. He was a victim of the Darbar attack that had left both his legs and arms in plaster. Once a yes-man to the Darbars, today he is spearheading his community's struggle. As it was already late, a charpai was put in the narrow street outside the house for me. Soon the entire length of the street was packed and blocked with charpais. People spoke to each other across the length of the street till they fell asleep. I woke up to the tune of Vande Mataram on a distant radio to find myself the only person blocking the street that had got transformed into a busy thoroughfare. I sat on the *otla* with a pitcher of water, brushing my teeth like the rest of them, all looking into each other's faces, spitting onto the street in front of them. The bathing place was a small space jutting onto the street with a three feet high wall around it. I decided not to bathe, rather self-conscious. I spent the next hour looking for an appropriate bush to sit behind, in the otherwise barren countryside. Later in the afternoon, I made the mistake of going to the well to bathe, to find a horde of women bathing there. I realized that the most private of my activities were here the most public.

The Unlearning

Things that I normally took for granted, as understood, needed to be explained here. Simple things like I had spent five years to become an architect was very difficult to explain, because they built their own houses. Or that I had come from as far as Punjab, away from my family, to be with them was considered both very brave and perplexing. I really did not know how to explain that travelling so far was not such a brave thing to do. Later I learned that very few in the village had even been to Ahmedabad, two hours away—it cost them two days' labour wages, and another day's labour was lost to be in Ahmedabad for a day, besides the expenses there. There were deeper meanings too. Their sense of belonging to the community was very strong. The reasons must have been most compelling, or my commitment very strong, for me to have left my community to come here.

They would be surprised when I asked basic questions or showed ignorance of issues of caste or crops. One person went as far as to say 'you people only know how to eat'. At other times we simply had to drop the conversation as it was impossible to continue. I was beginning to realize that words alone were not going to explain to them the world I came from. With it, I realized I was not going to understand them so easily.

One morning young Sava came and announced, with much fanfare, that he was going to show me Cambay. I was not really interested in seeing a small town, but he had put on his new shirt, and soon we were on our way to Cambay. He was much excited about eating in a slightly better restaurant than a *dhaba*, travelling in an autorickshaw, seeing a film, eating an ice cream—things that were quite routine for me. I decided to take back some sweets for Lala Mahetar's grandchildren and bought some worth 15 rupees. Sava and his friends were shocked: This incident made Sava suddenly conscious of the class difference between us, and from then on he maintained his distance.

Talking about money, I remember when I was working with them on the last phase of the housing, I had prepared an estimate of Rs. 1 lakh to be spent against the work schedules. This estimate slip was what I would constantly refer to all the time. One day Lala Mahetar said to me, 'You want to spend the one lakh, we want to save it.' I realized then that it was this attitude that had made it possible for them to develop innovative management ideas, to double the house area in the same money given to them by the government. Poverty had taught them how to extend the value of a rupee, and there I was not even using its full value.

I brought fourteen year old Ganesh to Ahmedabad. It was his first visit to this big city. We went to my cousin's house, and he could not believe that only one family lived in so many rooms of a house, and that we had a separate room for bathing only. At lunch he was surprised that we ate with so many items whereas he had been serving me only one vegetable with my meals in Golana. I realized how much I had taken them for granted, for what they were in the village, living in one room, eating with one vegetable, living in one set of clothes, and so on.

The significance of these incidents lay not so much in the knowledge of the difference between us. I might well have imagined it to an extent or read about it. But in every small incident I had to accept that I was faced with a value dilemma.

Once I sat listening to a woman relate how six of her children had died. Two from uncontrolled fever, one from a snakebite, another due to a split head with no doctor to stop the bleeding, and two others due to the local doctor's wrong medicines. The complacent acceptance of fate shocked me. She kept saying, 'It was all in God's hands.' I realized later that almost every family lost a few children like this. Then, during the rice season, Punja was explaining the importance of the timely second shower for a good crop. I asked him what if it failed. He looked up and said, 'It is all in God's hands.' One evening, while I watched a man possessed by *mata* convulse and shake violently, with people eagerly taking his blessings, I realized how secure my life was in comparison. And how much they depended on uncertain Nature for their security. For the first time I valued my education, however badly I was taught, for at least I was always assured of work and an income. For our system pampered the formal education and recognized it above any other form of learning. If belief in God is a function of fear, for the first time I was able to understand a person folding his hands to an unknown power upon whose uncertainty so much was at stake.

I had always believed that one's security came from within oneself, that the effect of our surroundings on us can be controlled. I saw that their security lay clearly outside themselves. Perhaps that is why they gave a great deal of importance to relationships. Almost every introduction of a person is accompanied by his or her relationship with some others. I began to understand that they held their society above the individual, and had developed a complex hierarchy of social structures. They had a clear understanding of what sorts of issues belonged in the realm of family groups, and what pertained to the *samaj* or the whole caste. Lala Mahetar was often called to arbitrate on a dispute or preside over celebrations pertaining to his family group (of fifteen families). He was also responsible for their wellbeing, in terms of getting work for them or arranging marriages. He would often leave for another village to discuss social, religious or constitutional matters pertaining to the *samaj* (twenty-seven villages of Vankar families).

I had always been confused by the devout confidence the people placed in the judgement of the *Nath* (the court of the *samaj*, where a bench of Mahetars from different villages pronounced judgement and punishments) and accepted their punishment. A punishment like excommunication had never made sense to me, because I did not appreciate the *sense of belonging* that the punishment invoked. The premise of their judicial structure, I slowly began to appreciate, was in the moral faith and trust of the community in one another and in their leaders.

Consider the exercise in which the suspects are made to eat uncooked rice. The person who cannot swallow the rice is the thief. The exercise rests on the faith the people have in the community, which creates fear in the thief, whereby his salivary glands go dry and he cannot swallow the rice. The first time I heard of this, I had labelled them superstitious and gullible. Later the realization dawned that this was the fundamental difference between us—their unconditional respect for fellow beings and my constant weighing of people in terms of gains and losses.

I think the first time I communicated with Lalakaka and his son on a personal level was when I expressed a desire to go to his fields during the rice season. He was touched that I should take an interest in his rice. I had always seen farming as something they would readily give up for, say, a government job, especially as the effort and risk was too much and the profits small. Besides, it was a preoccupation with basic survival, and not the higher pursuits in life, such as the arts and technology. Rice growing, I learned, was a craft that required an acute sense of timing and a keen understanding of the weather to get a good crop. During this season the entire *vas* is energized. I was surprised to learn that wheat, which requires comparatively little effort or skill, fetches a much higher price in the market. Rice growing was an expert's job, and they prided themselves in doing it well. I had not realized till then how strongly their identity was linked with farming.

When I prepared a plan for my rural exposure, I had decided that I would go and stay in a village and observe people at work and in their homes. I was cautioned on the plan: Was a village a zoo? Could I just go there and watch people without any accountability to them? It was only when I went there that I saw that the *vas*, unlike our cities, was like a big family living together. To be walking in their streets amounts to walking about inside someone's house. And so I began to realize the effort required to respect another culture. Even the different pace of a village was something to contend with. For almost a complete day on returning from or reaching a village, I would remain disoriented. It was only after I began to recognize this effect that I started preparing myself during my journey to or from the city.

Data, Information and Meaning

During the documentation process, my ideas of gathering information and recording them changed drastically. There were the obvious differences between their manner of expression and mine—in style, idiom, metaphor, and so on. I recognized these differences, and also the difficulties they posed for correct interpretation. But this recognition was not enough. There was much more to this communication gap between us. I could not see it all in the beginning. Looking back I detect, perhaps, three phases of development in my rapport with the community, in the bridging of the gap.

'If you want to know what people think about something, ask them.' A commonsense dictum, but loaded with all kinds of uncertainties. In the beginning I found myself doing just that—asking questions, for collecting data. It did not take long to sense that there was something wrong, something missing, something unreal in the transaction that followed between the respondent and myself. The responses were often stilted, as if the other person was looking for the acceptable things to say. Or there would be no response, a silence, a blank stare.

What was happening, I asked myself. What might be the explanations? Is this question–answer transaction unusual? Artificial? Have they some experience from other surveys, enquiries? Are they suspicious of something, do they not trust me? Perhaps there was something lacking in the *technique*—how a question should be constructed, what words and phrases to employ, how to begin, how to end. There must be expert advice on all this somewhere. I did some reading on the subject, met the experts, and returned to the scene armed with technique.

Whatever I did by way of new technique, the nature of the transaction did not change. I asked the questions. They answered. Was it possible, then, that it was not so much the sophistication or innocence in questioning that was the problem, but that the very act of asking questions was causing certain difficulties in the transaction? And therefore in response?

Thus began a second phase of enquiry, with a major change in approach. No questions. At least not to start with, and not directly. Instead, more listening. More deliberate and tuned in listening. I began to allow people to express themselves as they wished. People do have things to say, and do want to say them—but in their own terms. I had to allow that, and not insist on taking the lead by asking my questions. When it got going I had to only say and do things to aid the expression. It made a big difference to the volume and nature of response. But that was not all. It made a difference in me too, and in the quality of my communication with them. It was not merely some do's and don'ts in the conduct of a conversation. It was a question of my attitude and approach, and the major shift required in my relating to them.

The task benefitted too. I now had a more realistic basis (rather than an imaginary one) for providing some 'structure' for any probes or more formal, extended interviewing. I could see categories, subcategories and cross-references that had remained obscure earlier. I found it convenient to tape conversations as they occurred, and to later prepare the structured translations along the lines of my intended enquiry. I was happy with the breakthrough and the progress being made in data collection.

Alas, the joy was short-lived. I was told that the drafts I had prepared were consistently inadequate. It was pointed out to me that while the observations might be deemed correct, the findings were not acceptable—because they were *mine* and not *theirs*. In the process of converting the raw data into my format, I had missed the logic of the flow in their expression. Further, with my upbringing and education and training I had discerned only the logic of connections between words and phrases as I understood them—a cognitive logic. Could there also be, perhaps, an emotional logic? The full appreciation of the difference between content and process in human communication took quite some time to dawn. I began to see that there can be a whole *vocabulary of emotional expression*. I was only beginning to learn its alphabet.

'When this happened, we were confused, scared. We went to Gagan and Phily.' What they were saying was that there were areas in which they needed the support of the voluntary agency.

'They think they are bosses! That we don't belong to this village!' This was not mere anger at the other group. They were finally asserting their fundamental right for equality.

I was compelled to return to my tapes. I had to erase in my mind the pre-programmed translations, and listen to the original sounds afresh. I was amazed. There was so much there that I had not heard before. There was so much given that I had not taken. When I readjusted my sights, and shifted from my frames of reference to theirs, the meanings from within the words and phrases came out in a flood.

This reorientation in me also led to some practical changes in how to pose probe questions. For instance, 'What were the reasons that you had to fight for the land' was unhelpful. A blank stare. 'How did you feel about it?' 'Were you scared when you decided to fight for the land?' And the response contained all the reasons sought earlier. Similarly, seeking 'reasons' for their working on the housing project had to be replaced with an invitation to share their feelings about it.

The procedure I had adopted for recording data was the culprit, and I had to make a radical change. I decided to stay the translation, and first attempt a 'transliteration'—a word by word transcription with complete disregard for syntax, grammar and meter. When I read the transcription (and compared it to my earlier 'elegant' translation), I could see the difference. I could appreciate the nature of distortion introduced through translation. The explanation was only partly in the language itself—the conventions of usage adding ideas different from those intended. It was preceded by the principal source of distortion: the *translator*. The distortions caused by his perceptions of events, from his frames, were leading to the particular choice of words and construction in the translation.

The emotional vocabulary of a community can be very wide indeed. It is not heard directly and, therefore, not easily recognized as being there. Its significant (and legitimate) role in the totality that we call the language of the people becomes evident only when

Box 11.1: **Two Types of Transcription**

ELEGANT TRANSLATION	*RAW TRANSLITERATION*

Housing Design

Elegant Translation

We realized we would need the professional skills of an architect to help us design the housing, and to build within the budget. However, right through the building process, we kept the decision process in our control. We were helped by an understanding architect, Rajesh Shah, who realized that architecture was a process of human development in which he facilitated the evolution of a design with his technical knowhow and experience. Thus, by this approach, we gained in skills, information and competence. A large number of our people played responsible roles in accordance with their capabilities, interest and past experience.

Raw Transliteration

The plan Rajeshbhai brought was like this—slanting—like scissors, with corners coming out. Design in style! But according to our village living style, we did not like it. It works in cities. Here we have to tie buffalos, what not. The plan he drew his way . . . . In village, what kind do you want. We said, here you will have to measure 20 feet room—at the back 10 feet *vanjan*, in front 10 feet veranda—so 40 feet long, 15 feet broad we want. And at the back also 10 feet land we want. So he went back and drew again.

Why we were confident that in same amount given by government for small house we could make bigger one? Two–three reasons. From 7,000 rupees for each house that government gives, the contractor eats lot of money. We said if we make houses on our own then contractor robbing will be removed. Second, we said our own labour we will put into houses. Rajeshbhai said the estimate is going beyond 7,000 rupees, but if you give labour then we can do. So we said we will give free labour. A meeting of the *vas* was called, and they said one person from each house will work to keep income, and one we will give to *vas* for housing work. This will have to be said about people . . . . Every 15–20 days Rajeshbhai used to come and see how much we have moved—check against work done and say you are moving. Fine . . . so this way we got strength and said keep on working—there is someone to keep check and tell us . . . . Now if this project must be done again we can do all ourselves. Why? Because we have got experience.

Money and Accounts

. . . that we had the confidence to make an application asking that we maintain our own accounts on the housing required, that we had done some money keeping before. For mismanagement of the 15 lakhs would jeopardize the entire project and put us in a position of mistrust not only with the government, but also amongst our own people . . . .

We created for ourselves an internal auditing system

At first with regard to money our sight was very small. Now our sight has changed and become so big. For example, if we were asked, for this community hall say how much you want, we would have asked for 60–70 thousand. No? Why? Because can we think of asking for lakhs? But now, for getting community hall approved, how much we got? 2 1/2 lakhs. That means our sight has completely changed.

whereby our Daheda Centre kept accounts for all fair price shops of the *bhal* run by the Vankars. Only after the verification were the books made final. The Daheda Centre also became our training ground. For all the new ventures that we started the money management was taught to us at Daheda by trained staff of the Centre . . . . When the auditors came we were confident of our accounts and were not threatened. It was normal for the auditor to threaten us with the harm possible (from him) if there was some discrepancy in the accounts. He would not come to the village himself, but would call for all the books at Khambat. He would demand the use of a tractor and take grains from our stock, and address us with much superiority. So when we asked him to come to the village to do the audit, as he is supposed to do, he was most offended. Being confident of our accounts we refused to bribe him, and humbled him to speak to us as equals.

Now we have managed 15 lakhs . . . .

Co-operative money calculations Centre used to keep—we did not—Secretory of Co-operative used to keep. When our meeting came, we got together and we would work out in coming month how much money will be spent. The money—where it is, it stays there. A rough estimate we take out—like so much to be spent here, so much needed there—then that money we ask for, and bring. So we bring. So we all have knowledge. But in housing we keep complete control of money . . . . Auditors came and called for all books. Then he checked all books. But we were from the first principled—kept clear accounts, he could catch nothing . . . . First, in the village people were scared. So this advantage, who takes? The auditor. Why? Because he knows that here incorrect things are going on. So what the people say? 'Sir, whatever you say we accept, but please do the audit.' So auditor gets chance and asks for money, or whatever he wants. But here gets nothing. Then they had to take books to his office, because Secretary doesn't know how to write accounts, and he is afraid that their *mandali* will go. So there in the office, in secret, he will ask someone—the auditor—to write the books. Then the Secretary is who? A thumb impression. And the auditor is waiting for that to make money. But in our *mandali* all are powerful. Even the auditor has not studied like us. Then we have an internal audit, so there is no question of faults.

we acquire the sensitivity to emotional states beyond our limited experience.

I began to see everyday events in another light. I saw that the people here expressed emotions by letting it loose, rather than by verbalizing it in a complicated way. For instance, it was perhaps not childish, as I had felt earlier, that two persons should get into a fight, and then go and have tea together. They had successfully separated the argument from the relationship, while my urban upbringing would probably confuse the two things and, in the process, complicate future transactions.

Phase three had begun. Detecting the emotional vocabulary of a people cannot come from a lesson book, for it is intimately bound up with the unique history that they have experienced. The next phase in my reorientation began with the dawning of this realization and with the accompanying understanding of the community's history. Not too long ago, I had only a cross-sectional view of the housing programme. As an architect, I saw houses. I could document the achievement of the community in housing terms. I now had a slice of history before me. I could see various changes in the lives of the people in a longitudinal view, and I could see much interrelatedness among the changes. Around the housing I could see the achievements in community self-sufficiency, competence, togetherness. They understood banks, loans, credits, and the working of the paper money system. They had learned to manage it too, and stopped the exploitation of their ignorance. They had learned to hold together, stave off disruptive forces, take collective action. They took the crucial decisions themselves by good, rational analysis, relying on their competence, rather than superstition or fear or fatalistic submission. Where did these competencies come from? Could the housing structures be viewed, explained, evaluated in isolation? Did they 'cause' the housing, or did the housing programme, indeed, cause them?

I did not have answers for all such academic questions. But it was clear to me that the documentation of the housing would have little meaning of its own without an enveloping history of the people themselves. The information derived from the data before me would be of little use by itself. Only history would give it meaning.

Appendix 11.1

The Building Process

(*Excerpts from the people's documentation*)

When the work began there was a lot of enthusiasm. The housing finally took 12 months to complete, but at that time it seemed we would finish in four months! So much enthusiasm was there. Like Chagan, we must admit, worked a lot. Even at night he would sleep there on site and keep watch. And all this he did without any money, only because of his own attachment to the project.

Then, twice in between, the lime 'chakki' broke down. We had to send it to Ahmedabad to get it repaired. So for about seven–eight days all work with lime had to be stopped. We continued on other work, like watering of brick walls and foundations, and digging new foundations. Then once we said, 'everyone has been working so hard for so long, so let's take the next two days off. Let everyone wash their clothes and face and recoup.'

The reason for this tremendous enthusiasm was clear. For several years now, the people's need for housing had been increasing. The second reason was that this was everyone's need. For example, consider this: if 10–15 families were not a part of this process, they would have felt left out and got depressed. But here, because it was everybody's need, we decided right in the beginning that every household is to be given one house. No more, no less.

In other villages people don't work for ten days together, but here we worked for 12 months! Everyone here is thinking about this now. They realise that this would not have been possible with the enthusiasm of one or two people. This has been possible because of the combined enthusiasm of all 100. For this unity and cooperation, we had sown the seeds some four–five years ago. That is why this has been possible. Now that we have worked together, everyone's character has come out clearly. It has also brought out people's skills.

When we had finished the housing, the Sabarmati overflowed during the monsoon and there was three feet of water for three days in our houses. But no cracks developed anywhere! When the DDO came here after the floods, he said: 'You have done good work. For that this flood has proved to be a kind of report. There is no need to say anything else.' Even we had thought that at least some cracks would develop. Instead the lime became stronger in the water.

Upto the masonry work all the houses were done together. After that we first made a sample house to demonstrate how the rest of the roofs were to be made. In the plan Rajeshbhai had prepared, the wooden beam was placed slanting on the pillar, pulling it down. Because of this two or three pillars fell. So then we told Rajeshbhai: 'It won't work this way. You see how we have been building our roofs in the old vas. Along with the slanting beam we also put a horizontal beam, so that the weight of the roof falls vertically on the pillar.' We told him that for the kind of roof designed, they don't use such big and heavy wooden beams like we had used. They use steel angles which is much lighter. Secondly, in those situations the pillars are thick. Thirdly, they use sheets as roofing material. In our situation everything was contradictory—the pillars were thin, the beams thicker, and we were using tiles on the roof which were heavier. So then the roof design was changed. In the project this was the only place where we had some trouble.

In the Community Hall the truss for the roofing in the veranda was made too large. And because of that it came so low that one could bang one's head against it while walking. This was Rajeshbhai's fault, because he had designed it incorrectly in the plan itself. So when the truss was made and brought here, we realised even before it was put up that it was too big. We told Narendra, but he had not realized this. He kept insisting that they were according to the plan, and so correct. We told him that it was only clear we were all going to bang our heads on it. So finally it had to be sent back and made again. Because of this we lost about 10,000 rupees.

We also lost money because of incorrectly made foundations in the Community Hall. The back wall of the Community Hall that goes two storeys high had a foundation only three feet deep, and where the stage finished in the hall, upon which there is no load, the foundation was four feet deep. It should have been the other way around. Narendra did not notice this either.

Rajesh's supervisor used to buy material and ask us for the money by showing us the bill. We did not trust him, so we asked him to get Rajeshbhai's signature on the bills. Rajeshbhai used to sign, but he did not go to the market himself and check the prices. He used to trust his supervisor. So then we told him: 'You scout the markets, but for buying we will send one person with you.' Meanwhile, we used to check the price of the material in Cambay and get an idea of the costs.

We used to bring the skilled labour like carpenters, masons, etc., from Ahmedabad. But we took the precaution of providing the assistants to them from our vas. There was a reason. This way it was easy for us to keep a check on what they were doing through our assistants. And like Jainti, by the time the work finished, he had learned the skill himself. We used our people according to their area of expertise or interest. Like the person who worked on the lime 'chakki' had worked on it earlier in Ahmedabad.

Earlier we never trusted the village mason to set the stones in the flooring. Now we will give him the work in future. Because we have seen that the city mason, who did the Community Hall floor, takes four rupees per square foot, whereas ours takes two rupees, and the quality of work is the same.

Another place where we used our brains was with regard to the supply of water to the site. Our people used to find it difficult to carry the water on their heads from the pond every day. So everyone worked out the idea that if they brought the water from the pond through a pipe to the centre of the working site, they would save a lot of time. So with a pump we sucked the water through a 300 feet long pipe and made a 20' x 20' tank in the centre of the colony into which the water was collected. At one place where the pipe had to cross the road we even dug it up and put the pipe through a cement pipe, so it won't interfere with the traffic. Then in the monsoon the rains did not come and the main pond dried up. Then we got the canal opened to fill up the pond so that we could fill our tank on site!

In the beginning the people never gave any occasion to be reprimanded. But later they would become a little lax. To enthuse them, the Vadils would call a meeting and ask: 'What is the problem? Like this we won't be able to complete the houses!' And the following day you should have seen them work!

During those days a senior government officer came here. There were a hundred people working—with the lime 'chakki' working on one side and the water being pumped into the tank on the other. He saw all this enthusiasm and was impressed. So when we gave him an application to be granted a Community Hall for the colony he approved it! We did not even have to ask him a second time. He immediately said: 'Fine! it will be done.' Right there and then we said: 'We want the Community Hall, but we don't have any money to build it.' So he himself said that he would give us the Community Hall and the money as well. He felt that these people were working with so much enthusiasm, they deserved a Community Hall. This has been one of the main advantages of the housing. When important people come, they see that the government only gives the 'twin' design to be built, but these people have changed it . . . a hundred families have co-operated so well to make this possible . . . they have developed such a large space, it is such a clean place. This officer felt so happy watching us work that *he* asked us: 'What do you want?'

One other advantage of this housing has been on our mental health. With the coming of these new houses it felt as if five maunds of load had been lifted off our heads. From the narrowness of this vas, when a person goes to the new colony, he sees in front of his house: here is a road . . . a big veranda . . . in front of the veranda a courtyard . . . in between there are trees growing . . . so mentally one goes through a tremendous change. He becomes like 'free mind'! The place where one stays has a lot of effect on one's mind. For instance, consider Nathabhai. He used to stay in a space 10′ × 10′. Above his forehead he used to store wood. In front of him, his buffaloes were tied. Now imagine the effect this will have on his heart . . . one gets fed up! Now take Sava, in a room 5′ × 5′ he has his kitchen and his bed. One can never be at peace. You come back tired, you have no place to sit! The place is dark, so his mind also remains dark! Then a person always remains tired and disappointed. When there is no respectable place to stay and you tell him 'you must live with self respect' he feels 'where can any talk of self respect come from?' He looks at his surroundings and says: 'Where is self respect? Where is it?' So then all our effort to teach him self respect will have no effect on him.

Now in our Shahid Colony you have a large room of 20′ × 15′. There is so much of veranda and courtyard. A man feels he has come into a new world! So with increased awareness one's space also has increased.

Where we had earlier been hitting our heads against the Government for years and years to get money, in one single year we took three lakhs as subsidy for the cooperative farming and 15 lakhs for the housing. So from nothing the previous year, we took 18 lakhs that year!

Twelve

Notes on the Case Method

Vijay Padaki

Preparing the Case Lead
(Distributed Before the Workshop)

The response to the programme evaluation workshop has been very good. So has been the response to the suggestion that participants might bring *case leads* to the workshop. However, many have sought assistance in writing up the material to be brought. This note is meant to help. It is not meant to be a primer in either case study research or case writing.

Different End Uses of a Case

The two most common uses of case studies are:

* *To illustrate*: moving from the general to the specific—i.e., relating specific happenings in the case to a body of knowledge (or generalizations) available, as in medicine, law, public administration, etc.
* *To hypothesize*: moving from the specific to the general—i.e., a search for explanations, generalizations, in similar happenings, in other contexts.

There is a third use, less recognized and generally not pursued consciously in most cases—i.e., to explore and reveal the interdependencies and interlinkages across different things, events, structures, processes, etc., in the same *system*. This might come more naturally to the ethnographer–anthropologist, who seeks larger wholes, but it often remains beyond the nuts-and-bolts preoccupation of conventional case studies of the first two types.

It must be obvious that in relatively more complex and less understood systems—as in most endeavours of development and social change—we need many more of the third type of case studies. In programme evaluation, too, we need to look beyond pat cause-and-effect assumptions in interventions to more inclusive, qualitative/descriptive documentation as well.

Workshop Need: Case Leads and Not Full Cases

A good case study will obviously have good, rigorous research backing it. We do not expect a full, pukka case to be brought by every participant. That would be an unrealistic expectation.

A *case lead* is

* a summary narrative,
* of a potential case study, for a given purpose,
* based on considerable familiarity with the system (and processes) in question,
* and lacking only in the formal compilation of essential data, supporting evidence, crosschecks, etc.

In other words, a *lead* must provide just that much information that helps us decide (*a*) whether to pursue it or not for a given end use, and (*b*) if pursued, what directions the actual fieldwork in data collection would take.

What do We do with the Case Leads?

At the Workshop

Hopefully, there will be consensus within the workshop group on some things—perhaps some recurring issues, some methodological traps, some ideas for experimentation, and so on. We will then examine the case leads brought by participants, and select a smaller number representing this range of ideas for further development as full case studies. The 'adoption' of some case leads for further development will be purely on the criterion of supplementing the workshop deliberations, and will in no way be a reflection of the written quality of the lead or the importance of the programme/project it describes.

After the Workshop

Participants whose case leads have been adopted will be assisted by the workshop organizers to research them more purposefully and write them up. The completed cases will then form the valuable supplement to the proceedings of the workshop.

Types of Case Leads Welcomed

Since the workshop is all about programme evaluation, the case must obviously have something to do with PE of some real experience. This may be:

* In more direct terms, e.g., an actual PE exercise being the main point of the narrative.
* In indirect terms, e.g., a dispute regarding the 'benefits' derived from a given development project—in other words, the measure of benefit being inseparable from the assumptions about development, and conflicting views on the same.
* With an emphasis on the *concepts* of development and social change, e.g., criteria governing project selection.
* With an emphasis on *methods* of evaluation, e.g., 'measuring' the less tangible aspects of development, alternative indices of change, etc.
* About a specific project or programme, e.g., a milk cooperative or a food-for-work programme or a rural energy system.
* About an 'agency' whose function is social intervention and change, e.g., a government department, an NGO, a funding organization.
* About expected outcomes, e.g., achievements, 'success', 'products'.
* About unexpected outcomes, e.g., shortfalls, 'failures', side effects, 'processes', and so on.

Any Particular Structure/Frame for the Case Lead?

Yes and no. There should be no need to introduce 'rules' for writing cases/leads, and restrict the expression of questions/problems/issues as they might have occurred more naturally.

Yet, some tips and guidelines might be useful:

1. It is useful to first draft only a case *lead*. If it manages to reveal all that you consider as important ingredients, that should do. Two typed pages should be ample.
2. What is the *system* that we are trying to understand? Is it a village, a group of villages? A project? A voluntary agency? An interconnected set of governmental procedures? It is useful to be clear about the scope and bounderies of the system being referred to. Also, the other systems influencing what we are concerned with. The police? The collector's office? The temple? And so on. (An 'input–output matrix'.)
3. What is the *principal phenomenon* (as seen by the intervention programme) about which some development action was contemplated? How was it defined? E.g., as unemployment? As superstition? As ignorance? As malnutrition? And so on.
4. What was the intervention *rationale*? What was the reasoning behind the specific types of action contemplated/undertaken? Value bases?
5. Any 'model' of intervention invoked? Formally articulated? Underlying assumption?
6. Nature of 'evaluation'. Formal/informal? From within? External? Role/participation of people concerned? Nature/type of 'measures' to assess outcome? Who felt the need for evaluation?
7. What are the gaps? What other information/data may be needed for a full description?
8. Finally for the purpose of the *workshop*, it would be useful to know:

   * If the case is still 'live' or it is about events some time ago.
   * If there are other reports/documents on the same case, of direct or indirect value.
   * If the participant is in a position to 'go back' to the case for a fuller documentation study.

Preparing the Case
(Distributed After the Workshop)

Recap: Objectives

The general objective of the case studies in the present exercise may be stated as:

***To explore the validity of an alternative methodology in programme evaluation** consistent with an alternative set of premises in development intervention.*

As seen at the workshop, the prime requirement of the alternative methodology is the *sensitivity* to certain phenomena in the social system concerned that may be critical to the development process. In other words, the methodology packages of conventional tools and techniques might not have the required sensitivity for these phenomena.

Following from the above, the more specific objectives for the case studies may be stated as follows:

1. To explore the *relevance of the development criteria* listed (the alternative value premises):

   (*a*) Their presence or absence, in explicit or implied terms.
   (*b*) Their consequences for the conduct of the programme.
   (*c*) Their demands on the evaluation task.

2. To explore the *relevance of the evaluation parameters* listed (in the alternative methodology):

   (*a*) Prospects/difficulties in defining them.
   (*b*) Prospects/difficulties in observing them.
   (*c*) Prospects/difficulties in devising specific tools and techniques for them; i.e., moving towards standardized measures, indicators, comparability, reliability, etc.

3. To explore the *compatibility* between the development criteria adopted in a programme and the evaluation parameters assumed:

(*a*) The alternative criteria and parameters listed.
(*b*) The conventional criteria and parameters in common practice.
(*c*) The possibility of there being concept–method 'clusters', with some methods/parameters in evaluation 'going better' with some concepts/criteria of development.

It is, of course, unrealistic to expect every case to serve every one of the above objectives to the same extent and with the same conclusiveness. Each case is, in truth, an *exploration*. It must not be contrived to appear more purposive than it really is.

Finally, a few important supplements to the objectives above, to help plan the research and documentation work before the cases are written up.

No Need to be Defensive

Since some case leads have come from the programme involvements of participants themselves, there may be a natural, normal tendency to 'protect' features of the framework within which the case is being written. There is no need to do so, as the case

* *is not* setting out to evaluate the project or programme or the personnel or the agency concerned per se, and cannot in any way cast a value judgement on any of these, but
* *is* exploring dispassionately the merits and shortcomings of methodology—conventional as well as innovative, the prospects as well as the problems.

Cutting Both Ways

One important conclusion at the workshop was that a good alternative PE methodology should not only serve as a positive aid to programmes and projects with the alternative development perspective; it might also have a diagnostic value when applied as a package to any programme—to reveal sources of dysfunction and inconsistency in a programme where development is *not* taking place.

Thus it would be quite in order for the cases to confront areas of difficulty, conflict, failure, shortfalls, unexpected outcomes, etc., in the programmes being described, and attempt to apply the alternative framework from the workshop to analyze these difficulties.

Question Pat Assumptions in Methodology

An 'alternative methodology' has a long way to go from the first bursts of insight—where we are now—to a set of internally consistent tools and techniques. The cases can at best reveal some directions, some hypotheses, for more purposive research by others. One way in which a case can help is by exposing unquestioned assumptions, fallacies and pitfalls in prevailing practices.

For instance, we often put tools and techniques into convenient *dichotomies,* such as:

* Subjective vs. objective
* Qualitative vs. quantitative
* Process vs. product outcomes

Further, we *assume* intercorrelations among these dichotomized 'variables'; i.e., a process measure is necessarily qualitative and (therefore) necessarily subjective. Is this true? Must it be so?

Likewise, the case researcher may find other pat assumptions worth questioning as s/he proceeds with the documentation.

Don't Put Aside the Working Paper!

The working paper aided the workshop proceedings. The workshop proceedings reinforced the working paper. They are integral to the project objectives.

For sheer practicality, the workshop picked on a few and not all of the issues posed in the working paper, taking the proceedings in a certain direction. There are other points in the working paper that are pertinent—and closely related—to what was discussed and what emerged at the workshop. They would be quite in place in the case studies.

What Help To Expect

It must be clear that some jobs in the case study are best handled by the participants themselves, and no outsider can do them as well. There are such things as compiling the factual details, the historical details, the twists and turns in the course of events, the interconnectedness among events, and so on.

The help from the co-ordinator will be mainly editorial in nature, aimed at some uniformity across the cases in length, extent of analysis, clarity, meeting objectives, etc. He will not make any contribution of his own that is interpretative, judgemental or evaluative. Participants are welcome to subject any or all aspects of a case to any amount of discussion and analysis with him, at any stage of the case research; but the authorship of the final version of the case will remain the participants' only. The stages at which help may be sought are shown in the section below.

How to Get Going: Some Tips

Here are two maxims for starters:

* 'The best way to begin is to write something down first'—which means that not knowing where to start is a very common experience indeed, and need not become a paralytic condition.
* 'There is no one best way to begin'—which means that in a good case the interconnections among the parts will come out no matter at what point you begin.

The main value of these maxims is in the assurance they give us that it is safe to start anywhere as long as we know where we are going.

Yet, most case researchers find that some order and method always helps, and a completely unstructured approach to the task often results in directionlessness.

Here are a few steps, a sequencing of jobs, that might be useful to follow:

Step 1: First Sketch of the Scope

Consider the first three points of the starting framework (adopted for the case lead before the workshop) once again:

* What is the *system* . . . etc.
* What is the *principal phenomenon* . . . etc.

* What was the *intervention rationale* . . . etc.

Put down all your thoughts on these three aspects of the case as *points*—do not start writing essay paragraphs yet.

Step 2: Check with Workshop Framework

(*a*) Considering the workshop deliberations on criteria of development (alternative value premises), do we have enough descriptive material for the case *either* in line with the alternative criteria, *or* revealing what happens when there are conflicts or inconsistencies in the criteria?
(*b*) Considering the workshop deliberations on alternative methodology, do we have enough descriptive material for the case *either* in line with the alternatives sought *or* revealing the shortcomings/inadequacies in conventional methodology employed?

Step 3: Identifying Gaps

On the basis of the steps so far, it should be possible to list the different kinds of data/information/facts/figures/events/anecdotes we do not have readily with us, but which would be useful to make the case complete.

At this stage we should also ask ourselves:

* Is this case 'closed'? Can we go back to the project for more information? If not, do we have enough material for a case, *as per our case writing objectives*, even if incomplete?
* Is this case 'open'? If so, roughly how much time will we need for filling the information gaps identified so far?

Step 4: Interim Review 1

Whatever notes have been made so far may be sent to the co-ordinator at this stage. He will:

(*a*) Comment on adequacy/inadequacy of information available so far.

(*b*) Ask some questions about possible directions the case may go from here.
(*c*) Suggest alternatives on how best the information may be hung together.

Step 5: Filling Gaps

Complete the data collection as identified in steps 3 and 4.

Step 6: First Draft

Prepare a first draft of the full case as discussed at step 4.

Step 7: Interim Review 2

The first draft prepared may be sent to the co-ordinator at this stage. He will:

(*a*) Comment on the organization of the material and editorial adjustments required—sequencing, emphases, detail, etc.—essentially from the point of view of uniformity/comparability across cases.
(*b*) Suggest additions, elaborations on the narrative—hopefully unnecessary by this stage.

Step 8: Final Draft

(*a*) If editorial comments are many at step 6, prepare a fresh version, incorporating the corrections, and send it in.
(*b*) If editorial comments are marginal at step 6, send approval by post for the corrections to be incorporated by the co-ordinator directly.

About the Contributors

B.S. Bhatia is the Director of Development and Educational Communication Unit (DECU) of the Indian Space Research Organization in Ahmedabad, associated with the Kheda Communications Project from its inception.

C.R. Bijoy, a freelance consultant based in Coimbatore, is engaged in supporting grassroots organizations, with an emphasis on alternative community health systems.

K.S. Jagadish is a Professor in the faculty of Civil Engineering and a past Co-ordinator of the Cell for the Application of Science and Technology to Rural Areas (ASTRA) at Indian Institute of Science in Bangalore.

Sharada Jain is Co-ordinator of the Research Wing at Sandhan, a voluntary organization in Jaipur, and past co-ordinator of the evaluation research team at Institute of Development Studies associated with Women's Development Project in Rajasthan.

Subhash R. Joshi heads the Social Research Group at Development and Educational Communication Unit (DECU) of the Indian Space Research Organization in Ahmedabad, and has been engaged in all aspects of research of the Kheda Communications Project.

K. Ramakrishnan is a Professor in the faculty of Management and Entrepreneurship Development at Bharathiar University, Coimbatore, and past co-ordinator of the evaluation research team at Madras Institute of Development Studies associated with the National Adult Education Programme in Tamil Nadu.

Vanaja Ramprasad, a freelance consultant based in Bangalore, is engaged in research and training for development programmes, with current involvement in a project on biodiversity conservation for sustainable agriculture.

Amulya Kumar N. Reddy is President of International Energy Initiative, an independent, non-profit organization in Bangalore engaged in policy research for energy and development. He was earlier a Professor at Indian Institute of Science and one of the founders of ASTRA there.

Sandeep Virmani is Co-ordinator of the Ecology Cell of Jan Vikas, a voluntary organization in Ahmedabad, and was associated with the Khambat community housing project near Ahmedabad.

